"*My Little Skinny Greek Life: On Liberty Street is* a wonderful recollection of memories. Michael does a fantastic job of taking you by the hand and walking with you through his childhood memories. It is a fun and exciting read that keeps you wanting more! I urge you to find a comfortable spot and prepare for a joyous read! Michael takes you back to the innocence of life. He reminds us of the purity that comes with youth and the importance of family and friends, and that true wealth in this life comes from the memories we make and leave behind."

Rev. Fr. Gary Kyriacou
Pastor, St. Demetrios Greek Orthodox Church
Camarillo, California

◆ ◆ ◆

"Hitching a ride back in Mike's time machine was great. I'd forgotten about many things from my youth. I'm glad Mike remembered."

Tom Bednarik

◆ ◆ ◆

"Mike has captured the essence of growing up in a small Midwestern town in the 1950s and '60s! In today's world of planned activities and play dates, children no longer have the same freedom to explore, take risks and learn about life (and themselves), from those adventures. And, oh, what adventures he shares ..."

Beth Myers

◆ ◆ ◆

"Through the gauzy veil of time and nostalgia, Michael shares the charming heartfelt memories of his boyhood in Morris, Illinois in the 1950s and '60s. As you enjoy his many adventures, you will recollect and re-live your own childhood. A great read. Enjoy."

Jan Adrian

◆ ◆ ◆

"Mike's story of Greek immigrant life in our small town honors his parents and reveals the importance of family and friends for a young boy. It was a pleasure to read, and to reminisce of a simpler time for all of us."

Margaret Bednarik, retired teacher and friend

◆ ◆ ◆

"I believe anyone who grew up in Small Town, USA in the middle decades of the last century will find a soul mate in Mike Skopes. His vivid memory of such small details paints a beautiful Rockwell-like watercolor of what growing up in Morris, Illinois was like in the 1950s and '60s. This is a great read by a great friend; a thousand thanks for writing this."

Bill Fruland

My Little Skinny Greek Life

My Little Skinny Greek Life

♦

On Liberty Street

Michael H. Skopes

9-4-2016

Charlie,

For the child within. Enjoy the book and I hope you get a good laugh.

Michael

iUniverse, Inc.
New York Bloomington Shanghai

My Little Skinny Greek Life
On Liberty Street

Copyright © 2008 by Michael H. Skopes

All rights reserved. No part of this book may be used or reproduced by any means, graphic, electronic, or mechanical, including photocopying, recording, taping or by any information storage retrieval system without the written permission of the publisher except in the case of brief quotations embodied in critical articles and reviews.

iUniverse books may be ordered through booksellers or by contacting:

iUniverse
1663 Liberty Drive
Bloomington, IN 47403
www.iuniverse.com
1-800-Authors (1-800-288-4677)

Because of the dynamic nature of the Internet, any Web addresses or links contained in this book may have changed since publication and may no longer be valid.

The views expressed in this work are solely those of the author and do not necessarily reflect the views of the publisher, and the publisher hereby disclaims any responsibility for them.

ISBN: 978-0-595-48531-4 (pbk)
ISBN: 978-0-595-71955-6 (cloth)
ISBN: 978-0-595-60626-9 (ebk)

Printed in the United States of America

For Harrison and young adventurers everywhere

"Think about the other fella."
   Harry C. Skopes

Contents

Foreword... xiii
Preface xv
Acknowledgements xvii
Introduction... xix

Part I   Early Days

CHAPTER 1   Establishment 3
CHAPTER 2   The Basket................................ 35
CHAPTER 3   My Pal.................................... 41
CHAPTER 4   Carlson's Service Station 46
CHAPTER 5   The Farms................................. 59
CHAPTER 6   The Corn Festival 67
CHAPTER 7   Sunday Evenings 71
CHAPTER 8   Sidewalk Kindergarten...................... 74

Part II   Franklin School Days

CHAPTER 9   First Grade, 1958–1959 79
CHAPTER 10   Ace Hardware 85
CHAPTER 11   Second Grade, 1959–1960 87
CHAPTER 12   Monark and Coast King 91

Chapter 13	Third Grade, 1960–1961	97
Chapter 14	Holbrook, Cameron, and Halterman	103
Chapter 15	The Legend of Swimming Pool Hill	113
Chapter 16	Gebhard Woods	119
Chapter 17	Fourth Grade, 1961–1962	124

Part III Center School Days

Chapter 18	The Brick	131
Chapter 19	Pom Pom Pull Away!	133
Chapter 20	Music	139
Chapter 21	Chapin Park	143
Chapter 22	Fifth Grade, 1962–1963	151
Chapter 23	Combat	154
Chapter 24	The "Toe" Path	158
Chapter 25	Gorilla Balls	163
Chapter 26	Sixth Grade, 1963–1964	166
Chapter 27	Backyard Camping	175
Chapter 28	Free Goose Day	178
Chapter 29	Seventh Grade, 1964–1965	181
Chapter 30	The Gebhard Brewery	189
Chapter 31	Goold Park	194
Chapter 32	The Union Street Drag Strip	197
Chapter 33	Eighth Grade, 1965–1966	199
Chapter 34	Summer; 1966	215

Conclusion 225

Foreword

By
Tony Kidonakis

By late summer 2006, my grandmother was leaving our hometown ... Morris, Illinois. From the stage in front of the Grundy County Courthouse, I took a moment during my rock band's performance to ask the few hundred gathered there on lawn chairs and blankets to applaud Libby Skopes for fifty-six years of hard work as a homemaker and local restaurant owner. My grandparents had been the first of our family to arrive, and she would be the last to leave. Five years earlier, my parents had relocated to Ottawa, Illinois, to be near their family restaurant, and one-by-one my siblings and I had left for the Chicago suburbs to be closer to our jobs. My grandmother, now living alone with declining health, was prepared to move in with her daughter, Heidi, and her family in Des Plaines. Though I was excited for my young twin cousins, Emily and Evan, to learn our grandmother's native Greek language, Orthodox prayers, and bedtime stories, it saddened me to see our last family resident waving good-bye to the cheering crowd. My grandmother has always told me how her Greek mountain village was a community of families and friends that took care of each other. I feel lucky that my grandfather brought her to a small Midwestern town where that experience continued for her, her children, and her grandchildren. Therefore, I proudly proclaimed to the audience that no matter where our family goes, Morris will always be the place we call home, our family village in America.

Ultimately, it was my grandmother's son, Michael Skopes, who most contributed to my affection for Morris, Illinois. During my childhood, Uncle Mike had been like a legend to my brother, my sister and me—a cool actor living in California who made frequent trips back to Morris to spend time with family and reconnect with his hometown. I remember laughing with my little brother and sister until we could barely breathe while our uncle muted the television commercials and improvised his own comedic narration. We thrived on Uncle Mike's guided tours of Morris, where he took us to many sites of his childhood adventures: the parks, the pool, the canal, the *toe-path*. Once he brought us each a pair of ice skates and taught us how to use them on the frozen ponds at Gebhard

Woods. He'd buy giant ice cream cones from the Straightway Dairy and we'd eat them down by the Illinois River while he taught us to skip stones. We couldn't believe our eyes when he walked across the railing of an I & M Canal bridge as if it were a tightrope ... we thought he was fearless! He became practically immortal as he flew off the old high dive at the Morris Pool. We were too scared to attempt it, but there was our tall, strong, confident uncle diving off this legendary platform with multiple flips. We dreaded him leaving—the times he had to tear us off his legs to meet up with old friends, attend class reunions, or give the inevitable long hugs good-bye. He was utterly and completely our childhood hero.

In later years, our uncle's visits consisted of less sightseeing and more storytelling. In his book *My Little Skinny Greek Life* I learn how my hero, as a child himself, saved a life. I witness my grandfather as a Greek shepherd boy. I see my grandmother as a young woman dishing out French fries to hungry Morris teenagers at her restaurant, *The Basket*. I listen to my aunt and uncle giggle at sounds from Beatles records spun backwards. I welcome my sweet mother into the world and hear my grandfather whisper his last words.

As a child, I never wanted to say good-bye to Uncle Mike. Even at eighteen, I wasn't ready to say good-bye to my grandfather, and I don't think I'll ever be ready to say good-bye to my grandmother either. I hope remembering these stories will make it easier. Thank you, Uncle Mike, for this gift to our family, friends, teachers, and the generations yet to come. May your memories be eternal.

Preface

In December, 2006, at fifty-four years young, I opened my e-mail account to find a letter from one of my grade school and high school friends, Beth (Bednarik) Myers. She sent one of those emotion laden, perfectly suited for Christmas season stories. It addressed lessons learned during childhood and how people in general today could use a strong dose of compassion and man's humanity to man. Reading it reminded me of something that happened at about my twelfth year that mended my broken heart. I sent that story to Beth. It impressed her enough to write back encouraging me to pen a book about my childhood memories. Little did she know that about a year earlier, at fifty-three years young, I had already begun organizing (on paper) initial thoughts, mainly about my father. I had just finished reading Tim Russert's book about his father, *Big Russ & Me*. Many of Russert's descriptions of his dad sounded a lot like my dad, and I felt inspired to tell a story of my own.

That e-mail exchange with Beth started me thinking. For quite a while I had been thinking about comparisons. What is different about my life as an adult from my life as a child? What has changed? What is the same? I had hours and hours of time available to me for deep reflection. My commute to and from my job five days a week gave me all the time I needed to start this process of comparing.

Many of my thoughts were about old friends, my parents, two sisters, and how I missed them. I relived times of less complexity and certainly less traffic congestion. I compared the days of my youth to the days of today's youth while eying every graffiti paint job along my commute. Coupled with some of the current music I heard when channel scanning, I had to shake my head. When I listened to the news and talk, I heard things that made me long for a distant past even more. My world, my country, and my local environment were being tested, and the percentage of people flunking out disturbed me. I kept hearing about the polarization of people and nations, inept leaders and misguided opponents. I heard people speak about the degradation of the Constitution, loss of freedoms and rights, tragic loss of precious lives, and endless he said she said stories dominating the air waves. I came close to screaming.

What could I do to gain a little peace of mind? My answer to that question lies within the following pages. I had to create a place where I could go to be free from all the garbage … for a while and re-experience the good things I knew as a boy. Sure, the 1950s and 1960s had corruption, degradation, and injustices. I haven't forgotten them. Let's just transition into a neighborhood of solutions based on man's humanity to man rather than accusations, polarization, and inhumanity. Let's make use of those past good feelings and have some fun. That is why I wrote this book. To be sure, these are personal accounts of one man's youth, but they are also part of a universal melody enhanced with layers of harmony. A song we all can sing.

Acknowledgements

I thank my wife, Jan, for understanding the importance of this project, and what it means to me. Additionally, thank you sweetheart for your support. To our wonderful son, Harrison, thank you for waiting until the finished product before reading it. You are the joy in our lives. We adore you.

The following people have succeeded in jogging my memory with valuable bits and pieces; some large, and some small. To my family, beginning with my loving mother, Eleftheria (Libby) Skopes; I love you, Mom, and thank you from the depth of my soul. To my wonderful sister, Ann Kidonakis, my talented nephews Tony and Jim Kidonakis, my bright and lovely niece, Elaine Kidonakis, I'm honored by your support. To my cousin Martha Panos, much love and thanks to you. To my supporting cast of dear friends, Bill Fruland, Lee Randall, Steve Barkley, Beth Myers, Margaret Bednarik, Tom Bednarik, Steve Holbrook, John Halterman, Chuck Enger, and Gerry Carlson, each of you has a special place in my heart. To Elizabeth "Sis" Gabel, Morris historian Ken Sereno, Pam Wilson, and Debbie Steffes of the Morris Public Library, thank you all so very much.

Thank you, Father Gary Kyriacou for your blessing and capturing the essence of my story with your quote.

Thank you everybody!

Introduction

Beth Myers' suggestion to shift the focus of my story inspired me, and I gave serious thought during my drives to and from work about modifying my initial idea of writing a book about Dad. It made perfect sense because for years my friends had commented on my ability to extract colorful tales from the old days. This fundamental change in my story solved my problem of repeating the Russert book, something I would never attempt to do.

I am the only son of Greek immigrants who came to America for a better life. They were courageous parents who left their homes and families behind and traveled thousands of miles across the world chasing their dreams. Some dreams came true in a timely manner. Others took years or sadly slipped away in disappointment.

In this book I share memories—cheerful and sorrowful; comedic and dramatic. I'll focus on what I know best ... my own bit of personal Greek history. I'll present the philosophical curiosities of a little skinny Greek boy born in a small Illinois town in the early 1950s. I'll reveal thoughts (pleasant and not so pleasant) of a boy who loved his family and friends. I'll tell you about the world of a boy who loved music, make-believe, and most of the time spent in school. You'll learn intimate details about a boy who loved his childhood.

My young life's adventures on, and in close proximity to Liberty Street, the main street in town, meant everything to me. Although our actual residence address indicated Jefferson Street, Liberty Street received top honors. I say that because from my corner bedroom windows (there were two) I viewed several blocks of Liberty Street in each direction. Dozens of businesses lined both sides of this great thoroughfare, and my family owned and operated two—Harry's Cocktail Lounge and the attached restaurant—The Basket.

Two apartments made up the living space on the second floor of our building. At the time of my birth, we lived in the one further back from Liberty Street and over the restaurant. At about eight years old, we moved to the bigger front apartment situated right on the corner. I called this corner apartment above Harry's Cocktail Lounge, *home*, from my skinny eight year old days until 1976. That was when Mom and Dad sold the business and retired to a house just north of I-80.

Those two downtown apartments were the dwellings that sheltered my early times.

The following is a collection of stories; my memory chain of family, friends, and many of the townspeople from a small, picturesque, Midwest town ... Morris, Illinois. Although there are some references made to famous people within this book, I have no personal connections with them. I'm not friends with nationally known personalities governmental or otherwise (as is Mr. Russert). There are no interviews with world leaders or self absorbed, troubled, Hollywood celebrities contemplating rehab. This is a collection of many childhood experiences I shared with hard working small business people, factory workers, farmers, teachers, city officials, law enforcement officers, and students. I hope you enjoy the hilarious and sometimes heart breaking ride up and down Liberty Street where life was colored by (among a multitude of other things) the symphonic cheerful honking horns of the Chevrolet, Ford, Dodge, Cadillac, Pontiac, Buick, Chrysler, Plymouth, Studebaker, Oldsmobile, Rambler, Lincoln, and Mercury models we all used to drive.

PART I
Early Days

o o o o o o o o o o o o o o o o o o o o o o o o o o o o o o o
"Early times gone to rhyme …" Paul Cotton

SS Pannonia

1

Establishment

Early 1920s in Massachusetts

 Charalambos C. Skopis was born in April, 1903 to a poor family in a tiny mountain village named, Glena, in Epirus, the northwestern section of Greece near the Albanian border. As a strong, solidly built lad in Glena, in the early 1900s, Charalambos spent a good deal of his time working for his father. He led a quiet, uneventful young life of hard work. To say that times were rough in those days is a major understatement. People had very little in the way of amenities, appliances, tools, or even toys for the children.

One of the childhood chores given to Charalambos during the early twentieth-century included tending his father's sheep. One day, this shepherd boy sat alone upon a hillside rock as his sheep grazed nearby. The day was peaceful, hot, and dry; the mountain air—pure and clean. His shepherd's primary tool was a wooden staff he used to guide the sheep. On that day long ago, the staff proved dynamically useful in another task. A rogue pack of wild dogs rushed out from an adjacent stand of trees and surprised Charalambos. They had upset the peace, and sent the terrified sheep every which way in a cloud of mountain dust. The dogs attacked furiously. With no time to lose, the shepherd boy rose from the rock swinging his staff left and right clubbing as hard as he could to protect the sheep. One after another, he beat the advancing six or seven wild, mangy, mongrels with his staff as they fought back ferociously. One of them struck at the front of the boy's leg and tore open a huge gash near his shin bone. Determined and courageous, Charalambos fought for his life despite profuse bleeding and extreme pain. After an exhausting battle, he prevailed in turning the savages away. The marauding dogs high tailed it back into the woods without taking a single lamb. Victory!

Charalambos was my father. Looking at the printed Americanized spelling of his name, he could have taken the name Charles. But the *Ch* isn't a sound as in Charles. It is more like the *H* in Harry which is the actual translation. It is a heavily aspirated, guttural consonant similar to the German *ch* in Bach.

Having known my dad and his character well, it is easy for me to visualize how he fought for his life and the lives of his sheep. That was the only story my dad ever told me about his boyhood. I wish there were more. But what other kinds of stories could he have told? There were no Friday night football games or sock hops to tell and get excited about. He, his brothers, sister, and fellow villagers were probably lucky to own a pair of socks. Even then, they would have been homemade; knitted with coarse wool spun into rudimentary yarn by the local women.

"We didn't have anything ... nothing," Dad simply said whenever he referred to his early days.

Keeping today's standards in mind, the mountain life in Glena back then can be described as intensely simple and bleak—very bleak. Life for Dad most likely consisted of a day to day existence wondering what could be. When his older brothers Angelo and Gregory left the peasant life behind for America, the land of opportunity, I'm sure my dad dreamed of the better life for himself one day. Things would be different for his future family whenever that time would be.

The time for dreaming came to an end when Dad learned his brothers had made arrangements for his adventure to begin. He said goodbye to his parents, his sister, Olga, and set off for the port city of Patras. The fact that Olga stayed behind for whatever reason turned out to be an unfortunate twist of fate given the events and border changes following World War II. She lived out her life in third world poverty behind the *Iron Curtain* in Albania.

◆ ◆ ◆

Cinnamon shades of rust stains appeared to pour through the hawseholes of the SS Pannonia. The heavy anchors rose slowly, grinding, and dripping salt water from the Ionian Sea on the Western Grecian shore signaling an immediate departure. Her voyage across the Atlantic represented much more than just a point A to point B cruise. Pannonia's crew shouldered responsibilities that reached far beyond their careers. Their efforts helped to usher in the optimistic futures of passengers who adventured to America in the early twentieth-century.

On October 26, 1920 at the age of 17, Charalambos C. Skopis stepped off the steamship Pannonia onto the docks of Ellis Island in the Port of New York City. Dad's first order of business, aside from the formalities and institutional requirements upon entering the United States, was to get to Worcester, Massachusetts. There, he met up with his older brother, Angelo, and began his new life as a young American. Dad spent a few years in Massachusetts with friends and other family members; cousins who had made the trip to America before he did. They were all instrumental in either sponsoring his immigration, or helping him find his way in a strange new land, or both.

During these early days in New England, Dad studied English with a private tutor, an older woman who made it possible for Dad to acquire the language skills he needed to assimilate into American society. With her help he became a responsible United States citizen and started his new life. I don't even know her name. It would be an honor to thank her descendants.

On a Massachusetts muscle beach; note the scar on his lower left leg

After Massachusetts, he migrated west to Chicago, Illinois, where Dad and his two brothers, Angelo, and Gregory found work and homes. In just a few years, Dad had left Greece, resided in New England, and moved to Chicago. His search for the better life he dreamed about as a little boy in the Greek mountains began to take shape.

In 1929, Dad, at twenty-six years old, experienced prohibition from an interesting perspective. Turmoil characterized Chicago because of gangsters Al Capone on the south side, and George "Bugs" Moran from the north side fighting over turf, beer, and liquor. My young father found himself in some pretty eventful times. 1929, was the year of the St. Valentine's Day massacre in a warehouse at 2122 North Clark Street. Capone had arranged for a hit to be made on "Bugs" Moran and his gang. Moran didn't show up for the ruse which involved a truck carrying Canadian whiskey set to arrive at the warehouse garage. Moran's men were to then distribute the whiskey to their buyers. Well, instead of the delivery truck, a car carrying Capone's armed thugs showed up. They entered the garage and proceeded to gun down the entire Moran gang. My dad happened to be working close by on that day, and he (along with many others) endured probing questions by the Chicago Police following that gruesome crime. Of course he, his circle of friends, acquaintances, and co-workers knew nothing about the tragic circumstances. The questioning eventually ended leaving Dad and his friends to go about their business.

Shortly after those events, Dad left Chicago for the peaceful rural fields and farms of the Joliet, Illinois, area thirty miles southwest of Chicago. He didn't come half way around the world to get mixed up with gangsters. The big city had suddenly lost its appeal. He started working the fields for local farmers and eventually drove delivery trucks filled with vegetables to the produce markets in Chicago.

Unlike his two brothers, Dad disliked living in the city with its crime and congestion. He was a quiet man of few words. He avoided Chicago until he had to deliver or pick up farm related materials or drove into town to visit the brothers. More and more, he developed a belonging to the countryside which suited him better and reminded him of his homeland—simpler, and closer to nature. He loved the outdoors—the turning of the soil and planting crops for food. He continued this lovely connection with nature his entire life of ninety-four years.

After several years of farming in the Joliet and Channahon areas, he eventually settled temporarily in Grundy County on the Hornsby Farm in Mazon Township. Dad made many friends with farmers and small business proprietors from the surrounding towns. Soon, Morris caught his eye where an opportunity existed to go into a business there. As much as he loved the farming, he felt a need to make a change. So, Dad placed a *Public Sale* announcement in the Morris newspaper in 1937 stating his desire to quit farming and sell two horses, forty-five chickens, a Fordson tractor, disc and plow, a 1929 Dodge truck, a 1930 Ford coupe, and many other articles. Auctioneer, Arnold Tesdal, auctioned off everything and Dad went into the saloon business.

Dad's first business in Morris; *the quiet fella* sat at the far end

The early location of Dad's first bar was in the center of Liberty Street's 400 block. My guess—the picture is from the early 1940s. At the time, he also lived in the apartment above this bar. Going from left to right in the photograph, Helen Panish is seated at the bar followed by Art (Happy) Mahaffey, George Tolias, Dad, and at the far left on the floor—the resident cat. Other than the cat, I know the least about Helen Panish who worked for Dad as a cocktail waitress. Dad had met Happy in Morris and hired him to clean and also work behind the bar. Obviously he got his nickname from being a happy-go-lucky guy. Fellow Greek, George Tolias worked as a waiter at the Andan Café about three doors south until Dad brought him over to work with him. We respectfully referred to him as Uncle George, the Greek way of addressing a friend of your parents—a non-relative relative. He became good friends with Dad for life. In his entire long life, I only saw my dad weep tears of sadness twice; the assassination of President Kennedy and at the funeral for Uncle George Tolias.

Of all people, Bugs Moran actually sat in relative obscurity in this bar. He did so on occasion when he skedaddled out of Chicago in need of a place to chill out for a while. Dad told me how Moran had a hide out at the Peabody Coal Company strip mines just outside of Morris. Years later, the property became the

Morris Rod and Gun Club. "He was a *quiet fella*," Dad had said of Moran, who sat at the end of this bar minding his own business. "He never talked too much and kept to himself." Interesting—coming from Dad, it sounded as if he were describing himself—a man of few words. I also find it intriguing (not intentionally implying anything other than coincidence) that Dad worked near the Clark Street massacre and some years later Moran could be seen in Dad's bar in Morris.

What would a big time Chicago gangster be doing in a bar in Morris? Answer; thirsty of course, but he did have to keep a low profile while in town. He didn't want to draw attention to himself. I remember Dad describing Moran as a "regular looking fella" and that, "You'd never know he was a big Chicago mobster." The fact that this *fella* actually spent quiet, peaceful time in my father's place of business and spoke with my dad is quite a story in itself. I always found it spicy how Dad down played the fact and rarely spoke about it. I guess Moran's unassuming behavior paid dividends considering how Dad never made a big deal out of it. What a *fella*.

By the time I had grown enough to know and learn about Dad's friends, the early bar had long been vacated, and Dad had moved his business interests half a block south to 402 Liberty Street; the Louis Cocktail Lounge. Another fellow Greek man, Louis Nichols, owned and operated the cocktail lounge. Mr. Nichols first sold the business to two men from Joliet; George Dellos, and George Vasiris. They owned it for about two years until they sold it to Dad. Mr. Dellos went back to farming, and Mr. Vasiris returned to Joliet, Illinois, later becoming my godfather. His wife, Maria, my godmother, was sister to George Dellos. The George Dellos farm just northeast of Morris later became one of two frequently visited fun filled farms for my entire youth.

Up to now, you will notice the spelling of the last name—*Skopis*. That is the correct spelling of our family name used by every member of my dad's brothers' families to this day. Charalambos Skopis became Harry Skopes in the new world. It happened unintentionally when he endorsed checks and other documents necessary for starting his own business. *Skopis* appeared to be written as *Skopes* because of his penmanship. Hence, the new look and loss of one syllable.

The Louis Cocktail Lounge became Harry's Cocktail Lounge. The following picture is a post card rendering of the lounge. It shows the lounge from the front entrance on the Liberty Street end looking back toward the restaurant known as The Basket. The lounge, a beautiful room with booths made of a heavy textured orange/burgundy vinyl throughout, catered to distinguished customers who appreciated fine food and drink. Combination wallpaper and padded, textured walls were capped with a wall border of hand painted martini glasses near the ceiling. The bar itself; large, curved, and rectangular shaped accommodated twenty or so heavy, and very comfortable spinning barstools. The bar's top surface had a brown, varnished wooden hand rest raised above the bar about an inch or so and six inches in from the edge.

This post card shows the lounge in its prime

One of the most interesting elements built into the design of the lounge, was the front door; a heavy, aluminum colored, metal door with a martini glass shaped window centered on it from top to bottom. This classic piece of art has unfortunately disappeared. Dad had originally sold out to Mel and Agnes Peterson in 1977. When the Petersons eventually sold the bar years later, that next owner remodeled and the classic door was gone. If it is intact somewhere today, it might be worth a small fortune—a one of a kind piece I'd love to have now. Many nights as I lay in bed still awake at closing time, I heard the jingling of Dad's substantial key ring flopping around while he locked the old martini door.

My sisters, Ann and Heidi in front of the martini door

When Dad had established himself in this new location, he brought in a partner named Peter Panos. Peter had married Dad's niece, Martha, my first cousin. Martha was also born in Glena, Greece. Martha's father, my Uncle Angelo, was the oldest of the Skopis children born to Christopher and Anastasia Skopis, my paternal grandparents. When Uncle Angelo left Glena for America searching for a better life in the early twentieth-century, he left behind a pregnant wife. That baby was Martha. After establishing himself in Chicago, Uncle Angelo had arranged for his wife and daughter to come to America. It took ten years! Martha lived in Greece for ten years with her mother before meeting her father in Chicago. That is astonishing to me.

Martha and her mother boarded an Italian ship, the Rex, in 1939 and crossed the Atlantic, docking in New York on December 13, 1939. Martha described a tedious voyage in that the crew only spoke Italian, and the food they were served consisted mainly of eggs, fish, and oranges. Martha and her mother saved most of the oranges they received to give them to Uncle Angelo as gifts upon arriving in Chicago. That plan failed as the oranges were confiscated by the port authority in New York. They didn't allow produce into the country.

Cousin Martha crossed the ocean along with another Greek family whose patriarch awaited their arrival in New York. He then treated his family, Martha, and her mother to dinner on the night of their New York arrival. That same night following dinner, he took Martha and her mother to the train depot for travel on to Chicago. There, waiting for Martha stood her father, Mr. Vangeli (Angelo) Skopis, whom she had never seen before!

Time passed for Uncle Angelo, and Kalienthe (his wife), three children; Martha, second daughter Sophie, and son Chris. They lived together in Chicago until Martha married Peter, and the newly weds soon took residence in Morris above Harry's Cocktail Lounge on the corner of Jefferson and Liberty Streets.

◆ ◆ ◆

For roughly thirty years, my dad had lived as a bachelor until marriage plans were made with family back in Greece. In 1950, he left the lounge in Peter's hands temporarily and he returned to his homeland for an arranged marriage. It took Dad a long time to reach the point of marriage and eventually family. Circumstances had taken him to his forty-sixth year when he married my mother in the Northern Greek city of Ioannina (pronounced Yahnina) in January, 1950. The following photograph is probably the most meaningful picture in this book. It is an unknown photographer's vision of two young lives in the beginning moments of their commitment to each other as one. Here are my handsome mature father as a groom and my beautiful young mother as his bride. I may be prejudiced, but if there were a signature model for a lovely, young, classic Greek woman, this photograph of my mother in her simple elegant gown would be the one. She absolutely embodied the ideal, classical Greek female; her name, Eleftheria, meaning ... Liberty.

As a young girl growing up in Stavrothromi, in the mountains of northern Greece, Mom lived a hard life similar to Dad's—very much like the stories of the early American pioneers settling the Wild West. Families were large, and everyone had difficult chores and responsibilities. Mom learned sewing, cleaning, and cooking with her older sister. They (along with my grandmother) performed these jobs for a family with five brothers—a full load. My grandfather, a typical Greek mountain patriarch of a large family, had insisted on his way or nothing. He could be described as somewhat of a tyrant who knew that one day his two daughters would be given away to arranged marriages. He was especially protective of my mother; Eleftheria or Litsa (her nickname), the pride of the village. She was loved by everyone, and quite probably the most beautiful young woman there. Naturally, the father of such a daughter wanted to be sure the man taking her away lived up to his standards.

Stavrothromi

Limited education in Stavrothromi took place in a one room schoolhouse where students went as far as the sixth grade. Mom finished those six years easily enough. After completing school, her father made no effort to send her away to further her education. He wanted her home. Several years passed while living in Stavrothromi, and at the age of twenty-four, the arrangement of Charalambos and Eleftheria became final. The marriage soon followed.

All traditional Christian Greek weddings are in two parts; the Betrothal and the Sacrament of Holy Matrimony, or the Ceremony. During the Betrothal service, the priest blesses the rings and places them on their right hands. In the Bible the right hand is indicated as the good hand. The rings are then exchanged three times between the couple signifying their lives are intertwined forever. In the Greek Orthodox tradition, many rituals are in threes representing the Holy Trinity of The Father, The Son, and The Holy Spirit. Later the rings are placed onto the ring fingers of the right hands and vows are recited.

In the Ceremony section of the wedding, there is the beautiful symbolic wearing of the head crowns or *stephana* as a focal point. The two lightly adorned white crowns, or flower wreaths, are attached to each other by a long white ribbon and are worn by the bride and groom. The *stephana* symbolize a victory and the formation of a new household to which both bride and groom are charged to rule wisely with responsibility to each other and to God. The crowns also represent sacrifice of self, devotion to building up their marriage, and committing themselves as responsible parents to their children. The best man stands behind the couple and moves the crowns from the groom to the bride and back three times further representing a union of two becoming one. For much of the latter part of the Ceremony, the bride and groom are holding right hands. This grip is ended by the priest passing the bible between the hands symbolizing only God can take them apart. My parents were married in this fashion.

The reception and party that followed my parent's marriage had the folk music of Epirus as entertainment. The dominate instrument, the clarinet, I'm sure, created a festive atmosphere with bright song intros and solos. It is a truly versatile instrument able to reach deep resonating low notes as well. These lower notes do much to bring out Greek soul and blues. The clarinet was the instrument I heard most on the old 78 speed records Mom played at home. My memories of those clarinet trills filling our apartment when I was a little boy, along with my vision of watching Mom dance and sing, makes it easy for me to picture the wedding reception of Charalambos and Eleftheria Skopes in 1950.

For their very long honeymoon, the newlyweds traveled around Greece for three months by bus and boat. They visited friends and family for part of the time while exploring their beautiful Greece one last time before leaving her behind.

16   My Little Skinny Greek Life

The Honeymooners in Greece, 1950

With the promise of a better life, Charalambos whisked his new bride away from her family. He took her far from the donkeys ferrying water from a community well to a small stone cottage. He brought her decades beyond the rustic setting of rugged mountain labor, to the distant land where dreams came true ... America. This time, for Dad, the journey took only hours by plane and not days by ship—the final destination—Morris, Illinois.

From Athens they took a short flight to Rome where they switched planes for the Trans Atlantic flight to New York. Shortly after take off from Rome, one engine caught fire, and the plane's pilot made an emergency U-turn back to Rome. According to Mom, they didn't switch planes. Instead (unbelievably I might add) they waited for repairs to be made and then used the same plane for another try at crossing the Atlantic Ocean. The same plane! Excuse me, but I think I would have demanded another plane! In New York, they changed aircraft for Chicago.

Mom had visions of raising a family in the modern comforts of the great United States of America. Gone would be the labor intensive days of laundry in a tub with a wash board. No more baking in a wood burning stone oven without a door. None of those old cottage skills would be necessary in America. In America, they have machines to do the work. You cook with gas stoves and ovens with doors and thermostats. Motorized washing machines tackle the laundry. If you want to call someone, you don't have to cup your hands over your mouth and shout at the top of your lungs to reach across the hillside. No—never again; just pick up a telephone and speak normally into the black plastic handset across a system of wires like magic. These were conveniences unseen in Stavrothromi, and Eleftheria looked forward to taking full advantage; out with the old, in with the new. She wanted the new world; rich with amenities and opulence replacing malaise and barrenness. My mother welcomed with open arms an easier way of life.

◆ ◆ ◆

Of course Mom had been to large cities like Athens, New York, and Chicago during her travel half way around the world, but Morris, a town with a population of about seven thousand in 1950, still must have looked huge compared to Stavrothromi with maybe, and I stress the word *maybe*, eighty local citizens. Moving into an apartment right in the middle of the downtown area prone to honking auto horns was also a far cry from a tiny mountain village. The day to day pedestrians passing by headed for the Roth Bakery, the Straightway Dairy, Riz's Foodliner, the Morris Theatre, and many other small businesses up and down Liberty Street kept Mom visually occupied. They also frustrated her. She only spoke Greek.

Mom taught herself to read English by reading the Morris Daily Herald after learning a few basics from Dad. I have to admire such an achievement. Who wouldn't? I remember seeing her sitting at the first table of The Basket on many occasions thoughtfully going through the newspaper. She slowly did her homework while catching up on the daily events taking place in our small town.

The next picture shows Mom sitting in the bar reading the Morris Daily Herald. She is partially hidden behind the assortment of bottles, but it clearly shows her in study mode. This is actually an interesting shot. It shows the bar during a time when the stage was installed for organist, Gladys Tabler. Dad is in the foreground, and if you look closely in the mirror above Mom between her face and the paper, you can see Happy's profile reflection.

Many luxuries did come to Mom as a result of moving to America. In addition to the amenities, though, came years of unexpected hard work. It would be the biggest point of contention between my parents. Her hard work created a major disappointment for her that brought tension in later years. There may have been reasons unknown to me why this came to be. But for Mom, the commitment she had made at her wedding before God and family, her responsibility to family and husband, as defined by the Greek Orthodox Church, had to take precedence over any individual desires. Only by the hand of God could their vows to each other be broken.

◆ ◆ ◆

My sister, Anastasia Ann, (next photograph) was born in November of 1950 and named after Dad's mother, Anastasia. My paternal grandmother is a complete mystery to me. I've never even seen a picture of her. As for my paternal grandfather, I have seen two pictures of him at a reception dinner table on Mom and Dad's wedding day. I know nothing about their relationship, nothing about how they lived other than it was unbelievably difficult, and nothing about how, where, or when they died.

I, the little skinny Greek boy, was born in August, 1952. After one or two weeks of getting used to the new baby being around, Dad walked forty-five feet across the street to visit Dr. John B. Roth's office. What a convenience; having your family doctor thirty seconds away. Dr. Roth and Bernie Roth, the baker next door, were brothers. How cool is that? Fill up on cakes and donuts from one brother for a good stomach ache and see the other just inches away for the relief! Once inside Dr. Roth's office, Dad asked about paying his bill.

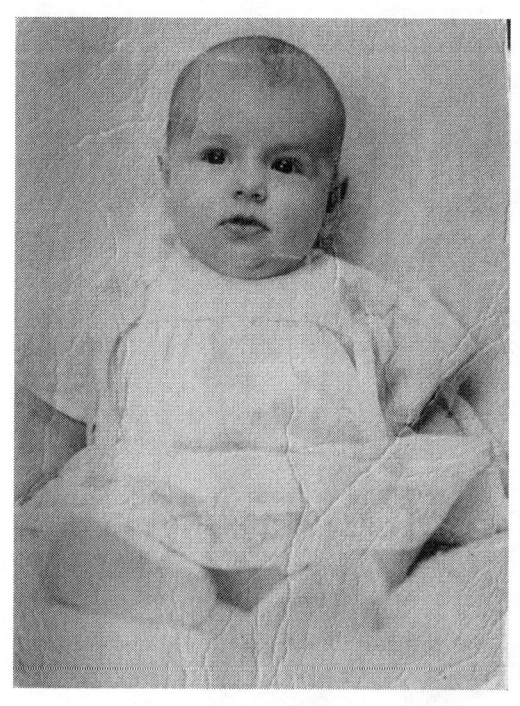

"Well, Doc?" Dad asked. "How much do I owe you for the boy?"

"The boy?" as if he'd forgotten all about me.

"Yes, Mike—my son."

Making a quick calculation in his head, Dr. Roth gave Dad the bad news.

"Oh ... fifty dollars," he said matter-of-factly.

With that exchange (as repeated a few times by Dad over the years), he reached into his pocket and pulled out his thick wad of bills held together by a rubber band. He peeled off the exact amount and promptly paid the good doctor for bringing me into the world that humid August night. Fifty dollars is all I cost my dad to be born. What a deal! Was I worth the expense? I'll take a wild guess and say ... yes.

My sisters and I were all baptized at the All Saints Greek Orthodox Church in Joliet. I guess you could say my sense of humor began on my baptismal day. Before my godfather assisted in dunking me, the fifty dollar kid, in the bath—I gave him a shower. I beat them all to the punch; the priest, godparents, and others in the immediate vicinity. As soon as they removed the white linen surrounding me, the geyser erupted—but not as an objection to the upcoming immersion. I simply insisted (in my infantile way) on establishing the terms of this agreement. If I'm getting wet; we're all getting wet. I had to be heard in some way.

The fifty dollar kid

Ann, which is the name she prefers in English, was lovingly given the Greek nickname, Tasia (Tah-see-yah) in the Skopes household. The English version became Tessy or Tess. My wonderful sister Ann has a calm, patient disposition much like Dad's. She has always been the one with a firm, realistic outlook on life; one filled with responsibility and maturity beyond her years. From an early age, she has been steady and well grounded. With that said, when anyone brought her to robust laughter, she exhibited the same affliction as Mom. They laughed themselves to tears when humor struck. They still do today. I inherited that as well but on a smaller scale. My specialty was more ... shall I say—slapstick? Sure, my eyes watered at a good funny, but mostly I'd scream out a symphony of sound and fall over in an uncontrollable body roll. When something struck me as funny; I mean really insanely tickling, I erupted without any self conscious reservations. These frequent outbursts created responses in kind from others in the immediate vicinity, and the laugh fests took on a life of their own.

Mom called out my name, "Mikey!" and cried some more with her hands up to her face, and Ann would run away into another room hunting for a tissue to get away from the dizzying madness. Dad, if he were any part of it at all, sat there chuckling. He pulled out his handkerchief and started blowing his nose which only trumpeted in the next wave of spasmodic Mikey floor rolling. Ann would stick her head back in the room for a peak at the nut case on the floor only to duck back out before her tears and Mom's flooded the place. Dad simply uttered an "Ah come on now ... don't you do that," and left for some place less crazy with his handkerchief in hand. He always had at least one handkerchief on him. You have to understand; just that simple phrase ... *Don't you do that ...* which he used in a variety of situations, ushered in a whole new level of comedy in my head. You see, Dad, even with a good command of Midwest American English, still spoke with a bit of a Greek accent. Combining his way of speaking and the few words he did speak whenever he made a comment, often slammed head on into my funny bone.

I think Dad, being an emotional reservist, took himself out of the absurdity loop for fear of encouraging a goofy, skinny, little kid who could find humor in almost anything. I could never really laugh *at* him; no way. He was my father—a man with a history of hardship and self preservation. The rugged mountain life he lived as a boy in the early twentieth-century deeply influenced his personality. So, I'm sure in his wisdom, he knew I could never laugh at him. He knew he had provided an easy life for his son; a life characterized with silliness and not burden; safety and not danger; comfort and not fear; fullness and not hunger.

On a hot August night in 1958, I remember standing inside the door to The Basket when the news came. Ann ran up to me with a big smile on her face.

"Mikey, Mikey, we have a new baby sister!"

Heidi was born only days before I started first grade. Ann and I were excited to have a new baby join the family. With our latest arrival, I witnessed a new custom. When relatives and other Greek friends visit a family with a newborn, it is customary to place silver coins in the crib next to the baby as a gift and as blessings for a prosperous life. I witnessed Uncle Nick do this for Heidi. For her first six years, Heidi had a sheltered life supported and protected by an older sister and brother. She stayed close to home.

Worry. Mom worried often, mainly about the safety of her three children. I can't recall the first time she mentioned or showed worry, but I do remember my first personal experience with worry. Heidi had started first grade, and I worried about her safety when she walked to Lincoln School on the west side of town. The school district borders had changed by then and instead of the short walk to

Franklin, she had to attend Lincoln. Her walk equaled six blocks. She had to cross the Jefferson Street Bridge over Nettle Creek. That worried me most. The roadway itself didn't present any problem, but the sidewalk and its fence railing needed repair. Being protective of my baby sister brought with it ... worry.

One day I had come home from one of my many adventures and asked for Heidi. No one answered. Worry. I looked everywhere in the apartment, the bar, the restaurant; no luck. More worry. I thought of the bridge.

(In Greek) *Where is she? Oh God, please help me find her safe.*

I ran outside into the alley, around Carlson's service station to the other side of the block; no sign of her. I started to panic and ran around the block from one end to the other calling her name. These tense minutes constituted the first time I'd ever felt the anxiety associated with such a fear; a physical discomfort too. My heart raced. A sickening feeling came over me. My search lasted a minute—two minutes—three—four. I have no idea. I thought about running to the bridge but instead, I ran back home hoping she would be there. She was. Heidi looked puzzled and surprised when she saw me in such a state. She didn't know her visit across the street to her friend Tammy's apartment could ever cause her older brother to appear so distraught. How could she know that? I took a huge breath to settle down. I felt relieved and at the same time frightened by the intense emotions and sensations that ran through me.

What was that I just went through?

I remember trying to save a little face but I couldn't hide anything. I thanked God for hearing my prayer and hugged my little sister. That day I got my first big dose of worry. Worry? No, it bordered on terror.

Heidi and I regularly played things like make believe at home. One of my favorite movies at the time, *The Three Hundred Spartans*, found us cutting a cardboard box into pieces. We colored and re-assembled them with string into an arrangement loosely resembling Spartan armor. Together, she and I made two wooden swords, and we re-enacted the battle of Thermopylae in the room we called *the hall*. She showed good sportsmanship in that she agreed to play those boy games with me.

We enjoyed playing records too. Somehow we got wind of the practice of playing Beatle records backwards. We especially liked *Everybody's Trying to Be My Baby* written by Carl Perkins and not Lennon/McCartney or Harrison. We cracked up when we heard *eba reba shnaben eba reba shnaben* coming from the speakers.

Heidi will contest this, but the two of us got along pretty well as kids even if I did inherit some of my grandfather's tyrannical ways. Then the accident came.

We were wrestling on Mom and Dad's bed and Heidi, about seven years old at the time, fell off the bed onto the floor. She fell facing up; landing on her shoulders and neck area. She cried out, and laughs turned into tears as she complained her neck hurt. Worry. Worry and fear. Again I felt an awful sensation cover my body. Only this time—thinking *I* had hurt my little sister badly. Her collar bone had fractured, and she needed to wear a harness-like cast around her shoulders for weeks. When Heidi had an itch under the cast Mom, Ann, and I took turns passing a handkerchief under the cast pulling it back and forth to relieve the annoying itching. I was responsible for the accident, and I have regretted it all these years ... guilt. I've never forgiven myself for hurting her.

◆   ◆   ◆

Mom used instinct when it came to rearing her children. With only a sixth grade Greek education, she couldn't rely on books written in English for guidance on how to raise a family. She didn't have that luxury. Her method for being a mom came from the old world ways passed on from one generation to the next. Just how well that method worked in a new world setting I can only determine in retrospect. Here is my brief take on it.

Mom's strongest character trait is and always has been her deep love for her children. Therefore, it was never an issue of major consequence to me when I met with punishment. If I needed to be set straight she implemented her method the best way she knew how. In one of my personal favorites, I had frustrated her enough with my antics that she threatened to get the κάλαμιδι (kalameethee) or, four foot long, one inch narrow, rolling pin used to make phyllo dough. To get the full humor of this you really have to picture a fuming Greek mom firmly stating in Greek that she is "going to get the pastry stick!" in order to clobber you with it. Dodging the κάλαμιδι always made me laugh which in turn got Mom to laugh, and the moment turned into a fun one instead of a punishing one. Knowing how much she loved me and the many ways she showed that love; with hugs and kisses, cooking, cleaning, and nursing my injuries minimized any ill feelings I may have had toward her way of setting me straight.

The majority of immediate disciplinary action came from Mom more so than Dad. These ranged from a strong scolding to a little slap on the rear end, or several combination shots to the butt and shoulders as I ran away. I'm pretty sure I deserved what I got from pushing issues a little too far. As time passed and I grew bigger, it occurred to me how to cleverly diffuse the blows. I took the pain. This convinced Mom that the pain in her hand hurt more than the pain inflicted upon me. We were in the apartment dining room one day, and I did something to anger her. She whacked me on the upper arm, winced and rubbed her palm. We looked at each other for a moment. It reached a point where we started to laugh, and that ended the hitting forever. I hugged her.

I suppose Mom's old world method of loving your children deeply, and sacrificing much of personal desires worked well in the new world. Our church required this of adults taking on the responsibility of raising a family. Regarding corporal punishment; some scholars believe it is harmful while others don't. Personally, I don't have any deep emotional trauma from my mother slapping me on the behind a few times because of disrespect. A time for punishment existed in our home, but it wasn't excessive by any means. In many ways, occasional physical punishment meant deterrence more than anything else.

◆ ◆ ◆

Dad's employee, Art Mahaffey, or Happy, worked many years for Dad. Happy lived up to his nickname as a likeable, friendly, old man. He played piano, and sang songs to us kids when we visited the bar to hang out with Dad. One tune in particular that I remember—*Pretty Baby*, an old Dean Martin tune. I remember him singing it to us as he accompanied himself on the old stand up piano in the bar ...

Everybody loves a baby that's why I'm in love with you pretty baby, pretty baby ...

If a contemporary Happy equivalent exists in some small town bar today, he might be performing a Lennon/McCartney tune for the kids.

Happy used his musical talents to entertain me and my sisters on a regular basis, and he even taught us a little tune that I have remembered all these years. Place a piano in front of me, and I'll warm up with that tune. It has no title or lyrics to my knowledge. It reminds me of the warm up tune, *Swanee River* that Art Carney played on the piano for an episode of *The Honeymooners*, *$99,000 Answer*. In fact, now that I think of it, Happy resembled the thin Ed Norton character Carney played along side the heavy set Ralph Kramden (Jackie Gleason). Incidentally, *The Honeymooners*, a favorite of Dad's, used to exasperate Mom. She didn't quite get the humor of a husband shouting at his wife for most of each episode. Mom left the room before the end of the episode when Ralph always apologized to Alice, his wife, and they embraced to end the show. This isn't to say Dad was anything like Ralph Kramden temperamentally, because he wasn't at all. Dad never shouted out in anger except the few times I needed a little taste of parental guidance. He did have Ralph's body shape though.

In addition to working regularly behind the bar with Dad, Happy also did the extensive clean up on Sundays when the bar was closed. This allowed Dad time at home with his family watching the White Sox and the Bears play on TV after driving us to the All Saints Greek Orthodox Church in Joliet.

The Greek Orthodox Church has always been a source of strength and stability for our family. However, my understanding of the religion wasn't easily learned during Sunday services. In fact, I learned very little because services were delivered in Greek terms I couldn't understand. Additionally, the distance from home to the church prevented us from attending weekly. We didn't have the luxury of walking as did many others. We traveled twenty-five miles one way. Sunday school, as a result, never happened for me or my sisters. Most of what we learned came from Mom. What I remember most about what and how Mom explained things to us is quite simple. Church provided a holy place where families went to profess their love for the child of God. I learned how to cross myself at a very early age, as did every Greek boy and girl. She explained an important reason (among many) why we make the sign of the cross—to ask for the Lord's protection. I grew up hearing about the sweetness of the Christ child, and how all of our Orthodox faithful cherished and loved him. Mom also explained, in her loving motherly style, how Christ loved and cherished us as well. Our adorable savior, for the longest time in my young life, appeared to me as baby in a manger or on the lap of Blessed Mother Mary. Who couldn't love and adore a baby?

Those Sunday mornings at home were an interesting routine for me as a kid. I woke up as early as possible attempting to be the first in the only bathroom shared by the five of us. Breakfast always proved to be absolutely the best. While I lay on the floor watching Sunday morning westerns such as *Gene Autry,* or my favorite interplanetary adventures of *Flash Gordon,* Mom graced a busy kitchen. She fried a package each of Oscar Meyer bacon, sausages, and a dozen eggs. She also toasted up the better part of a long loaf of white bread. A big jar of Welch's grape jelly, butter, grapefruit halves, and fresh Hills Brothers coffee, were set on the table. The eggs sizzled sunny side up in the bacon and sausage grease. Floating aromas that drifted out of our kitchen toward me in front of the television set on Sunday mornings made my mouth water. With every delicious item ready, Mom called us in and the fun began. Each of us sat in the same place every time. Dad and I sat across from each other next to the windows to my left. Heidi sat to my right. Ann sat next to Dad, and Mom positioned herself at the head of the table. My favorite way to consume this morning feast was to make a sandwich out of an egg (or two), bacon, sausage, and grape jelly on toast—three slices. After having seen my mother do this, it became a regular Sunday breakfast ritual for me. Just thinking about it makes me want one right now. My family enjoyed this breakfast tradition on Sunday mornings for many years.

As time passed, Happy's age forced him to retire, and Sunday cleaning days saw me beginning my contribution to the family business. Aw shucks! Some mornings I missed Flash Gordon, but never the outstanding breakfast. My job included lifting chairs and stools off the floor, sweeping, mopping, and about once a month ... waxing the floors. Tables, chairs, stools, and booths all had to be cleaned. Mirrors required serious tar and nicotine removal from all the smoking. Ash trays needed washing—large glass ash trays stained with the sticky leftovers from smoldering, smelly cigarettes. Of all my cleaning chores, ash tray duty totally disgusted me. With no mechanical dishwasher, the ash trays, about twenty of them, had to be hand washed in hot soapy water. The smell almost gagged me. I preferred to be in my pajamas on the floor watching Flash fight the evil monsters from Planet Mongo.

Much to the disappointment of my father, on many Sundays I did stay home for *Flash Gordon* and showed up late for cleaning. He wouldn't call up the long stairwell to get me downstairs to help. Mom did that, which made it easier for me to create some excuse delaying my responsibilities. You see, fear of Mom could never match fear of Dad. I'd get down there just in time to help put the stools and chairs back down on the floor. Dad gave me the silent treatment accepting the fact that his young helper couldn't match up to Happy. Boy did I feel guilty. In retrospect, I wish I'd skipped TV and helped Dad more.

◆　　◆　　◆

Many of my friends over the years thought my hours spent in a bar were interestingly different. I got to hang out in a bar every day and watch baseball games, football, boxing, game shows, and the news while sitting at my favorite booth in front of the TV. During lunch hour I watched the Chicago news with a news anchor named Jori Luloff. Female news anchors were not common, so she stood out. I remember a hair product commercial for young women called *Hair So New*. The scene featured a floating platform on a still lake. The platform supported a group of young people dancing. These people were energetic, attractive, and having good fun—of course ... that's what commercials are all about. Here is the hook line for the jingle ... *When you're out on the dance floor with Hair So New, your hair will look like its dancing too. Hair So New!* I guess the pretty young ladies caught my eye, and the jingle did its job as well. Go figure.

My favorite booth always seemed available to me. The TV set was up about seven feet and three feet forward from my seat. It sat on a platform giving the entire front of the room easy viewing. Not many people liked having to look up at such an angle, but I didn't mind. I could lie down as if it were my private sofa. My seat at the edge of the booth had a permanent dent in it from my hours of occupation day and night. Below the TV, a narrow short hallway led to the side door on Jefferson Street. From this side entrance came many of Dad's customers and friends who had to pass by my seat on their way to the bar. One I'll always remember was Mr. Fruland—my friend Bill's dad. After parking his car Mr. Fruland walked in, turned the corner and encountered me glued to something on the TV. He always said, "Hi Mike" and rubbed the top of my head. I thought it was cool to be greeted that way by my buddy's old man—or, *Fru*, as his friends called him. Mr. Fruland worked in the business office of the Morris Paper Mill also known as The Federal Paperboard Company. The Paper Mill functioned as one of the biggest employers in town if not the biggest. It's been said many times, that everyone in town, if they didn't work there, knew someone who did. I knew many. Years later I actually worked there for a while.

I think some of Dad's favorite times while working his own business included those nights when the Frulands, Fru and Helen, Bernie and Shirley Ravnaas, Orvel and Verna Larson, Bernie and Marge Roth, and Sam and Gretchen Johnson all got together during warm summer weekends, or cold Christmas holiday Saturday nights. Witnessing those festive evenings as I watched television in my booth, filled my senses with sights, sounds, and smells of camaraderie, laughter, cigarettes, and perfume. This was all so normal ... so ... home to me—a group of friends partying with my Mom and Dad. I knew them well and felt perfectly comfortable as a grade school aged kid walking behind the bar for a bag of chips and a 7Up or Coke. I exchanged smiles and greetings with the group. They were a fun loving crowd who held their alcohol well.

Never once in all the time spent in Harry's Cocktail Lounge, or at home for that matter, did I ever see my dad the least bit intoxicated. He would not drink during work except for special occasions such as one drink, a *Tom and Jerry*, for New Year's Eve or Christmas. He knew his responsibilities and his priorities. As for Mom, she never had more than half a glass of anything alcoholic (and diluted with water) if she drank at all. As a young boy, my role models—my parents and their patron friends—were wise and respectable in our environment of beer, wine, and hard liquor; a great lesson.

♦ ♦ ♦

Louis Nichols, who owned the bar originally, gave my sister Ann a watch for her grade school graduation gift. He purchased it at Bill Ostrem's jewelry store directly across Liberty Street. Mr. Ostrem, a tall gentleman in his late sixties, came in for a drink once in a while. He came in one day shortly after Ann got her watch. She approached him to show off her watch and he said …

"Yes, Ann, it's a lovely watch. Especially because of those Canardley Diamonds there," he pointed out.

My sister, surprised to hear that her watch had diamonds curiously inquired …

"Canardley Diamonds?"

"Why sure … Canardley … because you *canardley* see 'em," he joked.

Little bits like that, all in good fun, came from many of the adults over the years while my sisters and I visited the bar.

I listened to live organ music by Gladys Tabler when Dad swapped out the bar for the stage. I shared time (almost every night) with adults who drank beer, wine, and liquor while enjoying the organ music from Mrs. Tabler. Some of them were intoxicated to various degrees while most simply enjoyed a few drinks showing no inebriation whatsoever. Local merchants stopped in at the end of the day for one drink before going home. Others came later and stayed longer for the live music.

There were so many interesting characters I got to know, affording me plenty of unusual conversations my friends missed out on. I did, however, manage to pass a few choice stories along to them. One of my favorite Morris bar enthusiasts was an affable, thin, man of Norwegian ancestry in his forties named Henry Thorson. Hank, it seemed to me, did his excessive drinking to help soothe his broken heart. He and his wife were going through a divorce and he felt badly for his children. He missed his children, but got to see them as per his settlement in court. Hank entered Dad's place many times late in the afternoon carrying bags with groceries and gifts for his kids. I found that to be touchingly fatherly on his part. After his shopping, Hank managed to stop in several bars for a drink or two before going home. By the time he got to Dad's he'd be feeling no pain singing his favorite tune, snapping his fingers, and letting out his signature expressions of "Whoopee!" and "Here we go!" I got to be quite good at imitating him. Of course Dad, having the compassionate heart that he did, handled Hank with a gentle yet firm style. He simply said hello to Hank and told him to go home—Dad's way of saying no more drinks as soon as he walked in. Here is an example (from a few years ahead in time) of how the Hank Thorson visits went.

The front Martini door swung open and in sauntered a singing Hank.

"If you happen to see the most beautiful girl in the world, tell her to—hiya Harry!" sang Hank.

"Hellooo, Henry," Dad greeted.

"Whoopee, here we go!"

"Yeah, okay nephew." Dad often referred to some of the guys as nephews.

"Uncle Harry, gimme a Bud. Whoopee!"

"No, Henry. Go home now," Dad gently said.

"No? No Bud, Harry? Alright then; whoopee!" Hank managed to slur while feigning a look of drunken surprise. He knew Dad would not serve him. So, rather than sit on a stool and ask again, Hank, with his arms full of shopping bags, walked the length of the bar and back. He said hello to anyone there with a twinkle dance step as he sang …

"If you happen to see the most beautiful … Hiya Mike," he'd say to me when he passed me in my favorite booth watching TV.

"Hi Hank," I politely responded. I felt sorry for him even though his antics made me laugh, and I imitated him later for my mom and sisters creating one of our mini laugh fests. He spotted Mom through the door to the restaurant.

"Hiya Libby!" he called out.

"Hello Henry," Mom said with a touch of sorrow in her voice.

Hank made a turn back to the front door.

"Okay, Harry … see ya later … bye Mike."

"Good-bye Hank," I said.

"Bye now, Henry. Be good and go home now, okay? thaaank you."

When Dad said *thank you*, he didn't speak the words. He delivered them in a more sing-song-like fashion. He stretched it out—"Thaaank yoou."

"Okay … here we go … whoopee … if you happen to see the most beautiful girl in the world tell her to stick …"

The door closed; Hank moved on.

Dad had a good handle on keeping track of how much a customer had to drink. He knew when to stop serving and he politely refused to serve any more drinks when he thought a person had had enough. He ran the most respectable drinking establishment on Liberty Street. Everyone knew it too. Those who didn't, who may not have been regulars, found out soon enough.

My dad, the tough young man from Epirus who fought off wild dogs in the mountains of his youth; a young man who learned how to converse with Chicago mobsters, also managed to keep trouble makers out of his place of business. He told me a story of a young, local hot shot, fighter type fella who entered the front door one night and took a seat at the bar. He had been drinking elsewhere and had trouble on his mind from the start. The punk tested my dad—big mistake. The fella must have thought youth translated into superior strength. He learned the hard way never to come into Harry's Cocktail Lounge wearing a big *A* for *ass* on his forehead. After repeated verbal improprieties, Dad did his best to diffuse the hothead with calm warnings. The tension eventually reached its peak, and with a swift leap over the bar, Dad surprised this *mental giant* grabbing him by the back of his neck and the seat of his pants. In a few seconds the bum flew out the front martini door—so much for younger being stronger. In those days, bullies were treated with an immediate strong response and they got the message. Dad's countering move caused the fella never to disrespect him again. He showed up days or weeks later, and when he did, he actually apologized. From then on, the few times the fella returned—he behaved himself.

◆　◆　◆

Dad, a gentle man God bless him, showed respect for others. Respect always came first. Once while we were riding back home to Morris from a Chicago visit, Ann asked Dad ...

"Daddy, what does *considerate* mean?"

He thought for a moment as he drove his maroon and white, 1955, Buick Special along the highway. I waited to hear the answer.

"Think about the other fella," he said.

Douglas A. Hynds worked as a banker in Morris who came into the lounge late in the afternoons after banker's hours. Mr. Hynds was a stately, well dressed man about the same age as Dad; perhaps a few years older. He spoke with a deep and very old school voice—a robust gentleman. He always took a seat at the end of the bar where it came to a corner against the mirrored back wall. Visiting Harry's Cocktail Lounge probably gave him relief from the high finance headaches at The First National Bank one block away on Liberty Street. Mr. Hynds ordered beer—Old Style—and beer nuts. He sat quietly and read the newspaper as he unwound in his special corner of the bar.

In 1991, long after both men had retired, Mr. Hynds sent a thank you note to Dad. It says the following ...

> *Harry, you have the nicest ways of making other people happy. Thanks so much for all your thoughtfulness. God bless you. Thank you for the visit. I enjoyed it very, very much. My regards to your wife and family.*
>
> *Sincerely, Doug.*

My dad saved that card in his dresser drawer. I have the card now. Judging from a subsequently added sticky note which apologizes for the card's late arrival, it appears that Mr. Hynds was in some level of geriatric care. The sentiment looks to have been dictated to and written by a younger female. Mr. Hynds for sure wrote the closing, and his signature—*Sincerely, Doug*—is definitely written in the hand of an old man.

Dad never forgot his friends and would gladly shop for a few tasty delights such as fruit, bread, cheese, and wine to deliver upon visiting them. When Dad visited Mr. Hynds on that day in the spring of 1991, it may very well have been the last time they ever saw each other. Whether he brought a bag filled with treats for his old friend—I don't know. It may have been inappropriate due to Mr. Hynds' health. I am positive however, that Dad at least thought of bringing something.

Attorney, August Black, was also one of Dad's dear friends. Along with Uncle Nick, our fellow Greek friend and barber, and George Tolias, the men enjoyed day trips to Chicago's northwest suburban premier horse racing track, Arlington Park. After a day of fun at the races they drove to Greek Town near downtown Chicago for dinner, live music, and belly dancing at one of the several Greek restaurants on and around Halsted Street.

As Dad's lawyer and general consultant, Mr. Black never failed to advise my father with stalwart information when necessary. He helped Dad with income taxes and other legal business affairs. Augie Black, as Dad always referred to him, headed a large family. Together he and his wife, Marie, managed a busy home filled with seven children; George, Don, Frank, Jean, Ed, Linda, and Ritchie. During many of our family trips to Chicago's Greek Town and its ethnic grocery stores, Dad and Mom made sure to place several items in a separate cardboard box as a gift to the Augie Black family. Included in these boxes were many of the delightful Greek products we loved. Mom and Dad packed olives, olive oil, feta cheese, dried figs, bread, halva, pomegranates, honey sesame seed bars, wine, perhaps a bottle of Ouzo or Metaxa, even some of Mom's homemade Greek cookies—outstanding packages from the heart ... Mom's and Dad's. I remember the faces of Mr. and Mrs. Black and their family as they searched through these treasure boxes removing each item and smiling broadly.

As thoughtful and kind as my dad was with respect to others, he could also take care of himself in potentially threatening situations. If someone were to cross that *proverbial line,* well ... trespassers beware. Dad often walked away from the bar to run a quick errand to Matteson's Hardware up the block, or go into the basement for supplies leaving the bar unattended. People knew this. Even when working alone in the mid afternoon with a few customers enjoying refreshing drinks at the bar—if he had to go out for a couple minutes, he did.

A man I remember as, Scottie, a relatively new guy in town, showed up in the afternoons for a beer and got to know Dad. During the mid-afternoon lull, sometimes Scotty sat in the bar alone with Dad. After a period of time, Dad began noticing items missing after returning from his errands. Unable to prove anything for certain, Dad continued his regular behavior while at the same time building up his suspicion of this fella named Scottie. Weeks passed and Dad devised a plan. Apparently Scottie worked as a locksmith at some point. Dad kept an old safe in the basement and one day asked Scottie to take a look at the safe's *problematic* locking mechanism. So, with the skeleton key used to lock and unlock the basement door, Dad led the way into the dimly lit cellar. Dad kneeled down and began turning the safe's combination lock with Scottie behind him. When the safe door opened and Dad stood up, he turned to see Scottie poised with a gun in an attempt to rob him. In such a close proximity Dad quickly managed to disarm the bum. The details as to how Dad had accomplished this were never explained to me by my *father of few words* when he repeated this story some years later. He only said he took the gun away from the fella and told him to get out and never come back ... or else. We never saw him again. Not much longer after that event we learned Scottie found a new home in Stateville Penitentiary in Joliet for similar crimes. I guess he encountered others who preferred to call the police rather than take matters into their own hands like Dad.

◆   ◆   ◆

I grew up knowing my dad as a tough man who never complained about hard work. He carried out his labors with a quiet, patient, focus and rarely showed anger or frustration when things went wrong. I wish I had more of that quality in me. From an early age I realized I could blow my top if and when I was pushed enough, which on some occasions didn't take much. One such time came when one of my newly arrived younger cousins from Greece had pestered me long enough.

Mom's youngest brother, Milton, and his family emigrated from Greece and briefly lived with us before moving to Chicago. Their oldest child, Penny, a few years younger than I, had been badgering me for some time. After my repeated requests that she stop, it reached the point where I lashed out in frustration.

"Leave me alone you little son of a bitch!" I shouted.

I guess she understood that much English. She ran downstairs to tell my Dad. Shortly after her departure I heard the door open at the bottom of the stairs and a big voice.

"Mike?"

Uh oh ... I'm dead now.

I listened to the sound of my dad's footsteps climbing the stairs. He muttered a few choice Greek phrases, mostly to himself, until he reached the top of the stairs. I met him there, and I stood frozen in fear when I saw the look on his face. When my dad showed anger, his face turned red and this shade of red belonged to me.

"Don't you talk like that again," he fumed. He bypassed me, which I thought strange since I expected at least a firm grip about my shoulders. Instead, he went directly into the closet at the top of the stairs.

Oh boy ... I'm really dead now.

I knew exactly, the contents behind that closet door; coats, shoes—a barber's strop. A two foot long, three inch wide, double strip of brown leather that had long ago been retired, was about to become acquainted with a particular part of my skinny body. I couldn't move. For years Dad used the straight razor method of shaving before the Gillette, double edge, blue, safety blades hit the market. With new shaving technology in the Skopes residence, the strop found a new home in the closet until that afternoon when it came out of retirement ... lucky me.

In what seemed like a millisecond, the strop found my rear end for two well placed whacks. You know, I can honestly say it didn't hurt that much. What hurt me more, was knowing how I had upset my father. I deeply disappointed him. I mishandled a situation which to him seemed like nothing to get excited about—a little girl pestering an older boy. Not exactly a pack of wild dogs.

It ended with a stern look. He returned the strop to the closet and went back downstairs to work. My father couldn't or wouldn't strike me with his hand. It's as if there had to be something between us. Something else had to be the instrument of pain striking me, his son. He passed me and went directly to the closet. I stood right there in his path and he walked by me. Wow.

That one moment of corporal punishment was the first and only time my father ever inflicted physical pain on me. As a twelve year old boy, that incident helped me get the point. He knew it too. We never experienced another remotely similar clash in our relationship.

Dad was truly a humble man of few words; an honest man. I recently came across an obscure quote in my local newspaper describing a man so honest, you could play craps with him over the phone. That is a great way to describe my dad. His life's lessons of good character to my sisters Ann, Heidi, and me were taught to us mainly by demonstration and to a lesser extent—spoken. He showed us how to do something more so than explaining it. He simply got our attention and performed the task quietly; a sort of learn by osmosis. For example; in the basement of the bar preparing to go hunting one weekend (I couldn't have been more than ten), he showed me how to lace his hunting boots. A simple task you say—not really. They were the early 1940s army style boots that laced all the way up to the knee. That's a lot of laces to control without tangling them. The boots' lower halves had holes for the almost mile long laces, and the tops of the boots were all hooks. I stood and watched closely as he began to lace through the holes, stopping occasionally to pull the laces tight. Onto the tricky hook section; without a word he crisscrossed the laces—each time tossing the excess to one side. I watched intensely while sitting on an empty Schlitz beer case (his favorite beer). He laced both boots without a word of verbal instruction. It must have worked because afterwards, I never had a problem with hooks and bootlaces.

2

The Basket

The one place where Mom started learning English, "little by little" as she puts it, was The Basket. The restaurant which served breakfast, lunch, and dinner became a classroom and a social outlet for the new, young, beautiful, and auburn haired foreigner in town. It soon became her place of employment as well. She started working in the restaurant when I was about five. Up until that time she stayed at home, devoting her time and energy to the family and making sure her son stayed out of trouble. She didn't worry about her daughter because *mischief* wasn't her middle name as it was mine. Then a year later she had to stop because of being pregnant with Heidi. Mom worked the restaurant on and off a few times during the apartment years. She took time off for family, and when Dad rented the restaurant out to others. Honestly, The Basket did much better business when Mom managed it along with Dad.

The Basket floor plan included a counter with room for six or seven stools. There were three square tables for four in the center of the room and five small deuces along the three perimeter walls away from the counter. A doorway at the east end of the counter led into the cocktail lounge. From the outside, the most striking feature of The Basket was its large square window with *The Basket* hand painted on it. The only other significant item was the big yellow sign that hung over the sidewalk.

One of my favorite ways to spend time in the restaurant (besides eating) included sitting at the little table by the huge window and watching the events of the street outside—especially winter snowfall. Winter, being my preferred season of choice, provided excellent opportunities to sit by the long radiator next to the window to keep warm. I kept busy with such things as reading comic books and teaching myself how to shave. I had a toy, battery operated, electric shaver with a little cord sporting a suction cup at the end simulating the plug. I stuck the suction cup onto the huge Basket plate glass window and pretended to shave while I sipped a hot chocolate. After the close shave, I leaned back in my seat and fired up a fat, pink, bubble gum, cigar emulating my Uncle Nick. I called out for another burger and fries and went out to play in the snow after getting the, *you've had enough to eat*, look from the management. Imagine seeing a little kid doing that now. Do those shave toys still exist?

Many of the restaurant's menu items were served in a plastic basket lined with a sheet of kitchen paper which was the idea for the restaurant's name. I can't tell you how many baskets full of delicious burgers, fried chicken, tenderloins, grilled cheese *samiches* (as I playfully called them), fried shrimp, and fries satisfied my bottomless pit appetite. For as long as I can remember, I've been able to eat large amounts of food and never gain appropriately associated weight ... at least for the first forty-five years. Now, it is quite a different story. My body finally signaled me to stop, or else. For those restaurant years especially, I thank God for a high metabolism because I loved food so much. Mom often commented on the amount I could eat, and she got to the point of chasing me out of the restaurant because I so often wanted more. Seriously, she literally chased me out a few times, much to the amusement of many regular customers enjoying their lunches or dinners. Mom surely must have been thrilled to see me ride off on my bike headed for Chapin Park, or to ride all over town for hours. It meant not having to feed me. Then of course, I had to come home ... eventually. And guess who had built up a huge appetite? If not another cheeseburger and chocolate malt, I wanted more blueberry pie, or lemon meringue, or cherry, or whatever the pastry case contained. No, I didn't have a tapeworm.

Oh man, the pies! The most amazing pies came from the Fasano Pie Company twenty-five miles away in Joliet. To this day, they are the reason I love pie more than any other dessert. I made it my mission to be the first person to cut into any freshly delivered pie. I didn't care what kind; banana cream, coconut cream, peach, pumpkin, rhubarb, raisin, custard, chocolate cream, apple, cherry, boysenberry, anyberry, veryberry; pie! I had to have pie! Ala mode if you please. Don't forget the milk and two re-fills. Yes, milk disappeared in a hurry with me around. I could drink half a gallon a day. For this, Mom made it my responsibility to run over to the Straightway Dairy for double orders of milk.

"Don't forget the receipt, Mikey," Mom reminded me.

Did I mention French fries? Oh yeah. Let me tell you about the fries. These were not ordinary, long, thin, frozen, barely potato fries. Oh no ... no way. These were the best Idaho spuds purchased in bulk every two or three weeks from the greatest vegetable market in the Midwest. The wholesale market, just west of downtown Chicago, filled an entire neighborhood several blocks long with vendor after vendor. They provided every vegetable known to man. These foods were delivered to the market vendors by hundreds of trucks large and small. The trucks came from farms all over the state and other parts of the country as well. You'll recall earlier, that I mentioned Dad performed that job for a while. He delivered goods from his farm jobs around Grundy and other area counties. He knew his way around the market area just as well as he knew his way around country roads surrounding Morris. Dad had an amazing sense of direction. I often wondered how he found all these places. A true man, he never asked for directions. His own personal adventures as a young single man for so many years must have taken him on plenty of memorable road trips. Anyway, we loaded hundred pound burlap sacks of potatoes and other items into the trunk of his car. These were later stored in the restaurant storage room we called, *the back room.* The back room had storage shelves, a bathroom, and a twin size cot where Mom could rest when necessary. When prep work was done in the kitchen or in the back room, it always involved peeling those fresh, large tubers. Talk about KP duty; each one had to be hand peeled by Mom, Dad, Ann, or even me, little Mikey, when I wasn't away on some imaginative excursion. We placed the peeled potato into an antique French fry cutter—a sturdy, gray metal, industrial restaurant monster about a foot long. It was bolted onto the prep counter; a Veg-o-Matic on steroids. I didn't care much for peeling the potatoes, but I loved using the cutter. Customers watched as the device sliced long perfect strips. We inserted the potato into the open bay or slot parallel with the prep counter and pulled the handle. To the left was the sharp blade plate sectioned in 3/8 inch squares. To the right—the handle which when pulled, pushed the potato through the cutting squares and out into a waiting bowl; ingenious, fresh cut French fries ready for the deep fryer. These fries were known and described by many, as the best French fries in town. I personally can attest to that. I think I ate about a hundred thousand of them.

About every other day, Mom changed her homemade soups. These awesome tasting pots of gastronomical excellence included; navy bean, vegetable beef, split pea with ham, chicken with rice or noodles, and lentil—I loved them all. She served a daily special that sold out by the end of the day. Monday, customers could always expect beef stew, Tuesday usually meant Swiss steak, meat loaf on Wednesday, spaghetti and meat sauce for Thursday, fish on Friday, and liver and onions served on Saturday. During winter and other holiday seasons, the daily specials changed to include excellent comfort food dishes such as Mulligan stew, and corned beef and cabbage. For ninety cents, most specials included a small house salad, bread and butter, mashed potatoes or a side of veggies. I say most, because mashed potatoes and spaghetti didn't really go well together. By the way, the mashed potatoes were made from freshly boiled potatoes, fresh milk, salt, and pepper. No flaked, or boxed instant stuff there. What a great deal. Lots of good old fashioned hard work and care went into Mom's American fare menu. She didn't serve Greek food in the restaurant. Greek recipes were only for our home.

◆ ◆ ◆

The Basket had many regular customers of all ages. Young mothers came in with their babies and youngsters for early evening suppers. She had old folks very fond of the home style cooking from scratch for lunch and dinner. Old Ole Greenley seemed to never miss Monday's beef stew. Daily lunch hour saw our small business very busy with downtown shoppers coming in and local shopkeepers on lunch breaks. Local high school teens frequented the restaurant for the burgers, famous fries, and the juke box. The three guys I remember best, Jeff Peterson, John Sparks, and Gary Rose usually came in together. Jeff, a well behaved upstanding teen, lived around the corner on Wauponsee Street. He reminded me of Dobie Gillis from the sit-com of the same name. When those three came in together, The Basket became party time. They dropped quarters in the juke box, sat back and enjoyed cheeseburgers, fries and Cokes or Pepsi. Back then a quarter was good for three songs. They selected songs such as *Roses Are Red* by Bobby Vinton, *Hello Mary Lou* by Ricky Nelson, and for Mom they selected the instrumental version of *Never on Sunday* by the Don Costra Orchestra. She'd start singing the lyrics in Greek which entertained the boys. She loved to sing and showed no sign of stage fright as The Basket transformed into her stage. Singing came easily for her; a natural talent that always made her smile. Those guys had more fun making Mom laugh with their sarcasm and good natured humor, most of which Mom had a difficult time understanding. Her English had improved quite a bit by then, but the subtle clever banter the three boys offered up could frustrate her sometimes. The teens and Mom enjoyed good fun as they got a kick out of entertaining each other, and I took residence on one of the counter stools and watched the show between sips of my chocolate malt.

I met so many people while spending time with Mom in the little café. One young man in his late twenties, Dave Osmanson, worked for the city and spoke with an unusual high pitched voice; a real High Pitched Dave. He moved about in quick determined motions, slightly bent over, and pursed his lips often. Not as a show of disapproval of anything, but simply a nervous routine that went along with blinking his eyes and pushing his glasses up all the time. High Pitch Dave, a friendly fellow, usually came in for a cup of coffee to go. He seemed busy or preoccupied all the time. I picture him entering, saying in his high voice, "Hello Libby, cup of coffee to go please." Upon seeing me enjoying another wonderful meal, he gave a quick, "Hi Mike," then grabbed his coffee, pushed up his glasses, and promptly walked out the door.

Every time I hear an old song that I recognize from the juke box in The Basket, I see the tables and chairs, the tablecloths, the long counter and stools, the customers, and my parents working the entire day together. They moved back and forth between the bar and the restaurant taking orders, making drinks, cooking, serving, working the cash registers, and washing dishes—a constant almost choreographed flow of activities they performed as a team. I can hear the sound of the restaurant screen door swinging open followed by its return spring straining to close the door again. I hear the main door with its large glass window open and close with a shudder. My parents had help from Ann as she got older, but Mom and Dad basically worked those long hours alone. They took turns breaking each other out by going upstairs in the mid afternoon during slow time for short naps. This exhausting work schedule continued six days a week, and one day … it started. I saw a little disappointment in Mom's eye. She came to America for this?

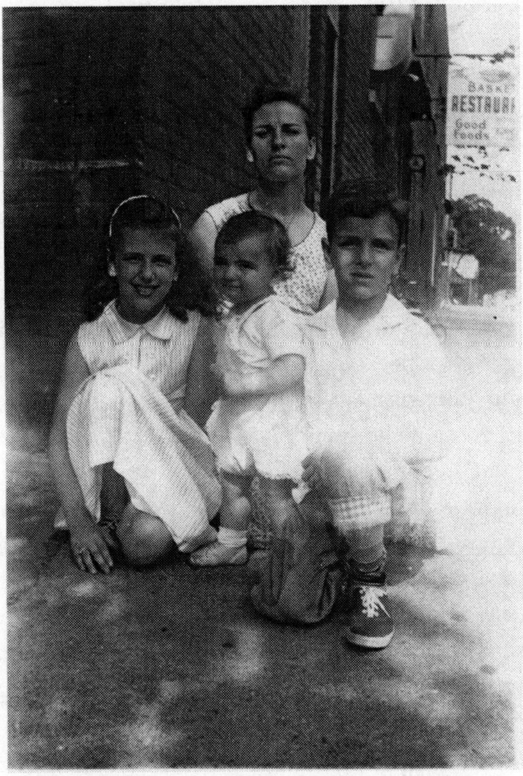
RESTAURA
Good
Foods

3

My Pal

$\mathcal{M}$om had one sister, Efthalia, and five brothers; Chris, George, Gus, Bill, and Milton. Of the four who made the plucky move to America, Mom arrived first. Her future efforts along with Dad's helped to bring her sister, Efthalia and two brothers Bill and Milton to America.

Uncle Bill followed Mom's lead after a few years and assimilated into American society. He came directly to Morris and lived with us for three or four years. In this next picture we are at the George Dellos farm. I'm wearing my Davey Crocket T-shirt, which I loved, and my favorite gun and holster set. Mom knew little boys and farm visits necessitated wearing the grubbiest pants available—so, as you can see, I did. I didn't care. The great outdoors, the Morris countryside my father loved so much and shared with me, continued calling out to me.

Uncle Bill (Theo Vassili in Greek), became my Pal. We called each other Pal. He spent time with me doing many of the things I might have done with my father who usually focused his attention on the business and not so much on playtime. In fact, I don't recall engaging in the simple father/son pastime of playing catch with Dad. Uncle Bill, younger and more playful, tossed the ball, pushed the swing, and carried me on his back. I remember Mom kneeling behind me teaching me to swing my bat as Uncle Bill tossed the underhand pitch from a few feet away. Her instructions on when to swing were in Greek of course.

Back in the fifties, baseball dominated sports talk in Morris and everywhere else for that matter. It consumed the attentions of every little boy and the big ones too. Games played on the TV in Dad's bar virtually every day during baseball season. At home, Dad, Uncle Bill, and I loved the Chicago White Sox. The bar had both types of fans, Sox and Cubs, exchanging animated opinions as to which was the better team. Dad loved the White Sox and naturally his influence carried over to Uncle Bill and me.

The first professional baseball game I attended turned out to be at the old Comiskey Park on Chicago's south side. At about five or six years old, I, along with Dad, Uncle Bill, and Uncle Nick (the barber), piled into Dad's old gray Pontiac, (about a 1950 vintage), and embarked on the first of many exciting adventures. Oh boy, my first guys only adventure—a road trip.

My memory of this road trip begins when the Pontiac bites the dust a few miles away from the stadium. I don't remember saying good-bye to Mom as we left Jefferson Street. There is no memory of the ride to the city; nothing, only the beginning of the Pontiac's demise. The car had stopped dead—unable to move another inch on that hot, muggy, summer day somewhere on Chicago's south side. Uncle Nick had his ever present cigar in his mouth and a non-mechanically inclined look on his face. What could a barber do for a conked out old car, take a little off the hardtop and dent the sides? Dad puffed on a Lucky Strike, and together with Uncle Bill they checked under the hood for any clue. I waited in the car breathing in the hot, humid, Chicago air. Nothing they did could resurrect the old Pontiac. It had conked out for good. A tow truck arrived, and I guess Dad sold it on the spot because from there we got into a taxi cab, and I never saw the old Pontiac again.

What a great adventure. The car died. I watched it get towed away, and then I sat in the jump seat of a taxi cab for the last couple miles on my way to see my favorite baseball team. We made it to Comiskey Park eventually taking our seats well into the game. At the park, we sat behind home plate slightly toward first base about twenty-five rows back. We were near one of those steel pillars that supported the upper deck. I vividly recall Nelson Fox coming up to bat, and I jumped up and shouted as loudly as I could, "Come on Nelly!" Dad bought practically every baseball treat available for me. Peanuts, a hot dog, ice cream, and who knows what else fueled my excitement. I'm surprised I didn't puke all over somebody as I watched our White Sox play the Baltimore Orioles and pitcher

Milt Pappas; a Greek like me! I even got a Milt Pappas autographed post card which I still have.

I have no memory of leaving the ball park after the game ended. Probably sleep walking by then, we caught a train back home to Morris. The Rock Island coach car rolling back and forth must have rocked me into an exhausted little boy sleep. My final memory of this swell adventure is waking up just enough to recognize my Pal carrying me off the train at the Morris train depot late at night. I got a whiff of his Vitalis hair oil and realized that I had become the baggage at the train station. The click clack of the train wheels rolling away, the creosote railroad tie smell, and the fuzzy sight of Liberty Street were my final sensory perceptions. Her humid, hazy, street light glow bathed our lonely footsteps in the night. My first adventure with the guys ended in a foggy vision of Liberty Street. My Pal carried me all the way home.

◆ ◆ ◆

Uncle Bill had landed a job at *Self Locking* and worked there for most of the time he lived with us. Working at the packaging manufacturing plant on Armstrong Street, he made egg cartons. I remember the black lunch pail that he carried to and from work every day. Mom usually stocked it for him with bread, feta cheese, a tomato, green onions, Greek olives, maybe a left over lamb chop, stuffed peppers or squash, and a thermos of hot coffee. Uncle Bill often wore a light, gray, zippered jacket over his short sleeved work shirt. He didn't know how to drive then, so he walked to and from work; about a two mile round trip. I remember saying good-bye to him in the afternoon and watching him walk off to his second shift factory job.

During off work hours, if we weren't watching baseball or football on television together, Dad, Uncle Bill, and I stayed up late on weekends to enjoy a little professional wrestling. My two favorite wrestlers were Dick the Bruiser and The Crusher. Both men were fun to watch as individuals, but when they got together as a tag team ... wow! The Bruiser and The Crusher had stocky muscular builds and snarling faces framed in light, blond hair crew cuts. They looked pretty fierce to me. They also chewed on fat cigars as they flexed and contorted their mugs for the cameras. We loved those guys. The Bruiser and The Crusher were always good for a big laugh after they beat the tar out of their opponents.

There is something to be said about having stayed up late with Dad and Uncle Bill, the camaraderie that developed between a little kid and his elders. Sharing that late night time together proved to be special no matter what we may have watched on the tube from *Shock Theater* to pro wrestling. Regardless, those late night moments past regular bed time had a special way of solidifying our relationships.

◆ ◆ ◆

Pal, handy with tools and making repairs around the apartment, put his carpentry skills to work for Mom by building a kitchen cabinet and counter top surrounding the kitchen sink. He built it from scratch with plywood, narrow pine boards, plain knobs, nails, and screws. I watched him design and build the whole thing off the top of his head with hardly a plan on paper before hand. When fully constructed, he painted it kitchen white. Uncle Bill's effort so pleased my mother.

Uncle Bill surprised me one day with an 8 x 4 sheet of plywood with railroad tracks attached to it in an oval configuration. My Lionel train set gave me hours of alone time. As I lay on my stomach on the bare plywood's center, my imagination filled in all the blank space on the plywood. I had room for every building, car, truck, crossing gate, mountain, forest, animal and whatever else I imagined to be there. In hindsight, that plain, simple set up was one of the best toys I ever had.

After a few years with us, my Pal announced his intention of returning to Greece to be married. Life charged on. Of course I objected to losing my Pal even if only for a short while. My sense of time wasn't too keen. I only knew his leaving brought me a profound sadness.

One Saturday morning some number of weeks or months later while asleep in my bed, a gentle shaking on my shoulder awakened me. The smell of Vitalis wafted through the air. I opened my sleepy eyes to see … my Pal! He had returned and I cried like a baby as I threw my arms around him and squeezed a hug of all hugs. Behind him stood this beautiful young woman I'd never seen before; his new bride, my new Aunt Frieda. Waking from a deep sleep and seeing my Pal kneeling at the edge of my bed literally left me speechless. In fact, my intense joy did nothing but make me cry and hug him so hard. I couldn't say a word as I listened to Mom, my Pal, and his new wife commenting on my emotional display. They knew how much I loved and missed my Pal. They knew how much it meant to me to have him back.

My Aunt Frieda, was then and still is today, one of the sweetest, kindest, women I've ever known. A bright and cheerful personality, genuinely pleased to accommodate guests in her home, she welcomes everyone with warm loving smiles. She and Uncle Bill, after their return to Morris, lived with us briefly. Soon afterwards, they moved to Chicago. Once again I had to say good-bye to my Pal. This time, however, instead of half way around the world he was only an hour's drive away.

4

Carlson's Service Station

lick, click, clunk, swoosh, and crash—in the distance. *Click, click, clunk, and swoosh, crash—closer—louder.* Those sounds were my warm weather, early Saturday morning alarm clock while the sun rose slowly in the sky. It cast long shadows on the pavement. I kept my two bedroom windows opened wide during the night allowing cool evening breezes in so I could sleep easier. In the morning the opened windows let in the early avian reports. Chirping robins, sparrows, and blackbirds sang their songs. Crashing flows of coins interrupted the chirping melodies and were the only other early morning sounds. One after another, the parking meters on Liberty and Jefferson Streets let loose their cascading rivers of change. Pennies, nickels, dimes, and quarters flowed like mini waterfalls into a metal pail. Loud and harsh as the noise may have been, I found it a comforting sound knowing an officer worked below making his collection rounds beneath my window. I looked out my bedroom window to catch a glimpse of old Officer Tony methodically inserting his magical key into each parking meter. He lifted the door to the change bin and out flowed cold, hard, cash right into his pail. From the pail, the change went into a long narrow metal container on wheels for easy transport along the route.

In every season, rain, freeze, or shine, someone had the meter collection duty. In my early years it was Officer Tony, the friendly elderly man who stopped during the day to chat with us as we played on the sidewalk. Each of those mornings with my window open, I heard the rushing coins; I awoke for another day on Liberty Street. If I ran out quickly enough, I said hello to Officer Tony before he got too far away. He was a kind old soul who didn't object to me following him part way along his route. He even let me turn the key to release the money.

With my first chore for the day completed, time came for my next breakfast of Maypo, or Cream of Wheat, oatmeal, or Malt-O-Meal, cold cereal, maybe some French toast, eggs and bacon, or whatever Mom had cooking at home or downstairs in the restaurant. Mom's wonderful food warmed my heart and satisfied my hunger. Reading about bursts of energy on the back of my Jets cereal box, got my motor running. My mind raced, fueled by the graphics and ad agency propaganda on the back panel. Visions of riding my bike into another day of adventure charged my imagination. Zoom!

Where should I go today? I know.

◆ ◆ ◆

Local gasoline stations or service stations were on several corners in the downtown area of Liberty Street during my youth. The station I knew best, Carlson's Standard Oil, operated across the alley from our building. Mr. Milton Carlson owned the business for at least thirty years until he retired and his son, Gerry (pronounced Gary), took it over. The following photograph is of young Gerry demanding of his father the rights to future ownership. How could any father refuse such an enterprising young man? It seems apprenticeship under the gun on the wild streets of Morris began at an early age for the Carlson family. Half a block away and a dozen years later instead of using a gun, I smashed a beer bottle over the bar and held it out toward my dad demanding the rights to serve spirits to the locals thirsting for a cold one ... just kidding. The following picture is Gerry Carlson starring in, *Stick 'em up Daddy!*

With the station only a few yards from the rear windows of our first apartment, I adopted portions of the property as my backyard. Just across the alley lay an area surfaced with gravel, shaded by two or three big trees, and large enough for two cars to park. One car parked in there belonged to John Panaiotou (also Greek) who owned the Andan Café next door to Dad's bar. The other car was Dad's. Dad and Uncle John must have had some kind of agreement with Mr. Carlson to use this space for parking. The details of that agreement had to be verbal and informal. But, knowing the way neighbors were neighborly back then, I'm not surprised to learn from Gerry how the conversation might have gone between Mr. Carlson and my dad. According to Gerry, Dad probably asked if he could park there and Mr. Carlson responded with something like; "You want to park there? Sure … go ahead." Ah the good old days. I like to think that in return for the favor my dad sent over a bottle of Mr. Carlson's favorite spirit or a six-pack of beer now and then.

A ten foot tall, three tiered, metal tire rack stood just west of the two cars. In addition to housing Atlas tires and other used brands, the rack gave me a great place for climbing around through the tires. What adventurous young boy wouldn't look at those rows of tires and want to crawl through them? Between the spiders, the pools of water collected in the upright tires, the chains locking them in place, and the height of the rack itself, *danger* defined this activity. Not only did risk of injury exist, but usually I came out of there covered in enough black face to rival the vision of Al Jolson singing his version of Gershwin's hit song, *Swanee*.

Luckily for Dad, he parked his car away from the tire rack. Unfortunately, though, for Uncle John Panaiotou, or more specifically his 1939 Green Plymouth, luck ran out. After years of rain and winter snows, the rack rusted badly near its foundation, and one day it tipped over onto the top of the Plymouth denting the roof. I dodged that bullet by not exploring the rack on that day. Uncle John had the repairs done giving the old car a two tone appearance. The newly painted roof made quite a contrast to the rest of the old car's faded original paint job. It remained that way for the rest of the time I knew Uncle John and his wife Gert.

Uncle John's old Plymouth served my family as well. In the spring when Dad couldn't drive us to Easter Service at midnight, we made the trip with Uncle John in his Plymouth. I recall vividly the drive back to Morris, holding my burning candle with its blessed light from church. When we got home we walked through the entire apartment, room to room, spreading the candle's blessing throughout our humble home. I continue this sacred ceremony to this day.

Carlson's Service Station 49

Ahead of the space for the two cars, Carlson's had more open area about twenty feet by fifteen feet along a wire fence behind which stood local jeweler, Mr. William Page's house. In that space during the summer, Mom hung laundry out to dry. We played around having fun doing silly things like the picture of Mom on the tricycle in this, the backyard we never had. Many times I watched Monkey, the Andan tabby cat, exit the rear door of the Andan chasing after butterflies and stalking birds in his jungle. As often as I saw Monkey, he and I didn't get along. He wasn't very friendly and I didn't care much for cats. We tolerated each other when we crossed paths in that small yard.

Leafing through all the family photographs during the time we lived on Jefferson Street, I get a profound sense of property sharing with Carlson's service station. For another example, between the sidewalk and the curb near the street, a small section of grass served as an outdoor family photo spot. We literally took dozens of pictures on that patch of green. Why that particular rectangle of grass acted as a magnet for family photographs more so than the *backyard*, puzzles me.

In retrospect, the space where Mom is pictured on the tricycle was much more attractive. On the other hand, the curb grassy spot, or berm, as some people referred to it, shows the station, vintage automobiles, and landmarks I'm thankful to have for viewing.

Our grassy spot served as a setting for relatives who visited from as far away as Peabody, Massachusetts. Check out this next lovely photo of Mom with my Dad's second cousin, Jenny Karademos, from Peabody. The ladies comprise the *lovely* aspect of the picture. What is interesting (if not strange) is the large service sign as a backdrop. It appears these two will be inspecting your muffler for free. Mom is on the left and Cousin Jenny is on the right.

May we install your next Maremont?

Sometimes there would be a service station sign on the grass, and other times it would be free of any advertisements at all. The entire section formed a perfect rectangle of grass and clover where Ann and I enjoyed beautiful spring days searching for four leaf clovers and picking wild blossoms. As always, the station continued to be busy with automobile activities and the island bell sounded off in the background. Mr. Carlson moved back and forth servicing the cars while we played. He pumped the gas and made change for the customers. All transactions then were in cash or the, *I'll pay you tomorrow* method.

◆   ◆   ◆

Coca Cola tasted better to me as a kid. My guess is the switch in the formula from using sugar to corn syrup as the sweetener made the difference. On hot days popping open that frosty old classic bottle really hit the spot. Coca Cola refreshed with a slight burn on the way down. And those sublime gulps led to a ballistic, satisfying belch ... yeah. Everyone sold those little bottles of pure American flavor. Ad campaigns were everywhere; billboards, TV, radio, magazines, and news papers. Carlson's Service Station had a brilliant red, metal, and stand alone Coca Cola sign probably worth its weight in gold by now. The red top section with *Coca Cola* written across it in that familiar script was a hollow metal shell. It boomed like a bass drum when I hit it with my hands. When I slapped the sign, it acted as a noise maker to attract business to the pumps. Mr. Carlson must have been one of the first to inadvertently employ a street corner mascot drumming in customers. I used to bang that thing to the rhythm of the good old Greek mountain folk songs Mom played for us at home. One afternoon I approached my favorite improvised drum and began my percussion solo with gusto. In doing so, I enraged the newly settled family of wasps who had found their way into the hollow cavern by way of a split in a seam. On this hot summer day, all I wore were shorts and a T-shirt. Not a lot of protection ... the wasps came right at me. They swarmed around viciously attacking the only one responsible for the ringing in their ears ... me. The creatures dived, attacked, and retreated only to circle back for another round. Dive ... attack ... sting, sting, and sting again. My upper left arm near the shoulder sustained three direct hits which caused an enormous, unfathomable pain. I ran screaming, terrified of more dive bombing wasps looking for revenge against the drummer. Luckily for me, I evaded any further stings by running faster than I ever thought I could. I don't remember if I ran upstairs to Mom at home or into The Basket for relief. What I do remember is the perfect triangle of painful swelling welts making their mark on my arm. Those three stings represented the most pain to date in my young life. There will be worse. The broken leg and collar bone I had sustained a few years earlier most likely caused me great pain. As I was a toddler then, I can't recall those pains, but the wasp stings, I certainly do.

◆ ◆ ◆

Many fathers with local businesses hoped that one day their sons or daughters would take over the family interests. Such was the case for the Carlson's. When time came for Mr. Carlson to retire, his son Gerry kept the station in the family. In the early sixties, it became Gerry's responsibility to carry his miniature windshield cleaner squirt bottle in his breast pocket. The time had come for Gerry to pump the gas, and service the cars. Those little pump bottles were always at the ready along with the traditional light blue paper towels giving each driving customer a sparkling windshield. So, Gerry, ten years my senior, became the friendly Standard Oil Man, and I began to see less and less of Mr. Carlson.

As I got older, I started hanging around with Gerry at the station in a more productive mode. Ringing the bell for the annoying fun of it with Mr. Carlson gave way to hands on participation and learning about cars with Gerry. Discovering how to change the oil in a car became one of the first services I learned by observation. On rare occasions, I actually got to pump gas once or twice under close supervision, and my favorite activity; operating the service bay lift lever. Watching the lift rise up to the ceiling with a car on board amazed me.

Another dangerous task, removing an old tire from the rim and replacing it with a new one, often entertained me. The stubborn old dinosaur tire machine of the era required much more muscle compared to the machinery of today. Watching Gerry and others struggle through that process of steel separating bars, and spinning center shafts, I knew to steer clear. Gerry kept me away from that job. More than a few times the steel bar hit the floor in frustrated disgust.

My first pseudo-job at the station had nothing to do with car knowledge and everything to do with extermination. I learned the discipline while at the Basket or Harry's Lounge; swatting flies! As a young kid hanging out at the station I wasn't old enough to actually be employed there. I simply conducted myself as a curious boy who liked to be with the older guys doing guy things like sweeping, wiping, cleaning, and swatting flies. Those pesky little critters buzzed everywhere, and I made it my quest to chase them all over the garage from the office to the bathrooms to the service bay. My credentials as a bonafide fly hunter were supported by the thousands of carcasses splattered against walls, floors, windows, and even Gerry's back and shoulders on occasion for a laugh. My efforts didn't go unrewarded because one simmering summer day, Gerry handed me a check for fifty cents; a whopping fifty cents! Now, I know you're probably thinking ... fifty cents!? How could that be right? Well, I didn't care. To me that check meant

Gerry appreciated my efforts in pest control—making me part of the Standard Oil team even if it appeared as somewhat of a joke. I gladly took the check from Gerry's hand and ran home to Dad in the bar to cash it immediately. When I handed the check to Dad, I saw the little smile of approval on his face. At the time, it never occurred to me the value of the check itself would one day be greater than the money it represented. I wish I would have saved it as part of my memorabilia collection. But I just had to have that money for a double dip raspberry ripple ice cream cone from the Straightway Dairy.

Maybe you think Gerry handed me the check that day because he knew I'd want to run home and cash it. Maybe you think he wanted to get rid of me for a little while. Well, in a recent conversation with Gerry he assured me that I was; "… Never a problem while at the station, Mike. You always stayed out of the way and helped me when I asked." When I heard those words over the phone from Gerry, they put me right back in that old station and made me wish I could reach through the phone to shake his hand and give him a hug. Validation like that from an old friend makes that fifty cent check memory worth a million dollars.

Spending so much time with Gerry at the station, I witnessed how some customers upon ringing the service bell, got a comical reaction from Gerry. One person in particular was a grouchy man who always barked his order to Gerry. "Gimme a couple bucks worth o' gas." So every time *Groucho* drove up to the pump and Gerry recognized his car, Gerry looked at me and imitated in his best grouchy guy voice along with the facial contortion; "Gimme a couple bucks worth o' gas." To which I laughed out loud as Gerry walked out finishing with a smile and a wink at me.

We also used to look at various automotive magazines, (the Playboys must have been hidden), and his old high school yearbooks, and talk about his old friends and classmates. I recall one guy named John Roberts. Gerry referred to him as "ol' fish face" for some reason. He didn't look like a fish to me.

I met several guys in their twenties, Gerry's age, and high school kids who officially worked for Gerry. The music these guys loved listening to on the gas station radio that really made an impression on me included The Beach Boys. *California Girls* got me wondering all about the beach life in California. I sang it to myself all the time as I scurried across the street to the Straightway Dairy for pizza and ice cream runs. I also found it interesting to listen to Gerry and his friends talking about the latest James Bond movie. The incorporated subject matter, not meant for my ears, intrigued me. As I hunted flies, I caught a few choice anatomical references from the discussions involving The Bond Girls. So, where were those Playboys anyway?

The one high school age employee I remember best during this time was Jerry Hunter. Jerry must have been about six feet tall. He sported the familiar blond flat top hair cut. Jerry loved a good laugh and we had many. Often, he and his pals who visited the station while he worked pitched in for a famous pizza from the Straightway Dairy across the street. Jerry called the dairy using the old black rotary desk phone to place the order. Then he and his buddies gave me the money to run across the street and buy it. Pizzas always took twenty minutes. After a while Jerry came in from pumping a tank of gas and asked me if the time had come for me to go for the pizza.

"It's about time to get that pizza, isn't it Mike?" Jerry hinted.

"It's only been five minutes," I replied.

"Five minutes?" Jerry laughed. "It's been at least fifteen!"

We could never agree on the time. No matter how long it seemed to be, and every time we ordered a pizza, I said five minutes and Jerry said at least fifteen. This became a recurring joke between us because after the first time it happened we recognized the humor of the situation. I couldn't gauge the passage of time that well, and Jerry ribbed me about it. Hence, the running joke developed, and I loved playing it out with Jerry every time. He ordered the pizza. He pumped a tank of gas. I swatted a fly, and we debated the time. Then we laughed like crazy while I ran off for the pizza. We popped open a couple bottles of orange Howdy sodas from the station machine, sat back and enjoyed the best cheese and sausage pizza in town. Often during the hot, pizza meals Jerry had to jump up when the island bell rang. He rushed out to pump some gas and clean a windshield while I sent a few more flies to the cemetery. We finished the pizza and orange Howdys, and then I walked or ran home daydreaming about California girls—pure, simple, small town fun. I loved every minute of it. Thanks for the pizza Jerry!

Bob Chally drove an awesome, black, 1964 Chevy Impala with a state of the art *four on the floor* Hurst stick shift. Now that was a hot car! It had masculine Mag racing wheels and huge slicks on the rear. Bob loved to burn those slicks often, and as a result, he wasted his rear end a few times. And who did he take it to for repairs? Carlson's Service Station and, Gerry, the Chevy rear end specialist of course. I didn't see any of those repairs being made since I most certainly sat in school finishing my insect collection, pinning a fly to my specimen board—one more dead fly.

Another neighbor and friend of Gerry's was Doug Fruland, a handsome sandy haired young man who resembled a young swashbuckling Errol Flynn. His father owned and operated the Fruland Funeral Home directly across the street from the gas station on Jefferson Street. Doug always smiled and had friendly conversations with everyone. One day at the gas station Doug and I were standing next to each other near the grassy berm admiring Bob Chally's smoking hot Chevy. Doug snacked on Fritos and drank one of those delicious Coca Colas out of a bottle. He attempted to have a conversation with someone several feet away from him (probably Gerry). He had a mouthful of crispy, crunchy, Fritos rattling his brain and had to stop chewing them in order to hear the other person's words. I, being much shorter, looked up to see him stop in mid-chew, crane his neck and smile realizing the only way to hear the other person was to stop chewing. It made him laugh a little. Then after hearing the message he responded and started crunching again recognizing the humor all the while. I distinctly remember his smile during this entire little scene.

Doug had recently married and no doubt must have been busy planning his and his wife's future when tragedy struck. I only just began to know him better, when he lost his life in a motorcycle accident. For that short time I knew him, I could easily tell he was a person of good character. Doug's loss greatly saddened my neighborhood and everyone in Morris who knew him. Doug Fruland is one of many sad examples of only the good dying young in Morris, Illinois.

One of my jobs for Mom at The Basket included delivering small *to go* orders. The one I liked best was taking Gerry Carlson his coffee. This afforded me the excuse to spend a few minutes at my favorite gas station. Gerry would be talking to a friend or working at his desk reading a repair manual (was there a Playboy hidden in there?) and I'd run in with my paper bag containing a cup of *cream no sugar*. We referred to the Gerry Carlson coffee order as *cream no sugar*. If it were winter and cold, I often stayed until Gerry finished and he would look at me and say ...

"Mike, how about a refill? Cream, no sugar."

"Okay Gerry. One *cream no sugar*!"

Back to The Basket—I opened the front door to Mom's busy little café, trotted to the counter and said, "Mom, *cream no sugar*." She knew that meant a Gerry refill and she filled the cup. I hurried once again to make the delivery and return home ... eventually.

Standard Oil Company had a product line using the name *Atlas* for everything from tires to batteries; everything automotive. Upon arriving one cold winter day at the station for my daily fix of watching the guys work and learning more car stuff, I noticed Gerry holding his hand up to his serviceman's coat pocket in an unusual manner. He had a smile on his face and leaned over to show me something inside the pocket. A tiny, short-haired, black and white puppy peeked out at me. I bonded instantly with that little guy and had to hold him. Gerry handed him to me, and I cupped him in my hands bringing him up close to my face for a little snuggle. He whimpered a cute puppy sound. He had puppy breath.

"What's his name?" I asked.

"Atlas," said Gerry.

From then on, the Carlson Service Station had a mascot dog named Atlas—just what I needed ... another reason to keep me at the station. Now I'd never leave! I loved puppies and dogs in general. I remember thinking how adorable it was to see Gerry working the gas pumps in the freezing cold with Atlas in his warm shirt pocket under his coat. From the warmth of the station office I watched Gerry and Atlas through the large plate glass window with a big smile on my face.

You sure are a cute little puppy, Atlas.

Gerry revealed to his customers this curious tiny puppy all safe and warm, protected from the winter. Little Atlas made everyone smile; even the grouchy, *give me a couple bucks worth o' gas* guy.

◆ ◆ ◆

Three distinct sounds filled the air in Morris, Illinois, during the days way back when. One, the Center School Buzzer, sent its oscillating waves roaring through the air indicating recess or the start and end of the school day. The second one gently entered my bedroom window from a block away; the First National Bank Clock that hung out over the sidewalk. Counting the number of chimes every hour gave me a reliable way to know the time of day. In fact, this clock also rang out every fifteen minutes as well making it easy for me to manage my daily kid schedule when within earshot. Too bad I couldn't hear it at Carlson's during the pizza runs with Jerry Hunter. But then I wouldn't have had the timing joke and all of that fun. The third signature sound in town roared each weekday precisely at noon. The lunch hour siren screamed out one long note. It started with a low pitch and peaked at a high energetic level. It then trailed away back to pre-siren peace meaning lunch time had arrived. Oh boy ... food! By the time the siren had finished, the final few twelve o'clock chimes from the bank clock ended. Each café downtown began its busy lunch hour. This midday siren also served as the klaxon notifying the volunteer firemen all over town that their services were needed. The siren peaked and retreated several times indicating an emergency and not lunch hour. By the end of the fire alarm, the cars came from every which way. Volunteer firemen honked their horns wildly, warning pedestrians and other drivers alike to get out of the way. I ran to the corner many times to watch the speeding cars come to a screeching halt in front of the fire house one and a half blocks away. The men were almost out of their cars before they stopped rolling.

I sat in my eighth grade English class in the fall of 1965, when the fire alarm interrupted the quiet day. Someone in class looked out the window and shouted out … "Smoke!" as he or she pointed in the direction of the rising column of thick, roiling black particulates. We all rushed to the windows for a clear view of what I surmised to be a fire very close to my home. My quick assessment of the evidence reaching high into the airspace above the buildings and trees worried me instantly. To my teacher, Miss Narrigon, I must have looked petrified because after I exclaimed the fire appeared close to my home territory, she didn't hesitate to allow me an instant excuse from class.

As I ran down Liberty Street I prayed hard the entire way to myself and aloud. I prayed that it wasn't our building, and that my mom and dad were alright.

(In Greek) *Blessed Virgin Mary, please protect my family and our home.*

The angle of my approach soon told me our home and businesses were not involved in the fire.

(Also in Greek) *Thank you, Lord.*

Fire truck sirens blared briefly and soon died down as the fire station was only a block and a half from the fire. Still, my heart raced as I feared for those affected by the beast. When I reached Jefferson Street, the humid, musty, smell of thousands of gallons of water mixed with the hot air and pavement, filled my nose. Turning the corner, looking in the direction of all the activity, it became crystal clear through the obstructing smoke ahead, that my favorite gas station had caught fire. It burned vigorously.

Oh no. Not my gas station.

Fire fighters set up a perimeter preventing onlookers from getting too close. A police officer stood in the intersection of Jefferson and Wauponsee directing traffic. Wearing their bulky fire gear, courageous volunteer firemen stood their ground. They wrestled with hoses amid the flashing red and white emergency lights of the huge red fire trucks. Water formed into puddles, flowed, or sprayed everywhere. It leaked in fine sprays from connections of hose to hydrant, and hose to hose. The massive fire department response—it was, after all, a gasoline station—produced a scene filled with confusing sights, piercing sounds, and acrid odors that completely bombarded my senses. Jets of water choked the flames inside Carlson's Service Station where the fire had been confined in the service bay section of the building where it started.

Gerry stood at a safe distance in front of the property watching his business go up in flames as other neighbors, friends, and I gathered around him in support. He appeared uninjured but obviously concerned about the damage. We watched in horror as the pungent smell of burning rubber filled the air.

To their heroic credit, the Morris Volunteer Fire Department quickly gained the upper hand. The building, although sustaining a good deal of damage, survived. The burning Atlas tires that lined the upper walls of the service bay had caused all the thick, belching, smoke making the fire look worse. When the smoke cleared and the event ended, we had a clear view inside the service bay. There, still up in the air stood the lift, but not held up by the air pressure. The pressurized lines were destroyed by the fire. A tall steel tank used to collect old motor oil had jammed under the lift. Gerry had shoved it under the lift just in time to keep it from falling to floor level and possibly striking him or anyone else who may have been in there. Even with safety locks built into the system to prevent a complete collapse, the frightening possibility still existed.

Inventory; mainly tires, belts, oil, and air filters took a big hit. Much of the tire inventory survived. In those days tires came wrapped in bands of light brown paper with stickers pasted on them indicating size etc. Gerry had no choice but to have a fire sale for all the salvageable tires even if the brown paper showed no evidence of fire damage. Anyone who purchased tires from the sale really got a great deal on perfectly good tires.

Not long after the fire (a period of months) Gerry closed up shop, and eventually a bulldozer plowed the property to the ground just as my high school days began. I stood in the alley between our building and the Standard Oil property watching the heavy bulldozer destroy one of my favorite places. My heart sunk knowing the island cord and bell were gone, along with Dad's parking space, and the adopted play yard. The pressurized lift lever I enjoyed operating and the spider infested three tiered tire rack were both history. The huge, heavy, office desk where Gerry and I sat looking at service manuals, magazines, and yearbooks disappeared. The room where Jerry Hunter and I laughed about pizza runs as we drank Cokes and orange Howdys no longer existed. Gerry's portable radio that blared Beach Boys music tempting us to move west became a memory. The corner where Atlas curled up inside his cardboard box until he outgrew it vanished. I wouldn't hear *cream no sugar* anymore. In the name of progress, they paved my paradise and put up their boring parking lot.

5

The Farms

Two farms in particular were Sunday afternoon playgrounds for me as a little kid. They were next door to each other, beyond The Rod and Gun Club (Peabody Coal Company) about seven miles northeast of town. Each owned and operated by fellow Greeks. The first farm belonged to the Tony "Shorty" Eliakis family, and the second belonged to George Dellos. We had a camaraderie amongst us that produced some of the greatest picnics known to man. These gatherings celebrated everything from the Fourth of July to breaking the Easter Lent fast. Our families savored some of the most delicious fresh foods imaginable. We butchered our own lambs in the morning, and cooked them whole over a bed of coals later the same day—a Greek tradition carried over from the old country villages of Epirus.

Uncle Angelo on the left and George Tolias on the George Dellos Farm

Many of these outings had the men roasting two or even three lambs at a time. Greek salads made with vegetables pulled right out of the ground that day complimented the delicious roast lamb. Rice pilaf, green onions, two or three kinds of Greek olives, and feta and kasheri cheeses added more delightful flavors to enjoy. Several of the women, including my mother, brought freshly baked spinach/phyllo dough pie called *spanakopita*, or a cheese version called *tiropita*. Dad filled the trunk of our car with a few cases of Schlitz, Old Style, and Budweiser along with Coke and 7Up bottles. The drinks ended up cold and refreshing after being covered with ice all morning in large, industrial size, galvanized, steel tubs. We even had a bottle of Ouzo and a bottle of Metaxa, both traditional Greek liquors, on the tables. These events were spare no expense, no holds barred extravaganzas fit for Zeus himself. What parties they were.

A delicacy, beyond my description here doing it any justice, called *kokoretz* was cooked on a three foot long metal skewer. The organ meats included liver, kidney, heart, and lung pieces skewered and wrapped over and over with the small intestines. To the unfamiliar this may sound awful, but trust me, *kokoretz* wouldn't disappoint most palates—superbly delicious. While cooking over the hot coals, the lamb and the *kokoretz* were regularly basted with a wild mustard herb bundle. The chefs in charge dipped this bundle into a mixture of olive oil, butter, salt, pepper, lemon, garlic and oregano. The basting went on for the entire cooking time, resulting in some of the best roast lamb I've ever tasted.

Nothing has ever even come close to the culinary delight produced over those barbeque pits, and complimented by the salads, pita, plates of sliced Italian bread loaves, and ice cold drinks. No other picnic feasts could match the farm picnics. Not even the Church sponsored picnics could compete with what my family and friends produced at these farm feasts. They were simply the best.

Mom and baby Ann at the Eliakis farmhouse backyard

The Eliakis farm prospered under the watchful eye of patriarch Tony, aka *Shorty*, Eliakis and his wife everyone called Mama. Uncle Shorty was … well … short. He wore glasses, had thinning gray hair and always … always could be seen with one of those thin black *Crooks* cigars in his mouth. Between Uncle Shorty and Uncle Nick, I don't know who smoked more cigars. For a small man who stood only about five foot five, Uncle Shorty had one of the loudest voices I ever heard. While I visited the Dellos farm down the road, I heard him yelling from a quarter mile away. The Eliakis farm funnies of hearing Uncle Shorty reprimanding someone from such a distance across an entire field, certainly cracked me up. He could have been shouting because the outhouse ran out of paper for all I know. Whatever the reason, his voice carried across that field many times tickling even my dad. On one occasion, old Uncle George Dellos walked past Dad and me on his way to repair a tractor. He carried a wrench in one hand, and with his other arm he wiped the sweat off his brow. I saw him crack a big smile and shake his head when Uncle Shorty had cut loose from across the field. Dad chuckled, I rolled, and Uncle George smiled as he worked on his tractor in the heat of the day.

Uncle Shorty's enunciation was distorted because of the Crooks cigar in the front of his mouth. His bellowing loudly in Greek on a hot summer day made for great *long distance comedy*. He may not have been raising his voice in anger at all. He did have a hearing problem and wore a hearing aid. Uncle Shorty often spoke at a high volume even when in close proximity.

Mama was this sweet little old lady who wore flowery farm type dresses covered with an apron. Her hands were the characteristically over worked farmer's wife's hands. She spoke slowly and stood a little bent over. She shuffled her feet over the sandy floors in her farmhouse seemingly without a care—happy to welcome us whenever we visited. Mama had a peculiar manner of speech which included the word *yes* in many of her sentences. She pronounced it in two slightly drawn out syllables.

"Hello … yayus … come in yayus," she would say in her tired old voice.

Mama wasn't Greek; therefore, many conversations included brief translations in English. I felt sorry for her being left out of so many details because of the language barrier. She never complained, though, and usually went about her kitchen chores unfazed by it all. She offered us drinks such as tea and coffee with Carnation condensed sweet milk out of a can instead of fresh cream. The old woman's warmth and kindness touched everybody who knew her and loved her. God bless you Mama.

In the cold winter months, we gathered around an old coal burning stove in the middle of the farmhouse living room. Uncle Shorty pulled the iron door open with a poker, stoked the fire with several quick jabs and tossed in a shovel full of coal. The stove kept the room nice and warm. I sat in Mom or Dad's lap in a big old comfortable fabric chair listening to the adults talk about farming, and sometimes stories from the old country. Some of it I didn't understand because of my limited Greek fluency. Regardless, the conversations held my interest because Uncle Shorty had such an animated old way of speaking. Knowing my somewhat limited comprehension, when I looked over to Mama I got a good understanding of what it must have been like for her.

Uncle Shorty and Mama raised two sons and a daughter; Steve, Louie, and Mandy. Together with their spouses, Pauline, Georgia, and Louie respectively, the extended family included six grandchildren; Danny and Andy, Tony and Teddy, and Gus and Maria. Gus and I were the same age. We had a knack for finding ways to get his grandpa Shorty all riled up. If we weren't chasing pigs or chickens, we were guilty as charged messing around on the farm equipment. If we got caught (and we often did), anyone within a quarter mile got an earful of Uncle Shorty's vocal ability, or *long distance comedy*.

Farm kids—Heidi, I'm holding Tony Eliakis, Gus Georgantas, and his sister, Maria

Gus lived in Joliet with his parents, Louie and Mandy, and his little sister, Maria. Since this was his family's farm, Gus dropped in much more often than I did. When I visited with Gus there, I followed his lead because of his familial seniority. He and I found plenty to do on his grandfather's farm. Whenever possible we helped his Uncles Steve and Louie with filling drinking troughs for various farm animals. Occasionally we slopped pigs and spread chicken feed. Mostly we ran around getting dirty by jumping into piles of hay or alfalfa. We threw rocks in the fields—or even more fun—used an old board or baseball bat to hit them into the stratosphere.

A long trail led away from the central farm yard north to a wide creek about two hundred yards away. Old discarded farm equipment, antique cars, and trucks littered most of the way along that path. Those vehicles gave us plenty of excellent exploratory sessions. Gus and I sat in the driver seats and pretended to speed around imaginary race tracks. We shifted the gear levers wildly and made crazy race car sounds. We bounced up and down on dilapidated old seats with springs that showed more than the fabric. We cranked old windows until they wouldn't budge anymore. Glove boxes were popped open over and over in the hopes of discovering bits of past valuables or paperwork. About the only things of value that we found were a few coins which we pocketed as if they were gold nuggets.

At the creek, we fished off the bank for catfish and blue gill using cane poles. Mostly, we spent time exploring and watching out for snakes; water moccasins, and garter snakes. Someone had kept an old row boat tied to a tree most of the time or turned upside down on the bank. On one of the trips to the creek, Gus and I took Mom with us. My godmother's nephew, Art, came along as well. He was in his twenties at the time, and I thought of him as kind of an older brother. Art used to swing me around while we grasped each other's hands, and he carried me on his back. You know—all the big brotherly type activities that thrilled little kids like me. On this creek day, he took the row boat out for a spin by himself. Mom, Gus, and I watched him from the shaded grassy bank when without warning he stood up and jumped into the water. Mom screamed as Art went completely under. She feared deep bodies of water because she couldn't swim. For a moment she stood petrified—at a loss for what to do. Gus and I stared at the water, waiting ... waiting when suddenly, Art, laughing wildly, reappeared like a missile launched from a submarine. The waist deep water sufficed in keeping him submerged just long enough to worry my mother. His little trick on Mom worked. We had little difficulty getting her to fall for stunts and jokes. Her innocence and trusting nature gave us little villains plenty of opportunities. Art grinned with pride. We all had a big laugh, and Mom soon forgave Art.

◆ ◆ ◆

Growing up in an apartment meant I couldn't have a dog as a pet. From Hornsby's pet department, we had a parakeet named Skippy, a little painted turtle, and goldfish, but much to my dismay ... never a dog. I loved dogs, and the closest I got to enjoying one as a personal pet, aside from Atlas, was informally adopting one of the dogs on Uncle George Dellos's farm. Uncle George had two dogs. The older all black dog, Ziki, for some reason unknown to me, didn't like me at all. Ziki growled at me whenever I got near him. My Pal could approach him and pet him all day long. Seeing Uncle Bill capable of approaching Ziki, I wanted to be his friend too—but it wasn't to be. Ziki rested under a small table in the farmhouse kitchen one day when I attempted to pet him. As I reached under the table, he growled ferociously and snapped—just missing me. He scared me almost out of my shoes. That frightened me to tears, and I trembled for several minutes afterward. I finally gave up on Ziki. He just didn't trust little kids, so I stayed away from him.

Fendeko with me and Heidi—Ziki with my Pal—behind us are Uncle Tony Fotos, Uncle Nick, Mom, Effie and Helen Fotos, Ann, and Julia Fotos—Effie, Helen and Julia are Uncle Tony's daughters

The other dog, Fendeko, possessed a completely different disposition. His affectionate demeanor attracted me immediately when I first met him. We got along famously which prompted me to tell my friends in town that I had a dog, but I had to keep him on the farm. Uncle George Dellos let me know with a smile how it pleased him to know Fendeko took a liking to me. This made me happy. We played together every day we visited the farm. I hugged him as often as I wanted, and he never objected. If for some reason Mom and Dad only planned to be at the Eliakis farm, I always requested to go visit Fendeko and usually got my wish. For some of those trips, Mom and I walked. The walking trips along the gravel road between farms turned into country wildlife safaris. Rows and rows of red winged blackbirds lined the power lines and fences along the way. The chirping in the afternoon sun gave a sense of endless open space as their echoes trailed away. The sound of our feet crunching along the gravel road scared out an occasional ring neck pheasant. A rare snake encounter always made for a good scream from Mom, and rabbits darted in and out of the roadside hedges. I loved those roadside safari walks and experiencing the wild animals along the way. A few minutes of walking brought us to Uncle George's driveway gate. Two concrete columns about five feet tall marked the entrance; one on either side. Upon entering the slightly upgrade entrance to the farm, Fendeko ran out to greet us. Ziki kept his distance and growled. Visiting with my dog friend, and enjoying a delicious cold drink of water from the farm well made my day.

Ann and I drink from the Dellos well

Then one day upon arriving at the farm, I jumped out of Dad's car and immediately went looking for Fendeko. He didn't come when I called. Uncle George sadly informed me my friend had died shortly after our last visit. I cried a deep river. The farm was never the same without him. I loved that dog.

6

The Corn Festival

*M*orris, Illinois, sits in the center of farm country surrounded by thousands of acres of corn and soybeans. They are the two major crops of the area stretching for miles in each direction. Other vegetables like tomatoes, squash, pumpkins, green beans, eggplant, and even melons can be found in smaller amounts. A few dairy farms dot the landscape as well as egg farms and some live stock establishments. But it's the corn that Grundy County celebrates with an annual Corn Festival the last week of September during harvest time.

The Corn Festival fills a week with festivities including parties, a soap box derby, live concerts and art shows. The week ends with a huge parade down Liberty Street on Sunday afternoon. To this day, Corn Festival is the single busiest week of the year. People from all surrounding towns and former Morris citizens who have moved away, return to re-acquaint themselves with old friends in places like The Lion's Club, The VFW, The Federation of Eagles, The Moose Lodge, restaurants and private homes all over town.

Life on Liberty Street during the Corn Festival in my childhood was outstanding for many reasons. First, we had the soap box derby on Saturday morning held two blocks away on Franklin Street directly in front of Franklin School. Only a day or two before the competition, local carpenters used lumber from the Beatty Lumber Company and erected a huge wooden structure fifteen feet tall by fifty feet long. Watching the men build this leviathan was almost as much fun as experiencing the race itself. I remember sitting on my bicycle at the curb near the school. The workers smiled broadly as they assembled, piece by piece, board by board ... *The Ramp*. Sounds of pounding hammers, buzzing saws and lots of wood slapping the pavement filled the air. A dozen or more skilled laborers gladly donated their time in the effort to build the thirty to thirty-five degree slope down which the homemade cars coasted one by one, racing against the clock.

The Ramp had to be built. No hill existed in town capable of providing such a perfect slope. Not until years later when the swimming pool hill underwent re-grading, did it qualify as a sufficiently angled slope for racing the soap box derby. Before the hill got its new look, repaved and modernized, it was too dangerous to ever think of using it for the race. It would have been a nightmare to see a little kid's car throw a wheel and fly out of control down the old swimming pool hill. The kid and car could have easily landed in Nettle Creek.

Although I never had the pleasure of riding down The Ramp, I'm certain it terrified some kids. I saw it in their eyes as I watched them roll down to the bottom plywood sheet and transition onto the street. Many unfortunate kids did side swipe the safety rails before they got half way down the ramp. The Ramp itself sustained thick black tire marks, a few blood drops from scraped elbows and hands, and teardrops as well. Those who made a clean descent rode off to the finish line where a stop watch awaited them. One lucky boy or girl coasted to victory a block away on Franklin Street. Trophies were awarded to the top three finishers.

I wanted to build my own soap box derby car and enter the race but didn't really know where to begin, and my dad had a very limited knowledge (if any) of how to build a car from scratch. I even wrote to my cousin Johnny in Chicago informing him of my plan. He flat out told me to forget it. "You will never make a go-cart," he said in his letter I have in my collection. "I tried before. It is too hard and costs too much." This disappointed me, and I abandoned the project after looking at the measly materials I had scraped together. During my initial steps creating the car, I had some boards, a bag of large construction staples I bought at Matteson's Hardware, a hammer, and a piece of rope. The rope would have been for the steering mechanism when attached to the front axel board. I had no clue what to do back then, compared to today when with a few mouse clicks, a plethora of *how to build derby cars* sites will pop up. With the parts laid out in front of me in the basement, I gave up and remained a spectator.

Another exciting competition that took place on Corn Festival Saturday afternoons involved the area fire departments for the water fight tournament. Fire department teams from surrounding Grundy County towns gathered up their gear in preparation for a unique competition. This event also took place on Franklin Street a few blocks south of the school and adjacent to the Grundy County Courthouse. Over the years, other street locations were used. However, this is the spot I remember most. The city street department, supported by the police and fire departments, closed a block-long section of the street with bright red fire engines at either end. Firefighters rigged a long steel cable about fifteen feet above street level with a *bucket* which actually resembled a small size aluminum beer keg. The bucket slid freely along the entire length of the cable. Hoses ran from the fire hydrants to the red pumping trucks. Their engines roared, building up pressure to shoot water aimed at the bucket hanging over the street. I got the biggest kick out of watching the bucket get blasted back and forth by men with big squirt guns. For a moment the bucket might go nowhere as water ammo from each team applied equal pressure. Then the bucket spun wildly out of control. Like a ball on a string it circled around the cable multiple times until one team got the best aim and angle. The crowd cheered on their teams as if watching a football game. "Go, go, go! Push them back!" Then, one team gained the advantage sending the bucket sliding back behind their opponents' heads so fast they couldn't keep up. It was quite a sight to see a team of able bodied fire fighters in full gear (helmets, coats, and boots), wrestling with a high pressure water hose. They struggled valiantly for position as they ran backwards through the water soaked street. The whole time, water sprayed high in the air all over the cheering audience. After a full afternoon of the round robin tournament, the winning team emerged, and just like the soap box derby, a trophy ceremony took place for the top three teams.

The crowning event of the Corn Festival was the Sunday afternoon parade. Six blocks of cross traffic along Liberty Street were closed off from Washington Street to Benton Street. Large, fifty-five gallon barrels draped with long boards made up the barriers. The slapping sound of the boards when they hit the ground, and the rumble of the barrels rolling away, let us know the parade was about to start. We took up our window positions. Popcorn, snow-cone, corn dog, and cotton candy vendors dotted the parade route below. Thousands of people lined Liberty Street five rows deep along the sidewalks. Young kids sat on the curb, and older folks set up their folding chairs behind them. My family, our guests, and I sat in the comfort of our own apartment and watched the Sunday parade pass right below us. We never had to plan or compete for a good seat. The best seats in town existed right at home.

This parade had everything that Macy's Thanksgiving Day Parade had except for Santa Claus at the end. It rivaled the Pasadena Rose Parade; perhaps not in grandeur and elaborate floats but in variety of entries. The Corn Festival Parade included marching bands from local high schools, grade schools, military bands, and drill teams. There were horses, tractors, floats, clowns, and characters on stilts entertaining the crowd. Beautiful young ladies tossed out candy for the kids. City and county officials rode in brightly decorated GM and Ford convertibles—not a Toyota in sight. We had precision motorcycle riders and champion drum and bugle corps performing elaborate routines several times along the route. Finally, an impressive display of law enforcement squad cars, the latest shiny red fire engines, and the still operating antique truck proudly maintained by the Morris Volunteer Fire Department, ended the parade. Clanging bells and wailing sirens put the final stamp on the Corn Festival Parade. I watched the crowd dissipate and the litter blow away into neat little piles until the sweeping teams came around to clean up. The festival ended, but there was still Sunday evening.

7

Sunday Evenings

As popular as the two farms were, on other Sundays, we stayed home for the day and later went out for a Sunday evening drive. My father knew the Morris countryside like the back of his hand. He could drive us to any area in and around Grundy County by way of the old gravel country roads or blacktops and never get lost. We piled into the family maroon and white, 1955 Buick Special on early Sunday evenings and drove all around the country roads. Fresh country air and stopping for ice cream highlighted these drives. If we took the northern route we stopped at the four way stop intersection of Illinois Route 47 and US Route 52. There, a little café next to a gas station sold ice cream cones. Mom ran in with the order for chocolate, vanilla, or orange sherbet cones. She returned after a few minutes loaded with the frozen treats, a pile of napkins, and off we'd go.

Those country rides were so refreshing after a hot humid day at home with no air conditioning. With frosty ice cream treats, windows rolled down, and cooler evening air filling the car, we were feeling alright. I can still hear the Buick's tires sticking to the hot blacktop road creating a steady sound like a sustained musical note. Cicadas buzzed in the trees adding their layer of nonstop bug vocals for miles. No sooner would one cicada end its song as we passed it, than another would overlap picking up the refrain. Rarely did the radio ever play music. If and when the White Sox had a night game, we listened to Bob Elson calling the game broadcast on WGN Radio out of Chicago. Elson's easy, low key delivery made listening to games on these outings feel like he reported to us personally—like another person in the car with us.

We made these trips often during the spring into the fall. Some families may have gone to movies together, or concerts, or other group activities. But, one of our favorites included the ride out in the country where Dad loved to be; in the great outdoors surrounded by corn and soybean fields—farm country.

◆   ◆   ◆

Our family spent just about every Sunday doing some combination of the following activities. We thoroughly cleaned the restaurant and bar in the morning, drove twenty five miles to church, attended church picnics, spent the afternoons out in the country at the farms, went out for dinner on occasion or usually finished the day with a great home cooked Greek dinner that often included Uncle Nick and his friend Joe Farrell.

Joe Farrell; a kind, polite, and handsome older man, had white hair with a distinguishing wave to it. His glasses added to my impression that he must have been well educated. He always looked so refined, well groomed, and impeccably dressed. Mr. Farrell traveled extensively as I recall and thoughtfully brought gifts home for us to enjoy. I remember one of the toys he gave me; a battery operated oil drilling rig, the kind that resembles a dinosaur head rising up and down connected to a set of gears.

Uncle Bill, painted by numbers Jesus, George Tolias, Joe Farrell, and Uncle Nick

After Sunday dinner, Ann and I usually walked together across the street and around the corner to the Straightway Dairy for a gallon container of chocolate ripple or chocolate chip ice cream. I recall the discussions in the kitchen deciding what flavor to buy. Just about every time we decided on chocolate ripple or chip. Mom made Turkish (Greek) and American style coffee to go along with her assortment of Greek cookies and of course the ice cream.

As in most families, the adults hung around the table for conversation and I dove into watching TV with my sisters. The line up usually included choices of *Bonanza, Mission Impossible, Ed Sullivan, Candid Camera,* and *The Wonderful World of Disney.* If we couldn't agree on the same programs (there was only one TV set) I had no problem retreating to my room for a comic book, or to play with a new toy from Joe Farrell—build a fort of sheets and chairs until our guests left at the end of the evening. Before Mom put away the leftovers, I dipped into more spanakopita topped with homemade plain yogurt, ate one last bite of stuffed grape leaves, or a piece of a roast lamb. If I had homework to do, I squeezed it into the schedule somehow. Bedtime came soon and the next day meant ... school. Burp!

8

Sidewalk Kindergarten

My parents simply didn't see the need for formal kindergarten. They thought it best for me to stay home until first grade. It didn't matter to me one way or the other so—I skipped it. As an alternative, my self-made kindergarten class met on the sidewalk in front of our apartment. For most of my time at home during the early years, Greek was my primary language. I basically learned English by playing on that sidewalk and interacting with the other boys and girls who lived nearby. One family in particular resided for a short while in the front apartment above the bar before we moved into it. They were the Rainwater family.

Mr. and Mrs. Rainwater and their three children moved into the front Jefferson Street apartment shortly after my dad's business partner, Peter, and his wife, my cousin Martha, moved away to Chicago. Larry Rainwater, who I rarely saw, was their oldest; about twelve at the time. Then Carol, roughly seven, followed by little Tina about my age (six) or maybe a year younger. Here are Carol and Tina with my sister, Ann and me. Tina was my very first kiss I'm proud to say. Mrs. Rainwater had called for Tina to come upstairs for lunch one day. We stood alone at the bottom of the stairs to her apartment just inside the door when we kissed good-bye. She giggled and ran up the stairs as I stood there watching her scamper away. I'm sure had anyone seen this childhood moment they would have called it cute.

Being surrounded by sweet, adorable little girls every day seemed normal to me. Look at my situation; a loving older sister whom I adored and still do today, plus two cute little neighbor girls right next door. We played together every day. We rode our tricycles, jumped rope, played jacks, and hopscotch. We colored the sidewalk with chalk pictures and sold lemonade for two cents a glass. As the only boy among the girls in our sidewalk kindergarten, I felt special.

Like most kids, we went back and forth to each other's homes several times throughout the day thinking nothing of walking in unannounced. I climbed the stairs to Tina's apartment and turned right toward the small kitchen softly calling for Tina—no answer. Moving on, I proceeded into the dining room where just to the left was the bathroom with its door wide open. There she stood, totally naked holding a towel; Mrs. Rainwater! I startled her into quickly pushing the door closed with a gasp. Oops!

My kindergarten suddenly had an anatomy class! The first time I ever saw a naked woman I was six years old and four feet away from her ... well ... you know where my eye level would have been at that age. I took off running. Some time shortly after my encounter with the female form, the Rainwater family moved away from Morris and Liberty Street. Tina went away. I never heard from her or saw her again.

Another outstanding sidewalk kindergarten source for learning English came with the flow of kids who walked to and from the Morris Theatre. Saturday afternoons were the best for this because of the double feature matinees. Some kids stopped and played a quick game of *Red Light/Green Light* or *Hopscotch*, maybe *Statue* or a game of *Jacks*. Whatever the game, I quickly learned new words every day from future classmates.

The best thing about sidewalk kindergarten was the fact that there were no schedules or time constraints. We played free home school all day long with Ann as our teacher. We made up our own rules and taught each other by sharing toys and games. The whole time during sidewalk kindergarten class, we learned an important lesson about how to be aware of cars on one of the busiest corners in town. A corner occupied by a grocery store, bakery, barber shop, photography studio, jewelry store, a doctor's office, a movie theatre, and a restaurant and bar. The people I met on this corner, the kids I played with, and the ones who passed by prepared me for official education; Franklin School and first grade.

Part II
Franklin School Days

○ ○
"When you see me fly away without you, Shadows on the things you know …" Neil Young

My first school

9

First Grade, 1958–1959

o o o o o o o o o o o o o o o o o o o o o o o o o o o o o o
"I'll never let you go. Why? Because I love you ..."
Frankie Avalon

*N*amed after Benjamin Franklin, the Franklin School building located at the northern end of Franklin Street is no longer a school. It now houses a few local businesses. It is comforting to know the building is still useful and has evaded the dreaded wrecking ball and accompanying bulldozers.

Every year near the end of each summer vacation when the *Back to School* signs appeared in town, I saw the excitement on Liberty Street. Every kid in town found his or her way to the primary stores for school supplies; Hornsby's, and Schultz Brothers. Shopping for back to school supplies with Mom at Schultz Brothers impressed me as a new first grader. My first personal back to school shopping experience gave me reason to believe school days would be filled with plenty of things to do and learn. Schultz Brothers advertised 5¢ to $1.00 merchandise. They sold everything from bulk candy to clothing. The poorly lit store had a dark array of aisles made of loose hardwood flooring that when walked upon, creaked loudly. Each floor board seemed to have its own pitch. When the store filled with busy shoppers, the foot and floor song rang out its melody like a full orchestra.

I actually enjoyed collecting all my fat, black pencils, erasers, crayons, paper tablets, three ring binder, scissors, ruler, and great smelling white paste in a jar. Do you remember the jar top with the paste spreading stick? I can also still smell the pungent oil cloths we needed for covering our class desks. I rolled mine up in a tube shape for storage in my desk. Organizing those supplies was so much fun. I liked the process of making everything fit just right in my briefcase.

I kept it all these years hidden away in closets with assorted keepsakes. Amazing, how my Franklin School briefcase from 1958 has survived the many moves from house to house, city to city, and state to state. It is in excellent condition; almost like new. Every fighter jet plane, propeller bomber, and white cloud in the pretty blue sky is there. The art work is so 1950s, while the craftsmanship is unlike anything made today. The bright red plastic handle looks like someone attached it last week. The interior vinyl lining has no cracks, and the leather strap

First Grade, 1958–1959   81

and brass buckle are hardly worn. Inside this unbelievably well preserved relic, I've stored equally well preserved homework assignments, report cards, diplomas, and other documents from grade school through college. The only report cards missing are grades one, two, and three. I'm curious to know my performance from those three years. It would be nice to have them for a complete set.

◆ ◆ ◆

School days had finally arrived. I entered first grade ready to go with English as my second language. I was the only Greek boy in town, and first grade made me aware of that fact. In the Greek language, the letter *r* is rolled, so when the time came for me to fly away from the nest for the first time, I took with me what I had learned. Many of you might recall the popular *Dick and Jane* reading books in early grade school. Along with Dick and Jane were, little Sally, Puff the cat, and of course my favorite—Spot!

"Rrrun, rrrun, rrrun Spot," I read aloud in class when my turn came. "See Spot rrrun!"

Right away Mrs. Coop, my first grade teacher, had to correct me.

"Remember Mike, in English we don't roll the letter *r*.

"Yes, Mrs. Coop," I said slightly embarrassed.

No one else had that problem when reading about Spot. At that moment, I felt different. It occurred to me ...

I might be the only Grrreek boy in town.

Newly aware of the rolling *r*, I focused on learning how to speak like the other kids. It took a while, but I got it because I had a good teacher.

Mrs. Coop conducted her class with gentle control—a comfortable place to be. When one of the little girls, Vicki Martinez, proudly proclaimed to Mrs. Coop and the class, that on the following day she would have a new look, Mrs. Coop supported her. She encouraged Vicki by stating the entire class looked forward to the exciting moment. I noticed the pleased look on Vicki's face from the attention Mrs. Coop gave her. Wheels turned inside my head as I wanted to receive my teacher's adoration and attention from something other than rolling the letter *r*.

The next day as promised, Vicki came to class with a new hair style and a brand new outfit. Of course Mrs. Coop did her job admirably by guiding everyone's attention toward Vicki. The girls clapped gleefully as the boys seemed to just go along with the flow. I, however, wanted that same adulation. I couldn't help myself and suddenly rose from my seat to steal away some of the focus—an upstaging if you will.

"Mrs. Coop," I projected. "I'm going to look different tomorrow too."

A hush fell over the room as I stood there not really caring that I had no plan for this eventuality. The moment ended without any real climax other than Mrs. Coop acknowledging my announcement much the same as she did the day before with Vicki.

Later that evening I pleaded with my mother to help me come up with my new look. Mom didn't quite get my sense of urgency, although I do recall her listening to my pleas. She gave it a good try, but considering the sudden nature of my request, there didn't seem to be a whole lot she or I could do. We came up with a formal outfit like the one worn in my class photograph. I couldn't change my hair like the girls could. I remember my disappointment because I wanted something beyond clothes. I had no clue as to what it could be. Moms are supposed to just come up with magical solutions for six year olds. I don't remember what happened the next day. Maybe things didn't turn out well and I tuned out the experience completely.

◆ ◆ ◆

Each day I walked to Franklin School in the sunshine, snow, and rain. With the changing seasons, I experienced numerous moments that jump started my fertile imagination. Hot days made me think of cooling off with a refreshing Popsicle, or cooking an egg on the sidewalk and then sprinkling the egg with street sand. On cold snowy days, I imagined traveling to the North Pole to meet Santa Claus for a candy cane and a load of toys. On rainy days, I played in the gutter along the curb. Years later I wrote these thoughts down in a children's song.

Popsicle Sticks

Walking down the street all alone
It's a sunny day

Just a six year old going home
With plenty of time to play.

I'm looking for Popsicle sticks in the sand by the curb
in the road, in the road
With plenty of time to play.

I'm looking for Popsicle sticks
On a Saturday after Friday with no more school
And plenty of time to play.

I'm looking for Popsicle sticks
Favorite flavors of grape and strawberry too
Any color will do.

Oh wouldn't you like to play the Popsicle game with me?
Oh wouldn't you like to play the Popsicle game with me? Me?

Walking down the street all alone
It's a rainy day
Just a six year old going home
With plenty of time to play.

I'm looking for Popsicle sticks in the sand by the curb
in the road, in the road
With plenty of time to play.

Oh wouldn't you like to play the Popsicle game with me?
Oh wouldn't you like to play the Popsicle game with me? Me?
Popsicle game.

Many of those days I walked hand in hand with my sister, Ann. Other days I walked alone. When it rained, I dropped the flat sticks in the stream of water along Liberty Street's curb. I watched them sail away to a far away harbor. I imagined myself as the tiny captain of the Popsicle stick as it rode the rainwater current hugging the curbside. These water journeys could potentially become tragic. You see, up ahead in the chilly, wet, distance loomed the sewer grate with a one way trip into the Illinois River or worse, the local water treatment plant. My busy imagination, however, got me out of those jams easily enough. I simply jumped ship and used my super human strength against the current to safely swim away. I grabbed up the sticks in a jolt of reality and shoved them into my pocket. I didn't want to be late. Mrs. Coop promoted me to second grade.

10

Ace Hardware

Living downtown had advantages for little boys seeking fun. For me, a popular, and some may have thought unusual place, was the Ace Hardware Store. Unusual, only if they didn't know about the second floor. Half way through the store, past the hammers, pipe wrenches, nails, screws, and toilet seats, a doorway led into a stairwell. The door was partially hidden by layers of hardware store products decorating the wall on both sides and the aisle shelves in front of it. Entering this door, I imagined myself climbing the ante-chamber stairwell to Santa's attic workshop. Old wooden stairs moaned and creaked with every step up, up, up to the huge second floor area almost entirely devoted to … toys!

More like a warehouse than anything else, I spent hours in that room when not at home or in school. At the head of the stairs management had assembled a row of bicycles. Next I recall the long aisles of multi-level displays holding enough toys to rival the entire toy section of the Sears Catalog. Unlike the excitement of turning the Sears Catalog pages, the Ace toy room meant hands on real toys. Everything I could possibly want sat right there in front of me waiting to be picked up and thoroughly tested out by professional kid hands … mine! I discovered battery operated cars and trucks, airplanes, tons of wind up toys of every description, models, cowboy six shooter holster sets, western style rifles, WWII M-1 rifles, machine guns, army helmets, football gear, and balls of every kind. As much as I loved to eat, I passed on the Easy Bake Oven sets, companionship with Chatty Cathy dolls, strollers, and whatever else the girls played with. I declined to look at that stuff and went directly to the boxes of slot car racing sets.

I had my eyes on the Strombecker box that sported a race official waving checkered flags. I wanted that road race set more than anything. It came complete with two XKE Jaguars; one red, one black. The wide, black, track with metal power contact strips gleaming in the center, beckoned my attention. The power strips flanked each of the two slots that held the cars on the track. Two sections of the track had a cross over for lane changing. On one track section, the lanes squeezed close together, called a *chicane*, only allowing one car at a time to pass through. The cross over and chicane sections caused quite a few accidents as the pictures on the box indicated. The totally awesome Strombecker race track could be set up as an oval, or a figure *8*.

The next Christmas, a big flat package had my name on it. I ripped it to shreds first to reveal the Strombecker road race set I had been drooling over for weeks. Whoa, what a feeling. I had been given the best gift from the entire top floor of Ace Hardware. I gave Mom and Dad big hugs as happy tears streamed down my cheeks. My new Strombecker race set thrilled me with several years of crashing, rubber burning fun.

The Ace Hardware second floor toy section only a block away from my bedroom became my adopted play room. I spent so much time there, and it didn't seem to matter that I rarely purchased anything. I must have been a respectful browser. The store employees and owner never objected to me taking advantage of the treasures they displayed. They saw me each day when I was there and smiled as I proceeded up the groaning stairs to Santa's toy land. I tested everything of interest and made sure everything worked. I guess you could have called me a quality control specialist; a quasi-employee with free reign as my outstanding compensation.

11

Second Grade, 1959–1960

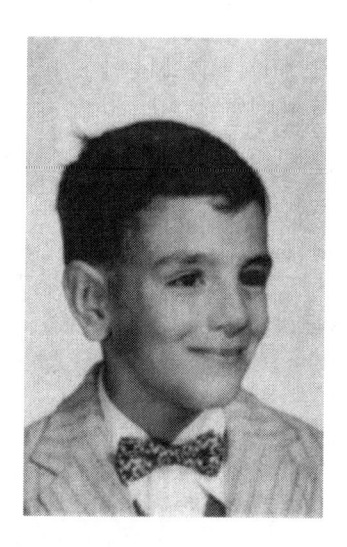

o o o o o o o o o o o o o o o o o o o o o o o o o o o o o o
"There's a man in the funny papers we all know, Alley Oop ..."
Dallas Frazier

*C*lass photo day had arrived, and I still felt the ill effects of the mumps; notice the somewhat forced toothless smile. Mom insisted I go to school that morning regardless of how I felt. Her little boy would not miss class picture day. At the time I didn't care one way or the other about having my picture taken, I only wanted to stay in bed. Looking back on the experience, I have to thank Mom for her imperious nature. I have this great photograph to keep the picture chain in tact.

Much older than Mrs. Coop from first grade, Mrs. Windsor, my second grade teacher, had curly gray hair and looked like a grandmother. She and Mr. Windsor, a Grundy County judge, lived on Union Street across from the high school in a large two story white house. I remember they kept a horse, Queenie, on their property. My sister, Ann, and I along with her friends used to stop by to visit Queenie. I remember wondering what it would be like to live in such a big house with a huge yard. Having a horse to ride every day seemed like something I could never have. Funny—in Stavrothromi, Greece, Mom and her family had a horse. In America, I didn't.

If I had paid more attention to the other kids during those Queenie visits, I might have been introduced to Beth Bednarik sooner. She lived only a few houses down from the Windsor house. We must have spoken to each other at least a little bit. Here she is in second grade; adorable isn't she?

By second grade, I had long since mastered the English *r* and moved on leaving the rolling ones for when I spoke Greek with my family at home. In our second grade school year, things got serious. Now I had to compete for class ranking in such a way that I didn't quite recognize at first. But it didn't take long to figure out the ranking system for what it represented. There were three groups; Blue Birds, Yellow Birds, and Red Birds. The Blue Birds constituted the outstanding students. Yellow Birds were those of mid-level achievement and Red Birds for the slower learners. I belonged to the Yellow Bird group, a middle of the road type of guy.

Each group had its desks arranged in private, segregated, semi-circles. Mrs. Windsor moved from group to group after having made her general instructions to the class as a whole. She spent more time with red birds that needed the most help. When I finally understood the reason for the grouping I didn't like it, mostly because I felt sorry for the Red Birds and one boy specifically.

One part of my character that was most profound to me was the often overwhelming feeling of sorrow I felt for those less fortunate. It didn't have to be a richer or poorer observation though it could have been. I discovered this about myself while sitting in the Yellow Bird circle in second grade. It broke my heart way back then to see other children struggling with what I thought were simple daily activities. I continue to have this trait today. I'm convinced it came from my father and his generosity with those who were down and out. As an eight year old boy on a visit to Chicago with my family, we exited the main entrance to Union Station on La Salle Street. We passed a man sitting on the cold pavement cradling a cup for donations in front of him. Dad didn't drop in coins, he dropped bills.

Getting back to the Red Birds, I still get teary eyed thinking back to my Red Bird classmate, Freddy Pfaff. Freddy, a gentle soul, unfortunately had a degree of mental disability that back in those days was referred to as *retarded*. I knew Freddy all through grade school and he, more than anyone I knew then, brought those feelings out in me. I couldn't call him retarded. Like my compassionate father, I described him as being slower than the rest of us. He spoke in labored drawn out words through his ever present smile exactly like the one in this picture. At times, Freddy had a little drool on his lower lip when he spoke which made it very difficult for me to hold back my sadness. I felt pity for him because of his sweet, trusting, personality that transcended the bad break he got in life. Only recently did I learn something new about Freddie. On a winter's day a few years after second grade, he loaned his fur-lined gloves to Billy Fruland. Billy didn't have his own gloves, and Freddie shared his.

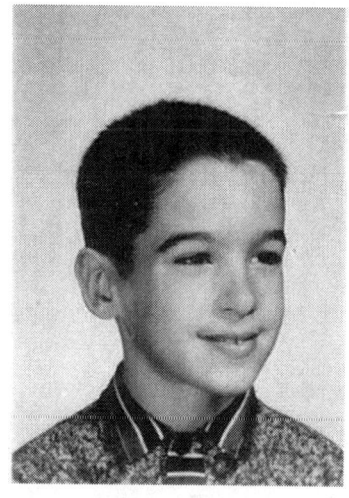

As a mechanic, Freddy's father worked at the Buick dealership garage located on Liberty Street. I used to see Freddy in there with his dad as he worked on the cars. When Freddy got older, he helped out in the garage wearing mechanic's coveralls like his dad. It made me happy to see him proud of himself and wiping the grease off his hands with a shop towel.

In those early days on Liberty Street, I really did know myself pretty well—a healthy self-awareness. I recognized the compassion that lived inside of me. But I didn't let anyone else see that in me. I internalized it. Freddie didn't know, and I kept at a distance most of the time because I couldn't handle the sorrow. I'd break down and cry. I wanted to be his full time friend, but I couldn't find the strength within myself to be more than a kid who could be kind to him whenever our paths crossed. I just wish I could have had the strength to manage my feelings better—for Freddy.

12

Monark and Coast King

For my eighth birthday, Uncle Bill surprised me with my first bicycle—a twenty four inch Monark from Gambles. During my childhood I proudly rode that bike, followed by a twenty-six inch Coast King three years later. Each single gear machine fulfilled my cycling dreams. Sure, some of my friends had multiple geared, Schwinn Sting Rays fancifully styled with banana seats, and sissy bars. That was okay with me. I enjoyed my bikes just the same, and together they performed handsomely as my main mode of transportation.

I learned how to ride a two wheeler by using my sister's big blue girl's bike. Despite its size, I easily stood and pedaled because it had the girl's dip in the frame. A real treat to ride, Ann's bike felt sturdy, and with fat tires it rode smoothly. The feeling of freedom I got while learning to ride that large bike excited me beyond belief. For a seven year old, experiencing such speed and wind-in-the-face exhilaration, couldn't be beat. I felt somehow addicted to the activity and had a difficult time relinquishing the bike to my sister. I had to ride, ride, and ride! Freedom!

The Jefferson Street kindergarten sidewalk from Liberty Street to Carlson's service station had become our bike riding path. From the time we first began riding, we had to watch out for cars pulling in and out of Carlson's driveway. Caution came as part of the deal when rolling past the gas pumps, over the black bell cord and ringing the service bell. We got the biggest kick out of that bell. While hosing the service bay, Mr. Carlson got his kicks as well by shooting the water at us as we flew past. He knew we were coming, but he pretended not to know. Suddenly he turned toward us and fired away full throttle. Sometimes he got us, and sometimes he missed. Either way, the screams of laughter seemed to tickle him too. I could tell we entertained rather than annoyed him. He was after all, the friendly neighborhood Standard Oil man who cleaned your windshield, checked the oil, topped off the air in your tires, and filled your tank with gas. Mr.

Carlson personified service with a smile even as we rang that bell over and over, day after day. And when my bike tires needed air, Mr. Carlson gladly pumped them up too.

◆   ◆   ◆

While away on one of our many day trips to Chicago, some criminal stole my Monark from the sidewalk in front of our apartment. I will never forget the emptiness and anxiety I felt as we drove by the apartment late one Sunday afternoon upon returning from the city. With daylight fading, I saw well enough from the car, that my Monark bicycle had vanished. After Dad parked the car, I ran past where I had left my bike and stormed up the stairs. I flopped onto my bed devastated. My birthday gift had been criminally yanked out of my life forever. I remember wanting to search the town from one end to the other to get my bike back. Dad quietly assured me any such attempt would be futile. I felt guilty and angry with myself for leaving it out unlocked which is what I always did. People in small towns don't steal other people's property ... or do they?

One of Mom's regular customers in the restaurant, a construction worker named Bernie Hansen came in for lunch at least twice a week. Mr. Hansen, in his late thirties and single, lived in another small town, Mazon, approximately ten miles south of Morris. He worked various construction projects throughout the area. He was a kind and generous man, perhaps a bit melancholy for being unattached and without a family of his own.

Mr. Hansen had a large vascular birthmark, or blood vessel abnormality called a *port wine stain* on his lower lip and chin. The aberration was large enough to cause people to react uncomfortably upon first sight. Mom taught us well by explaining the importance of not staring and having sympathy for Mr. Hansen. I certainly did. She and Dad were sensitive to people with handicaps. With both my parents owning such a capacity for sympathy, it is no wonder I had such an acute sensitivity for it.

One lunch hour, while sitting at his regular booth at the rear of the lounge, Mr. Hansen stopped me as I passed by.

"Hi Mike," he said. "Hold out your hands."

"Hello Mr. Hansen."

I held my hands out in front of me. He reached over placing one hand under mine. He opened his other large clenched fist above and unloaded a fistful of change into my waiting palms. Wow! The sheer weight of the coins indicated to me I would later count out several dollars in mostly half dollars, quarters, dimes and nickels. I recall this happening several times back then. It always brought a huge smile to both our faces. Even later, when I anticipated his generosity, it still thrilled me to get all that cold, hard, cash. I'm sure Mr. Hansen got a kick out of the look on my face.

Mr. Hansen outdid himself one day at lunch time. I had entered Dad's bar through the side door as I often did on my way into the restaurant. That route took me past the booth where Mr. Hansen, always sat. When he saw me he stopped me with his deep voice.

"Hello Mike, I'm sorry about your bike," he said.

The memory saddened me, and it surprised me that he knew. Without verbally responding, I nodded and continued into the restaurant to see Mom and put in my lunch order. Mom must have told him about my loss. I walked back toward the bar to sit in my booth to watch TV when Mr. Hansen stopped me again. This time he put out his hands, and with an understanding look in his eye, held my hand with both of his while pressing something into my hand.

"Mike," he said, "go buy yourself a new bike."

This took me by complete surprise. I opened my hand to find a crisp, folded fifty dollar bill! I didn't know what to do or say. I stood there frozen and excited at the same time. He helped me out of my stupor.

"It's okay Mike. Go ahead. Go pick out a nice new bike."

I don't remember if I even thanked him because of my excitement. Four choices entered my head immediately, the upstairs of Ace Hardware and its row of bikes at the top of the stairs—no, too much trouble with the stairs. How about Gambles, one block east where my Monark was purchased?—no again—too much pain remembering my Monark. Perhaps the Coast to Coast Store two blocks south on Liberty Street would be good. Choice four, Swanee's Schwinn Store four blocks away—no, too far. I darted across Jefferson along Liberty Street headed for the Coast to Coast Store where I knew of the bicycles they had lined up inside. Coast to Coast; easy, close, and harbored no bad memories. I asked the sales clerk if I had enough to buy a bike and she said I did, so I picked out a twenty six inch bright red Coast King. I must have taken all of ten minutes to select, pay for and exit the store with my new wheels. Mr. Hansen mended my broken heart. That story is the one I mentioned in the preface that I sent to Beth.

I have no way of knowing how my father felt about another man giving me so much money. Did he resent it? Did he even care? Maybe he paid Mr. Hanson back the money because he felt guilty for not replacing my Monark soon enough. Either way, the two men were friends and they must have known the importance of mending my broken heart that day.

◆ ◆ ◆

For several years, I rode my red Coast King all over town and even once tried to take it on a day trip to Minooka, east on US Route 6. A group of us wild and crazy kids decided to make this hastily planned road tour one morning. To the best of my recollection, Steve and Denny Holbrook, their cousin Rob Enger, Roger Roth, Jack Cameron, Pete Butler, and I made up the group. On a warm summer day, we convinced ourselves we could get to Minooka a full ten miles away without any problem. Off we went without any supplies; no helmets, bicycle gloves, water, or even telling our parents about our plan. For those of you who have never taken a long bike trip, there is a huge difference between riding a bike all over town for a day of goofing around, and that of riding along a two lane highway through open countryside several miles without water or snacks—huge.

We got as far as the Rock Island Railroad crossing about five miles out. A freight train happened to meet us at the crossing adding a thrill to the ride. Just past this crossing rose a long, fairly steep, uphill grade; a difficult climb for me to make on a one speed bike for sure. Reaching the summit, we assumed the Minooka city water tower would be visible, a major morale booster. Parched, sweaty, and pretty beat from the hill climb, we stopped to catch our breath and feast our eyes on the Minooka water tower. Seeing it meant only a few miles remained. We couldn't see the water tower—a *Twilight Zone* moment. The tower had to be there. I saw it every time we passed by on Interstate 80 driving to Chicago. Confused and let down because we expected to see progress, we searched for an answer. The only sight was more of the road and a long row of trees ahead to our left. At the time we had no idea those trees hid the water tower. Minooka lay ahead only two or three more miles. We miscalculated how far we had actually traveled, and were probably only twenty minutes away with flat ground ahead and just three miles remaining. Three miles to reach cold water, pop, candy, and chips in downtown Minooka. We argued for a few minutes—go on or turn back. We opted for turning back—so much for inter-town bike travel. We gave it a gallant attempt but the road won, and our group returned to Morris hungry and thirsty.

My red Coast King lasted several years through mud, rain, and even snow. I particularly enjoyed the unusual challenge of trying to make it through snow. Slipping, sliding, and spinning my rear wheel brought back memories of learning to ride all over again. As fun as the snow could be, it was mostly an effort in simply trying to stay upright and soon lost its appeal.

In addition to street riding, we rode our bikes up and down the hills in the old abandoned strip mines. Strip mines existed all around Morris. A series of hills stood out west just beyond the high school football practice fields. Our bikes hit those hills often enough, but they mainly served as a good place to play army. Our favorite hill climbing spot found us in the area of strip mines near the new city water tower on the east side of town off Armstrong Street. At the end of First and Second Avenues, a little service road curved around close to the water tower. Passing the tower and continuing for several more yards brought us to the entrance of the best hill climbing paths in Morris. The entrance hill reached high into the sky, tempting and certainly terrifying. The trails beyond this first hill wound through the hills as far east as the city landfill or *the dump*, half a mile away.

These old dry hills had excellent trails packed into the dirt by the older boys with their motorcycles. On any given day, the trails filled with forty or fifty kids on bicycles and motorcycles of all kinds. It took plenty of energy to ride the acres of hills and trails out there. Many of the hills were close to twenty feet high. Those of us with only one speed bikes had to jump off and push uphill more often than not. The best rides, though, were when enough downhill momentum on one hill sufficiently carried you up the next hill ahead. This activity wreaked havoc on most bicycles. The stress often cracked frames, blew tires, bent rims, and broke spokes, front and rear. Bikes then weren't equipped with shock absorbers, advanced frame design, and construction materials like the mountain bikes of today. My rims sustained a few dents and I lost a few spokes resulting in the dreaded wheel wobble. Perhaps the most feared crash was landing hard and slipping off your seat onto the top bar and experiencing your basic groin smash. It happened often. Rough riders that we were, we rode on. Nut cups would have been a good thing for sure, but no one wore one. Honestly, I don't think anyone really thought about it.

The intimidating entrance or first hill coming into the area was also the last as you were leaving the property. Once, on the way out, an accident occurred involving one of my classmates, Gary Matteson. He rode down the huge exit hill too fast and hit the bottom of the hill … hard. He had injured himself badly. A small group of guys took off to phone for help. After a few minutes an ambulance showed up and took Gary to the hospital. He had sustained an injury to his neck and also broke a collar bone or an arm. Gary's crash reminded us of just how dangerous this adventure could be; dangerous but one heck of a lot of fun.

I rode my Coast King pretty hard as a kid until it finally gave in to old age—or abuse. I eventually gave it away to charity, a fitting gesture since I received it under similar generous circumstances. How could I ever forget the generosity of Mr. Bernie Hansen?

13

Third Grade, 1960–1961

ooooooooooooooooooooooooooooo
"I'm a walkin' in the rain, tears are fallin' and I feel the pain ..."
Gary Allan

"Can she bake cherry pie, Billy boy, Billy boy? Can she bake cherry pie, tell me Billy?" This is a line from an old 19th Century English song originally known as *Willy Lad* or *Charming William*. I first heard it from my dad's employee, Happy, who played it on the old piano that used to be in the bar. I sang this perfect little ditty to my pal, Billy Fruland, in Mrs. Sykes' third grade class. Mrs. Sykes had gray hair, long facial features, and was in her late sixties I would say.

She must have been very near retirement as Mrs. Windsor was the year before. She was tall and I recall her voice having a deeper tone than most women.

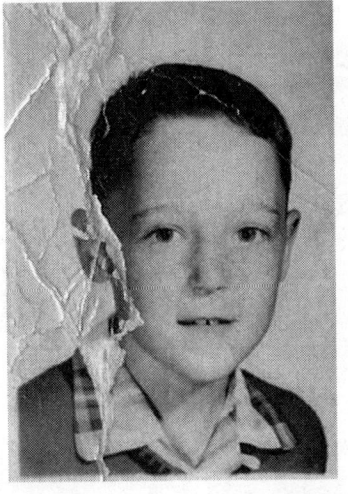

Although we met in second grade, third grade is where Billy and I began to interact more. As the only Billy in my class, he naturally became the recipient of the tune. I crossed paths with him in the classroom and out of the blue started singing the song to him. The melody must have been in my head because Happy had just played it for me the day before. It's funny in hindsight how the picture in my mind of this serenade shows Billy politely shrugging it off. I suppose a third grade boy singing some strange song to another third grade boy would be somewhat annoying. What else could he have done; punched me in the nose during class? I'm glad he didn't.

◆ ◆ ◆

Out on the barricaded Franklin Street playground, two forces of opposing armies took aim at each other. For days, rebellious Confederates led by General Steve Barkley battled it out with the Union Army led by General Billy Johnson. These two fourth graders built up their armies with volunteers from all grades. Billy Fruland joined the Union army under Billy Johnson's leadership. He didn't like that Barkley kid, so he elected to go Union. The two armies lined up at either end of the playground and followed their Generals into marching, charging clashes.

Wearing their ragtag, incomplete uniforms, each loyal group of soldiers followed their respective leaders into wild heated battles. They wore authentic looking felt caps purchased at Schultz Brothers. Some kids (including General Barkley) carried cap pistols and holsters while others wielded swords—a sight quite different from today's playground scenes. Try taking a cap gun to school these days and well, you get the picture.

General Steve Barkley dove into his leadership role like a boy on a high level government operation. Steve gathered his men around him on the battlefield and rallied them with motivating oratory filled with inspiring rhetoric. Prior to the first bell calling everyone to class, he prepared his men.

"Men ... we have to get this school business out of the way ... now. Be ready for the battle at recess!"

The Confederates cheered as the bell sounded. Franklin Street emptied. Inside, teachers conversed about what to do with the growing problem of violent army battles out on the street. Children were suffering disfiguring war wounds; skinned knees and palms, bleeding elbows, ringing ears from cap blasts too close for comfort, and plastic sword bruises about the arms and legs of the poor little soldiers. One of the teachers took Steve aside and lectured him.

"Now Steve, these civil war battles are an interesting method of teaching your fellow students American History. However, we believe it is more important that students come to school and learn their lessons in the classroom. Every student needs to learn arithmetic, English, and history in class," she said firmly.

"Okay. So let's get school out of the way because I got stuff to do. I gotta send out scouts. What's all this arithmetic stuff about anyway? For Pete's sake I got battle plans to make. I don't have time for this. I've gotta attack at recess!"

That was a pretty good speech for a rebel. But it didn't work. General Barkley caved under the pressure from higher authorities, and when recess came, he, General *Bully* Steve Barkley, surrendered the Confederate Army—his army—to General Billy Johnson. The Union Army rejoiced victorious. The rebel soldiers were shocked and quite noticeably upset with General Barkley for surrendering. The war games had stopped due to injuries on the battlefield of Franklin School playground.

◆ ◆ ◆

Third grade offers very little in the way of interesting or funny in class factoids. My pal John Halterman had a crush on Marne Davis. I learned Patricia Enerson had an eye on me which at that age elicited a less than favorable response out of me. I rudely scratched out her picture in our class group photograph. Sorry Pat, girls didn't figure into my equation just yet. In third grade, we paid close attention to the cursive letters that bordered the ceiling above the blackboard. Lining up at the blackboard and learning longhand with Mrs. Sykes that year was a primary focus, and the activity I remember best. Just one student picking up the chalk and dragging it along the blackboard's surface without creating a massive, vibrating, screeching, noise was an art in itself. Creating readable symbols out of this procedure proved to be another thing entirely. Furthermore, a long row of students produced a concert of variable squeals and screeches that made it even worse. Who can deny many of the ear-splitting shrills weren't deliberate? Mischievous side glances at each other while facing the board started the fun. After all, I was in there with my companions fully capable of that mischief. They were John Halterman, Jack Cameron, and Vince Hodgson.

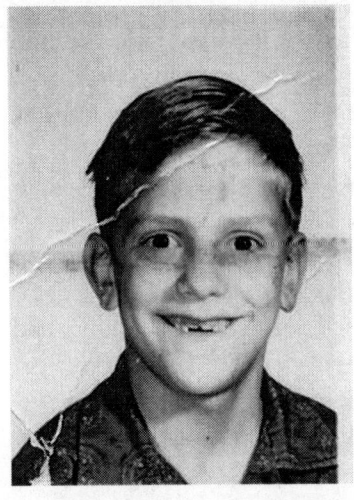

Vince lived with his family in the very last house on the west end of Washington Street six blocks away from me. Vince and I started hanging out together sometime around the third grade, but my guess is we probably cried or laughed face to face much earlier than that in the nursery or the halls of Morris Hospital back in the year 1952. Our mothers gave birth to us within hours of each other. I like to think we did, somehow as newborns, hear each other within the walls of the hospital. I like to think we winked at each other as if we were working out preliminary details for the future mischief to occur in elementary school.

Vince had a plain, simply designed tree house in the side yard of the Hodgson home facing the old flour mill. With each visit I made, Vince and I climbed up the wooden rungs that were nailed into the tree trunk to the humble little hut. We gazed at images in the clouds as they slowly blew by, trying our best to identify the usual dog with floppy ears, or Godzilla swatting a plane out of the sky. In those moments high up in the tree, we had plenty of time to wonder about the heavens above the clouds and what lay beyond the moon and our solar system. It became an inspirational highlight of every visit to Vince's home. I loved the tree house and the imagination it inspired.

◆ ◆ ◆

Franklin School had its gym located in the basement. In addition to P.E. class, the room served as a setting for music class with Mrs. Hammer where we learned to play a variety of instruments such as the sand blocks, wood blocks, triangle, and small cymbals. My favorite choice, the tonette, similar to its larger cousin, the recorder and the most difficult to learn challenged me for sure. I mean, how long does it take to figure out how to rub a sand block? Everyone looked forward to music class and Mrs. Hammer at the piano. We dug into a large box of various percussion instruments and took our places on the risers for daily hot licks as aspiring rock stars. I don't recall trying to tackle the current hits of the time such as *Runaway* recorded by Del Shannon, *Alley Oop* by The Hollywood Argyles, or *Hit the Road Jack* by Ray Charles, *Big Bad John* by Jimmy Dean, or *Never on Sunday*, a good Greek tune. Hey, I could have sung it in Greek for everyone and rolled the *r* to my heart's content too! We basically played the usual *Twinkle, Twinkle Little Star*, type tunes. Then, for the Christmas season, I remember *Silent Night*, and *Jingle Bells*. For me, music class, with its assortment of *dive into the box instruments*, lived up to what creativity in school meant—having fun. This outlet for the arts became the official place where my life long interest in performing live music actually began.

Our basement gym also served as a safe refuge when strong storms blew into town. Thunderstorms were normal for Morris, and some rumbled in quite violently. Huge thunder blasts that shook whole buildings happened all the time. The entire student body took cover in the basement gym one day while a storm raged outside. We huddled together waiting for it to pass. Looking up from my place on the floor, I saw Mr. Johnson, the janitor, walking down the gently sloped ramp into the gym's southwest corner. He wore knee high rubber boots with his coveralls tucked into them and a mop and bucket in one hand. He looked kind of silly. Mr. Johnson had apparently been cleaning up some rain water and entered the gym to inform the presiding teachers the status of the situation. Panic didn't enter my mind at all. We'd been through dozens of storms without any major damage in town, and this one eventually blew over as well. The end of the school day saw a bright sunny sky for my walk home. Finding any Popsicle sticks along the way would be a bonus.

Of course the main purpose for the gym was physical activity. The shiny linoleum tiled floor measured about sixty or so feet long by perhaps thirty five feet wide with a low ceiling. Activities were limited because of the low ceiling so the games mostly involved running from one end to the other. Games like *Stone,* for example, where the game starts with a few kids in the center of the floor and all the others run past them. If those static center stones (kids) touched a runner, that runner became a stone in that spot; pretty elementary stuff.

Buying new gym shoes meant requests to get the latest PF (*Posture Foundation*) Flyers, US Keds, Red Ball Jets, or Paul Parrot shoes at one of the shoe stores in town on Liberty Street. Of the three commercial jingles on TV for each brand I only remember … "Paul Parrot, Paul Parrot, are the shoes you ought to buy. They make your feet run faster as fast as I can fly."

The Morris Shoe Store on the 200 block of Liberty Street was where Mr. Lee McCullom worked. Mr. McCullom had a high level of energy about him. He had an eager to please approach for customer satisfaction—an admirable business ethic which when coupled with his growling breathy laugh, created an unforgettable town character. I watched him tie my shoestrings so rapidly and with such technical precision that it seemed to me (even as a third grader) that he found humor in his own idiosyncrasies. I certainly got a kick out of hearing him growl his unique laugh. Visits to his store were always beyond amusing. Mom and I exchanged glances every time during his shtick of quick tie skills and crazy laughter. Tears welled up in her eyes while attempting to hold back out of politeness. But, she couldn't keep from losing control, and we laughed together. Mr. McCullom had to know his odd laugh got us going and not necessarily his jokes. Maybe he didn't know, but I didn't care. I had a blast witnessing his personality. Buying shoes since then has never been anywhere close to that much fun.

In third grade we learned good penmanship, a little music, and physical education. During these noisy activities we slowly started the lifelong degradation of our precious sense of hearing. Miss Davies instructed us as to the importance of taking good care of our ears. She encouraged this when preparing to administer hearing tests on her sound machine. We gladly sat there listening closely while wearing headphones and raising our hands up and down identifying sounds (most of which I wouldn't hear today). And yet, at the third grade blackboard, we wreaked havoc on our ears with shrill chalk stick vibrations. Early stages of hearing loss continued with the sand blocks, cowbells, wood blocks, and various other noise makers in music class. In gym class we squealed our PF Flyers, Red Ball Jets, and US Keds over highly polished linoleum tiles as ear drum piercing screams bounced off the walls. We were having the times of our young lives. Mrs. Sykes propelled me into fourth grade.

14

Holbrook, Cameron, and Halterman

Though sounding like a rock band or a law firm, these three names belonged to my closest friends in the grade school years. All three families had their homes on the perimeter of Chapin Park. I remember the very moment I first saw Steve Holbrook. I pedaled my Monark near the Methodist Church. Steve rode his light green bicycle on the Jackson Street sidewalk directly in front of the church. I turned left onto Jackson and we passed each other right there. We didn't say anything during the quick passing, but I astutely noticed he had red hair, fair skin, and freckles. Because Steve was one year younger we didn't cross paths in early grade school. We were destined, however, to meet again because of the existence of Chapin Park. I don't know the actual event that solidified our friendship, but it may have been a bike race around the dirt field in the park, or perhaps a baseball game. Whatever the milestone; we became buddies. Soon after our official introduction to each other, I met his older brother, Denny, a year my senior.

Denny, the oldest of the four Holbrook siblings including Steve, Cathy and Mark, radiated confidence and physical strength. He advocated organization and preparation; something I noticed early on as I watched him doing his homework on their kitchen table. He wrote in small, precise letters, and his work always looked perfect to me.

At two years younger and less solidly built than his older brother, Steve often had to endure the dominating ribbing that inevitably came his way. Denny nicknamed his younger brother, *Duke* or *Dukey* (pronounced Dooky). Actually they called each other Duke out of brotherly love and in good fun. It must have come from John (*The Duke*) Wayne movies.

As brothers often do, they had different ways of seeing things. One silly example I remember involved the best way to get warm when first climbing into bed for the night. Steve's method utilized the wriggle around creating friction technique to heat up the bed. Denny's idea called for tightly packing the covers around you and remaining still. I recall that exchange one afternoon as the three of us talked in their bedroom. Don't ask me why I remember that one—just a goofy moment during my observations of two brothers and how they interacted with each other. There were many times I felt envious watching brothers interact. Not having a brother bothered me sometimes, and I often wondered what it would be like to have one.

◆ ◆ ◆

Jack Cameron and I were together in Mrs. Coop's first grade class and also second and third grades with Mrs. Windsor and Mrs. Sykes respectively. Given the amount of time we shared in class and the fact that he lived across the street from Chapin Park, it's easy to understand how we thought of each other as best friends during those early years. Jack and I went so far as to one day cut our fingers and press them together as blood brothers. For obvious health reasons, I don't think this ritual is practiced anymore.

Energetic and small, Jack had a somewhat rebellious, pugnacious, attitude about him at times. He liked Bugs Bunny cartoons and the annoying way Bugs tormented Elmer Fudd. That said, it's easy for me to understand where and how Jack might have adopted his Bugs Bunny-like acerbic attitude. It came from *dat wabbit* himself! His family had a little, black and white, Boston terrier named Tina (nothing like the adoring Tina I used to know) who always barked viciously at me. Jack exhibited good control over Tina (the dog). Many times, I thought Tina would rip into me for sure, but she never did thanks to Jack.

◆ ◆ ◆

John Halterman shared the first three years in grade school with Jack and me. Before moving close to Chapin Park, John lived near me just one and a half blocks east on Jefferson Street. Of all my close pals back then, John held a special place in my world for two reasons; a handicap, and his ease of expressing himself. First, in those days John suffered from a mild form of epilepsy. I felt sad about that, but he did eventually overcome it. At the time, my other friends and I didn't quite understand it medically, and his parents skirted explaining it to us. In hindsight, I find it easy to understand why they didn't go into detail, given the relationships between boys and adults in those days. Adults never told us much. Personal matters such as those were kept within the family. Other kids simply didn't need to know. We had been made aware about John's problem and that's about all.

John's handicap manifested itself in a truly fascinating manner. At any time, and for no apparent reason, he drifted into this trance-like state with his eyes staring off into space. We called it *daydreaming*. His face showed no emotion whatsoever, but in his eyes I always saw something that made me think he experienced some kind of nirvana. Whenever this occurred, wherever he drifted, nothing could be done to help him back. We waited for the *daydream* to run its course which might have been only seconds or up to a minute or more. If we were playing a game or out running around, we made sure he wasn't in any environmental danger.

In the northwest corner of town, a small bridge on Johnson Avenue passed over Nettle Creek near Lisbon Street. A group of us; John, Jack, Steve, Denny, and I rode our bikes to the bridge and left them at the side of the road. We took a little path through a stand of bushes and trees to a tranquil curve in Nettle Creek where we liked to wade in a series of gentle rapids not far from the Johnson Avenue Bridge. We gave this place an unusual name; *Trenches*. The place looked and sounded similar to what you might expect out of a fairy tale. Trickling water in the narrow stream wound through a meadow of low lying plants, wild flowers, and of course ... nettles. Larger cottonwood trees shaded the entire meadow. We had spent several minutes that afternoon splashing through *Trenches* and cooling off in the rapids. Morris didn't have a beach with waves large enough for surfing, but on a hot summer day the next best thing was a flat piece of plywood underfoot through the shallow rapids of *Trenches*.

After attempting to surf the rapids with little success but ingenious loads of fun, we headed back to our bikes at the bridge. Parallel with the bridge and about a foot below road level lay a section of steel pipe perhaps eighteen inches in diameter that crossed over the creek bed. Several basketball-sized rocks and jagged chunks of broken concrete littered the creek bed, eight free falling feet below. Our next improvised adventure stared us smack in the face. We couldn't resist traversing the pipe by straddling it with our legs and scooting across. The other guys had already made the trip ahead of me without any trouble. I followed next and then behind me, John ... the last. After I got to the other side Jack shouted for me to look back at John.

"Mikey! John is daydreaming!" Jack yelled.

He had started to daydream halfway across. Without hesitation, I got back on the pipe and walk/crawled as fast as I could to reach him before he fell off onto the rocks below. I held him in a bear hug for what seemed like the longest daydream ever. My legs grabbed the sides of the pipe to keep my balance. Cramping set in, but I ignored the pain as I heard the rushing water flowing over the jagged concrete slabs. I wouldn't look down ... I couldn't look down because of the angle my head took in the bear hug. I remember thinking ...

Wake up John, wake up.

My legs began to tremble from the strain of holding us both in place. The whole time in his distant, peaceful place, John sat absolutely still and relaxed—completely unaware of our predicament. The other guys called out to me in a collage of words, most of which I couldn't understand except for—"You got him?" and "Hold on!" I just wanted them to shut up. I had to concentrate on the precarious balancing act for as long as it took. John and I sat there on that pipe locked together for about two minutes, to the best of my recollection. He finally started coming back from somewhere out in the galaxy. I felt his arms move first and I spoke to him softly so I wouldn't startle him.

"John, you're okay ... I got you and we're alright. Just don't move ... okay?"

When he became lucid again, he looked into my eyes and almost started to cry. The first words he said to me were ...

"You saved my life."

"I had to," I said.

I don't think I ever expected to hear anyone say those four words to me in a real life situation.

In a few moments, John had regained his grasp of the pipe. I turned around slowly on my sore legs so he wouldn't have to turn, and we shimmied across to the waiting hands of Jack, Steve, and Denny. The fact that no one else scrambled out to help me never entered my mind until a while afterwards. Pedaling away from the bridge, I exchanged the usual insults with the other guys for not helping. You know, just the usual stuff ...

"You guys are real buttheads. Thanks for helping."

In response I heard ...

"Takes one to know one!"

"You're still a butthead," I repeated.

And followed by the all encompassing ...

"I know you are, but what am I?"

From that rescue moment on, John Halterman couldn't thank me enough. He wouldn't let me forget that I had saved his life once. I'm glad I did.

The second reason for my closeness to John involved his ability to express himself so effortlessly. We sat among the buckeyes that had fallen off the trees in the yard of his first house discussing Flash Gordon. We contemplated outer space, questioned life in general, and the nuances of friendship. During these conversations, he found it so easy to let me know how much he valued my friendship—pretty heavy stuff for two little kids. His intelligent, caring nature filled John with wonder about the universe, and like me ... he loved watching Flash Gordon. We had a great childhood friendship.

◆ ◆ ◆

"Let's go to the show." That was our Morris way of saying "Let's go to the Morris Theatre and see a movie." Only half a block separated me from the Morris Theatre and the same for John on the theatre's other side. John, Jack, and I went to the show many times along with Frankie, John's little brother. We particularly enjoyed the Hercules movies starring Steve Reeves. Why not ... Hercules was Greek! Even the Three Stooges made a movie about Hercules and time travel back to ancient Greece entitled, *The Three Stooges Meet Hercules*. Being Stooges fans, that silly film rattled our funny bones. I remember other films we watched such as *Rodan*, a giant airplane gulping bird, *The Time Machine*, *Jason and the Argonauts*, *Journey to the Center of the Earth*, *Gorgo*, and the *Godzilla* movies. Also lots of Jerry Lewis movies cracked us up. As much as we enjoyed laughing we pretty much craved the science fiction adventure films. *The Mysterious Island* and *The Time Machine* were two of my most favorites.

I mentioned John liked *Flash Gordon*. We all did and discussed the episodes in detail. Buster Crabbe played the role of Flash, the hero battling his evil rival, Emperor Ming the Merciless, played by Charles Middleton. We poked fun at Ming, his evil ways, and his emperor's clothes. As much as we liked the *Flash Gordon* series, we always thought the shots of the space ships circling, spewing sparks, and smoke looked pretty cheesy, especially in the shots of several ships flying in formation. Those special effects from the old days of the 1930s were dreadful. However, the absolutely beautiful Dale Arden character, and love interest for Flash, played by Jean Rogers more than made up for the funky special effects. I fell in love with her every Sunday. Later in the series, Carol Hughes, another fine looking woman who found her place in my growing line of actress heart throbs, took over the role of Dale.

Sunday morning black and white TV also filled my head with musical jingle phone numbers from the commercials that played between the programs.

Remember these examples?—a carpet company that played—*Mohawk four, four one hundred*—sung to a Native American style drum beat. Or how about—*Hudson three two seven hundred*—sung by a deep voiced announcer for a mortgage company. I entertained myself by singing along with these fellas every week. The things I remember!

Left to right; Frankie Halterman, John Olson, yours truly and John Halterman

When our group of buddies got together, we didn't always create crazy, reckless adventures in mischief. We played *Clue*, *Life*, and *Monopoly* where John Halterman loved shouting out "Pay doctor's fee!" with glee whenever one of us drew that Chance Card. Another board game we played, but only once, was a U.S. Civil War game. I say once, because after the first time, we could never figure out how to play it again. John owned the game that required logic, strategy, and use of statistics. Crazy as this may sound; the game seemed possessed with a life of its own and wouldn't let us play it again ... creepy. We tried many times. No amount of time spent reading and re-reading the instructions did any good. A degree in enigmatology would have been helpful. We really kind of freaked over that bizarre *Twilight Zone*-like anomaly.

John, Denny, Steve, Jack, and I had created an outer space club where we studied the solar system, our Milky Way Galaxy, and contemplated the size of the universe. We knew all the planets and their order from the sun. We learned distances, diameters, how many moons each planet had, and talked about these statistics at length. Our little un-named club studied as many pictures as we could find from library books, Life, and National Geographic magazines.

Another constructive and historically educational activity we undertook had us embroiled in dinosaur study. Like the outer space club, we memorized all the dinosaurs we could and facts about each one. Inspiration for the dino club came from watching a short series called *Journey to the Beginning of Time* on the *Garfield Goose Show*. The story followed a group of four friends who visited the pre-historic hall of New York City's, Museum of Natural History. After their visit, they went on a Central Park river tour in a row boat. They passed through a cave and came out the other side in the Jurassic Period of the dinosaurs. At the beginning of their adventure they encountered a saber-tooth tiger, a pteranadon, and a brontosaurus. Later they witnessed a fight to the death between a stegosaurus and a tyrannosaurus-like creature called a ceratasaurus. This fascinating fantasy motivated us to learn interesting science information without having to be in school. This is also where I first learned about the Greek roots to so many scientific terms which in turn helped me to learn them. My Greek background sure had interesting applications and advantages. Again ... I felt special. My cephalous (head) swelled with Greek pride and my heart smiled.

The Camerons eventually moved south of the river to Pine Bluff Road. A certain degree of difficulty needed to be overcome for us to get across the river to visit each other. The trek over the river bridge had to be made by car. There was no sidewalk for pedestrians on the narrow two lane bridge, and no way would we ever venture to ride our bikes across the long span—way too dangerous; even for us. When we arranged for visits, Mrs. Cameron or Mrs. Holbrook taxied us over and back. My mother never learned to drive and our dads were usually at work.

While living out there in the sticks, Jack had discovered a new place to explore. It didn't take him long to find the Aux Sable Creek. It meandered about a quarter mile from the new Cameron home. A short hike from his house took him to a huge log jam in the creek. When Jack told us about this log jam, we automatically had to go. This conglomeration of trees and debris created a twisted, tangled, dam the likes of which we had never seen or played on anywhere. And, if negotiating the thirty foot long, and ten foot high log jam weren't enough, an exciting new place to explore lay just on the other side of it. We called it ... *the tunnel.*

A bend in the creek near the tunnel made the natural choke point for this huge log jam to form. We carefully selected the passable logs, root clusters, and dead branches as our pathway to the other side and the tunnel opening. Maneuvering proved a little tricky. Dozens of spaces between the jammed trees sat like traps to catch an errant foot possibly snapping a leg in the process. Some of those gaps were large enough for a one way trip into the water below. In some sections with nothing to hold onto, a balancing act had to be performed on smaller diameter branches.

The tunnel opening could be easily seen across the log jam. The size of a small window, the menacing black hole tempted us to enter. It hovered near the top of the ten foot tall creek bank. We had prepared ourselves ahead of time for the darkness inside the tunnel. In our pockets, we carried matches, several short candles, and a flashlight or two. Jack, Steve, Denny, and I made it safely across the precarious log jam. Next, we had to crawl up part of the steep, black dirt, creek bank to reach the tunnel. Exposed dangling tree roots added to the creepiness of the tunnel opening that loomed before us. And who knew what kinds of spiders or even snakes lived inside. We pulled out our candles and matches. Who would be the first to enter?

"Don't look at me," muttered Steve.

"What's the matter, Dukey ... chicken?" big Denny poked.

"No."

"Sure, Dukey ... you big chicken."

"Shut up."

"I'll go ... fatheads," Jack boldly interrupted.

Denny followed. I wasn't too keen on entering this foreboding cavern first either, so I didn't object to the volunteers. Hanging curly roots and possible slithering critters convinced me that safety and comfort came with the third place in line followed by Steve. The tunnel started with a straight ahead crawl of about four or five feet—so far so good. It didn't take long for Jack and Denny to disappear up ahead after a ninety degree left turn for several more, nerve wracking, feet. One of them placed a lit candle in a nook carved out of the dirt wall lighting the way for me. I saw just how this maze took shape. With the muffled sounds of Jack and Denny already way ahead, I looked around me noticing the engineering. Above my head, by only inches, plywood formed the ceiling. The walls weren't supported by anything, just carved out dirt with the little shelves cut for candles; claustrophobic to be sure. The narrow passage way allowed only one person at a time. Making a U-turn in this tight squeeze was next to impossible. After the first left turn, came another ninety degree turn—this time to the right. This segment of the underground route led us in a straight line for about another ten feet of knee scuffling. Then, we came to the last right turn which immediately opened up into a small, square, room about the size of a king size mattress. There, I found Jack and Denny sitting up in the *home room* well lit by the remaining candles and their flashlights. The floor had dropped a few inches allowing more comfortable headroom. The four of us took our positions around the perimeter leaning against roots, crumbling dirt, and spider webs.

"Okay … now what?" I asked.

"This is it," said Jack matter-of-factly. "Ooga booga!"

The burning candles began taking their toll on the oxygen content of the air further exacerbating my claustrophobia. So, after only about two minutes of sitting around doing a whole lot of nothing but staring at each other in dim light, the novelty wore off. Then … somebody farted; long and loudly. We decided by instantaneous, unanimous decision to beat it—out of the tunnel. Off we went, scrambling one by one, barely in single file out of the king size home room. Our shoulders scraped against the dirt walls further deteriorating the integrity of the tunnel and churning up clouds of dirt.

"I hope this thing doesn't collapse," I managed to choke out.

"Just shut up and go, go … go," Jack coughed.

It was quite an effort to see anything in this dungeon of darkness. Rushing past any wall sconce candles we had placed earlier blew them out. Now we added smoldering candle smoke to the already foul air. I tucked my head and ran straight into a wall missing a turn. Jack slammed into me from behind.

"Watch where you're going will ya?" I called out.

"You watch where you're going you idiot! I can't see a thing in here," wise guy Jack spewed out in his sharp tongued way.

"I can't see anything either ya lame brain, gimme a break."

Regardless of the kicked up dust, candle smoke, dirt, bad gas, and dangling roots—laughter filled the tunnel. We coughed for fresh air. Brrrat! Another fart—more laughing.

"Shut up, and get a move on will ya? I'm gaggin' back here!"

That sounded like Denny.

Finally ... light at the end of the tunnel. A sheer drop awaited us at the exit hole—nobody cared. We were starving for fresh, breathable air—laughing—coughing—spitting; clambering for the right to breathe.

"Who's the gas bag?"

"Who do you think?"

"Who cares? Move it!"

Four goofballs launched themselves out of the tunnel opening like turds squeezed from a foul smelling, wretched colon. We rolled down a few feet of the dirt bank grabbing for the nearest log jam branch. We were free of the foul air but still losing breath from laughing so hard. We must have been a sight; four filthy, kids sliding down the dirt embankment reaching for any branch to keep us from landing in the creek—excellent.

That ended my interest in returning to the tunnel of Pine Bluff Road. We never found out who built it, how, or why. We could only assume a farmer's son with a backhoe devised a plan to construct a fort of his own. We found it. We explored it and left it ... quickly.

So, the basis for most of our adventures had roots in films and television. Whatever the pastime, there always existed the possibility of real life danger. John Halterman's unpredictable daydreaming episodes kept us on our toes. Our imaginations knew no boundaries when it came to diverse scenarios such as crawling along the suspended pipe near *Trenches*. Perhaps we were running away from Ming the Merciless, and braving the pipe gave us our gateway to safety. Maybe crossing the Aux Sable Creek log jam to the tunnel led us to another dimension in time. We could have been trying to get away from Godzilla when we pedaled our bicycles at full speed down swimming pool hill.

15

The Legend of Swimming Pool Hill

The official street name is Northern Avenue. During my childhood days, Northern Avenue had a much steeper grade without curbs. On either side of the old street, were two to three foot deep ditches carved out over the years by rain and melting snow runoff. We used to walk up and down those mini canyons for the sheer adventure of it. It was a gas to take the hill on a bicycle as fast as you dared. An old bridge lined with narrow pipe-like hand rails spanned Nettle Creek at the bottom of the hill. One summer day, just past this old bridge, I came upon the aftermath of a nasty bicycle crash.

Minutes before me, two boys rode together on one bike; one driving it and the other sitting on the handle bars. The passenger had his feet on the two nuts holding the front wheel to the fork. I've never known the kid's name driving the bike, but I'm sure the handle bar rider was a boy named Kevin Woolridge. One of Kevin's feet slipped and went into the fast spinning spokes of the front wheel sending them crashing to the blacktop. This chopped off Kevin's little toe. I arrived on the scene only a few minutes after the crash. The two boys involved had already left the site; probably in a car headed for the Morris Hospital. For some reason, they had left the severed toe behind. I stared at it … in the middle of the street with a number of others gathering around looking at it … a toe. A toe, once part of a foot connected to the leg of a boy we knew. The crowd grew. Kids coming from and going to the Morris swimming pool stopped for a curious look.

"Not something you see every day … is it?" somebody said.

A pinky toe lying on the hot blacktop of Northern Avenue was not exactly a pleasant thing to see. Still freshly severed, it looked so out of place … almost cooking, simmering on the hot tar. I rode away on my bike before I puked. As for the toe and its host ... I don't know if they ever got back together. I kind of doubt it.

◆   ◆   ◆

We literally lived at the municipal swimming pool during the summer months. The pool functioned as the best baby sitter a parent could want. My friends and I walked or mostly rode our bikes to the pool for the one o'clock opening time. We stayed for the entire session ending at five pm. Every pool excursion began at home with getting a bath towel and folding it lengthwise to about a foot wide. On top of that towel at one end, we placed our swim trunks. We then rolled the whole thing from one end to the other. Next, we jammed the roll between the top bars of our bikes or in a basket if you had one. Most guys used the manlier jam method, and we rode off for the pool.

We often had to stop and re-adjust the roll or secure it again and again on the fly. Once in a while, the roll fell out onto the street. This necessitated an emergency stop to gather up the items quickly in order to catch up to the other guys. For the most part, those of us who held onto our rolls kept riding. If we felt the least bit considerate, (*thinking about the other fella*), we stopped forward progress and rode in a circling pattern of bicycles in the middle of the street until *the other fella* retrieved his lost roll. Sometimes the bikes circled around the kid who had to stop. Either way, the playful insults flew from the circling boys until one of *them* lost his roll and laughter and insults came from all over the place. If your roll never fell out in transit, you were lucky ... real lucky.

A full day of biking, swimming, and diving off the boards did wonders to keep us in great shape. We splashed thousands of gallons of water high into the air from a set of diving boards at the pool's deep end. At fifteen feet deep, *the pit* had plenty of depth to accommodate assorted dives, cannonballs, can openers, gainers, and flips; front, and back. Together, they created a nonstop chorus of screaming fun and excitement. Those happy summer sounds could be heard for hundreds of feet around the immediate pool area of Goold Park.

An assembly of four diving boards stood at the deep end of the pool known as *the pit*. The lowest spring board, referred to as *first board*, near the corner of the pit could launch a diver high into the air. The second highest board known as *second board* had been built on the opposite side of the pit about fifteen feet away and three feet off the ground. Between those two boards stood a steel frame structure that housed the two coolest boards; *third board* and the king of them all ... *top board*.

The bravest divers attempted their tricks from towering ... top board, a good thirteen feet above the water's surface; the best diving board ever. A two tiered system of ladders leading up to ... top board, made getting to it a trick in itself. The first set of silver painted steps leaned at about a sixty degree angle from the pavement to a small waiting area at the rear of third board. This waiting area held as many as ten kids. We huddled, and shivered with purple lips and goose bumps waiting our turn. We waited to fly off third board or change our minds and move up to the awesome ... top board. From this waiting area, climbing the second ladder invited none but the brave.

Making the ascent to the top meant concentrating on getting there safely. From third board's waiting area, a ladder consisting of five or six rungs went straight up in an awkward climb to the upper level waiting area for ... top board. In hindsight, the ladder seemed like an afterthought instead of a priority for safe passage to a high diving board. Difficult as it may have been negotiating this ladder, I never witnessed anyone slipping and falling off of it.

After finishing the climb to the top, we beheld an awesome view. From this vantage point, every kid in the pool was subject to scrutiny. If you were looking for a friend, this was the place to be on lookout. But gazing back down that treacherous ladder gave us a terse reminder of the effort it took to get there.

The first time up there was a frightening experience. Any fear of heights easily created a dilemma; go out to the end of the board and jump or retreat to the dreadful ladder; a chicken's way out? For a first timer, either choice involved a heroic effort. I made my first climb to the top at age eleven. Wow, what an exhilarating feeling. I walked ever so slowly out to the end of the board. My hands held onto the guard rail for as far as it would allow. Even then I leaned back as much as I could to regain some semblance of security while out there in open space so high above ... the pit.

To better understand this eleven year old first timer's predicament, consider this. From eye level to the water's surface, had to be fifteen feet or more. Now, add another twelve or fifteen feet through the crystal clear water to the bottom of the pit. That's thirty feet of optical illusion. Enough to scare the athletic supporter off of most any boy! I wanted out. And jumping seemed out of the question. With nothing but air around me and my wet feet gripping the non-skid texture of the board beneath me ... I ... stood ... frozen. What do I do? I started thinking of the Three Stooges and the *step by step slowly I turn* routine. Not funny. Then, I considered simply backing up. No way! Others impatiently waited their turn. Voices called out for me to ...

"Get on with it!"

"Yeah, come on ... jump."

I pictured a mean kid running out a few feet on the board and feigning jumping at me. They sometimes did that stuff you know; stomping their feet in an effort to scare the daylights out of you and make you fall off.

Oh boy, I'm really in for it now. I'm so glad Mom isn't here to see this. Hey Mom, look at your little chicken Greek boy now! Watch this!

I prayed silently as I pictured her watching me shivering in fear. My goose bumps had goose bumps, and my lips must have been so purple they were black.

Dear Lord, help me get off this diving board.

Anyway, I had a major problem in need of a quick solution. I bent down to grab hold of the board.

Maybe ... just maybe, sitting down at the board's end is the solution.

Nope, couldn't do that either. The board bounced a little while I crouched for the sitting position. Meanwhile, the other kids behind me started spouting impatiently.

"Jump already, will ya!"

"Let's go ... I gotta take a leak!"

They laughed at me.

Aw ... man, shut up.

Tuning out everyone's jeers, I finally hit upon the solution. Crouching as low as possible without sitting, I attempted to shorten the optical illusion distance to a more manageable one.

Yes!

It helped considerably as I slowly stepped off the high board dropping ... dropping ... dropping and finally contacting the cold water in an exhilarating splatter.

"I did it! I did it!" I cried when I surfaced.

Suddenly, every kid who had waited behind me bombarded me with all forms of bomb dives, cannon balls, butt busters, can openers, and Chinamen. The life guard almost choked on his whistle in objection to the rule breaking onslaught while I fought for my fair share of air. My first high diving experience had finally ended successfully. From then on it got easier.

After a full day of swimming, the time came for having an after the plunge treat. The ice cream boy sat at the top of the concrete stairs which led down to the front of the bath house. We had a choice between Popsicles, ice cream bars, orange creamcicles (a personal favorite), orange push ups, or drumsticks. The other source was the little candy store at the top of swimming pool hill.

First ... the ice cream boy; a small vending business in town operated a fleet of dry-ice-refrigerated, white boxes on tricycles. Each one had an older boy riding it—literally peddling frozen treats. The ice cream boy had at his fingertips, a bar lined with bells that he tapped with his fingers to attract attention. That rack of bells signaled the Pavlov's response in every kid hungry for a cold treat. The ice cream boys could be found at the little league games at Goodwill Park, and riding all over town. Mainly, they parked one at a time by the pool. Kids who swam all day built up an enormous appetite, and those boys sold a lot of cold satisfying goodies.

Our second choice was the little candy store high up on the hill above the pool; Mrs. Neal's Candy Store. Mr. and Mrs. Neal lived in the house only a few feet from the store which, as far as I know, never had a name. Some kids referred to the store as Mrs. Neal's Bug House due to the fly strips hanging from the ceiling. They were coated with so many flies they looked like black furry poles. A gravel driveway wound through that section of Goold Park directly in front of the store. Sometimes I would find loose change in that gravel and spent it in the store to satisfy my sweet tooth. For years, I had these awesome dreams of finding lots of change in that gravel.

The bug house had every kind of bubble gum, candy bar, and sweet treat you could imagine. Among many others, there were sour grape bubble gum balls, sour apple, the powder blue Satellite bubble gum balls, Bazooka, Slo Pokes, Clark bars, Milky Ways, Snickers, Baby Ruth, O'Henry bars, and my favorite, Bonimo's Turkish Taffy in three flavors; chocolate, strawberry, and banana. We placed the taffy in the freezer at home for a few minutes and then slapped them on the table while still wrapped and feasted on the little ice cold pieces. Mrs. Neal also stocked those colored candy dots on long strips of white paper, wax tubes filled with colored sugar water, tiny wax cola bottles filled with the same stuff, bright red wax lips, wax buck teeth, Lick-a-Made, Sweet Tarts, red shoe strings ... everything. Mrs. Neal sold sodas, or *pop* as we called it in the Midwest. She had ice cream for root beer floats, and in the back of the store, behind the little counter, she had a grill for hamburgers and hot dogs. During the school year at lunch time, she made burgers for the high school kids who crossed the street to sneak a cigarette. In the summer those same sandwiches were prepared for intensely hungry swimmers.

Herein lies the legend in the *Legend of Swimming Pool Hill*. Legend has it that one sweltering summer day, years before I ever knew of the store, a young boy left the swimming pool after a full day of water fun. He ached with hunger from expending so much energy splashing and diving to his heart's content. Mrs. Neal wore sleeveless dresses under her apron during the summer heat to help keep cool. Her hair was tied back in a bun and when she lifted her arms reaching for something overhead, her armpits shown hairy. He could have ordered all the candy in the world, but he wanted real food. The boy ordered a hamburger and sat at the counter eagerly waiting while she prepared the sandwich. From the corner of his eye, the boy saw the woman reach into the refrigerator and remove a fresh, bright red, ball of hamburger—his bright red, ball of hamburger. He could almost taste the well done meat layered with lettuce, pickles, ketchup, and mustard. Then, she tossed the ball of meat way up into the air and caught it on the way back down right in the center of her hairy armpit. Her arm clamped down tight with a juicy, squishy sound flattening the meat against her sweaty, dripping, ribcage. Then, with an almost witch-like grin, she peeled the well seasoned paddy from her glistening wet skin and tossed it onto the hot sizzling grill.

"That's it—I'm outta here!"

The boy ran out of the store screaming, never to return.

I never ordered a hamburger at the bughouse—because of the legend? Nah ... not really; because Mom had her own restaurant with the best fresh cut fries in town, great hamburgers, sandwiches, and everything else. By the way, Mom used a metal hamburger patty maker bolted to the work shelf behind the counter next to the potato cutter. She preferred the correct way to flatten fresh balls of red hamburger meat. I rode home for a feast I could never get anywhere else for the price ... free! Thanks, Mom.

16

Gebhard Woods

Thinking back to some of the best expeditionary times of my youth, I'd be remiss if I didn't detail time spent in Gebhard Woods. No matter what the season, the thirty acres of Gebhard Woods State Park provided my friends and me with countless hours of adventures in nature. In the spring, wild flowers bloomed everywhere; including blue bell, white trout lilies, and violets. Living among the kaleidoscopic blossoms, we saw raccoons, beaver, muskrat, and deer. Hundreds upon hundreds of walnut, oak, ash, maple, hawthorn, cottonwood, and sycamore trees filled the park. Flying through the trees were gorgeous scarlet cardinals, the state bird of Illinois, fat orange breasted robins, screeching blue jays, and the ever ubiquitous sparrow.

Between the four distinctly different fishing ponds stocked with bass, crappie, bluegill, and bullhead, Nettle Creek winding through the woods, and the Illinois Michigan Canal, water based escapades were plentiful. If we weren't spending an afternoon fishing in the ponds wrestling with hooks and huge night crawlers from Valerio's Bait Shop, we could be found wading in the creek. We didn't just step into Nettle Creek with our pants rolled up; oh no. We made grand entrances from above by way of the vines hanging from a stand of tall maple trees lining one shore. Skimming along the water's surface, then letting go into waist deep running creek water best describes one of our many Gebhard Woods outdoor delights. The creek bed here consisted of pebbles, sand, and many softball sized rocks. These conditions made the water sparkle in the sun. On a hot summer day, this was just as much fun (if not more) as the Morris swimming pool. The pool had treated, clean water, diving boards, and life guards but Nettle Creek through Gebhard Woods had the vines! John, Jack, Rob, Steve, Denny, and I had a blast splashing among crawdads and minnows in the somewhat less than swimming pool clean water. And we didn't mind. We enjoyed a free of charge scene right out of Huck Finn; boys, swinging vines, and a running creek.

Swinging vine battles involved fists grabbing T-shirts, body slamming close calls, and crashes into the water. No doubt, we ruined a few shirts and ripped holes in our jeans. Shoes and socks sometimes drifted away in the current saved by sand bars and branches downstream. Bumps and bruises gave way to fits of laughter when firm grips were lost and flailing arms and legs slapped into the water. Events such as this helped define small town outdoor living for me as a boy.

Keeping in mind these water purity levels, I now present to you the filthy, muddy, and downright creepy Illinois & Michigan Canal water. Any sane person after taking a look at the water in the I&M Canal wouldn't dream of swimming in it. But you guessed it—we weren't sane.

John Halterman, Jack Cameron, Steve and Randy Meister, Steve and Denny Holbrook, and I lived on the edge. We certainly proved that one day. The Nettle Creek stone aqueduct, barely ten feet wide, still channels the I&M Canal over the creek twenty feet below. A small wooden bridge used to span the canal where the concrete wall still meets the ribbed steel pilings leading up to the narrow aqueduct. This wide area in front of the narrow aqueduct and the old wooden bridge hosted the scene of an epic sea battle. We brought with us boards, nails, a hammer, and three short logs about four feet long. With those items we constructed a raft on the spot and set it into the murky, disgusting water. We went in with the raft while holding on and kicking our feet. Nice. Everyone swam in the water except for Denny who stood on the concrete where it joined the steel pilings. He was the only one brave enough to stand on that concrete wall and entertain the thought of a very shallow dive into the canal. We didn't know the canal's depth. Did an old barge lay in waiting just below the surface? We didn't know that either. Perhaps he would impale himself with the front wheel spokes of a dumped, stolen bicycle. I used to think my Monark ended up in the canal, and one day I might see it poking out of the water.

I watched Denny closely from the opposite shore as the Meisters urged him on. He took his time studying his options with arms folded. His face showed his dilemma.

To dive or not to dive? That is the question. Whether 'tis nobler to go through with this dive or regain my senses and walk into the water from the shore like the other wimpy chickens.

It took Denny a minute or so until he finally dove in. We applauded; right there ... swimming in the I&M Canal of all places. To this day I don't know what in the world ever made us think of actually swimming in the Illinois & Michigan Canal. It really is mind boggling thinking about seven daring knuckleheads, one small raft, and a host of unknown amoebas and other protozoa capable of sending us to the hospital. Protozoa—another word derived from the Greek, *proto*, for first and *zoa*, for animal.

Well, our three log, four board yacht could barely serve two swimmers at a time. We struggled to keep afloat. At one point Jack lost his spot on the raft while in the middle of the black water. The shortest of the group, Jack, could still touch the slimy, oozing mud bottom with his feet. Yuck! I tried desperately to keep away from the bottom mud. If anything gave me the creeps, stepping through the muck at the bottom of the Illinois & Michigan Canal most assuredly did.

"I'm standing on something!" Jack yelled.

"What is it?" John asked.

"How should I know you moron? It's flat ... and hard."

"Well get off of it you idiot," goofed Denny.

"Yeah, come on. Get off of it you idiot! It might be a snapper!" we all shouted laughing.

"It's not a snapper ... and you guys are the idiots!"

Jack stepped aside closer to shore, and like a rising sunken ghost ship this six foot long, narrow, black, wooden raft slowly broke the surface.

"It's a raft!" Jack exclaimed.

We watched this ancient, water logged, ugly thing barely stay above the surface.

"I wonder how long it's been down there." Steve said.

"Look at it Dukie. Years ... it's been down there stuck on the bottom for years," Denny jabbed at his younger brother. "Wudaya think?"

We looked on in amazement. We weren't the first ones to brave the repulsive canal water. There were others just as courageous or ... stupid. We had resurrected someone's long lost raft from the murky depths of the I&M Canal. A former rafter's pride and joy had been lost to the thick, black, bottom gook; mud that reached to our knees.

Our imaginations quickly took over and we commandeered the old ghost ship into our sea battle. It became the ideal derelict ship for us to ram with our newly launched raft. The old ghost stayed afloat long enough for us to smash into it two or three times. Then ... it disappeared into the darkness and sunk back into history ... once again.

By this time, we'd had enough of the mud, enough of the disgusting water, potential rusty nails, the possibility of snapping turtles, and bottom dwelling catfish with large stabbing fin barbs. Imagine the infections from those potential injuries. The whole scene begged for a responsible adult to walk by and end the fun. The adult didn't show up and we abandoned our raft ourselves, collected the hammer, the leftover nails, and went home. Oddly enough, we never saw our raft again. I wonder if it met the same fate as the ghost raft. That was the first and last time I ever set foot in the Illinois Michigan Canal ... voluntarily.

Gebhard Woods basically could be divided into two parts; the main entrance, fishing ponds, and picnic area on the west, and the wild undeveloped wooded section on the east end. In a spot near the pseudo-border between these two distinctly different park lands, stood a stone chimney/fireplace about nine feet tall. Obviously the park authority intended it to be a place for warmth and outdoor cooking, but we saw it as another adventure—a portal to another dimension. The hearth at ground level, large enough to crawl into, led to the inner chamber of the chimney. Once our group of adventurous, make believing, daredevils gazed up into the long dark cavern, we immediately determined that we should climb up through it to the top. No problem at all. No fire seemed to have been in the works recently. The inner stones felt cool to the touch. Up we scaled, one at a time like little chimney sweep brushes cleaning out the soot and ash. Such a tight fit with only an inch or two of space between our bodies and the stone lining felt a bit claustrophobic. Gaps between the smooth stones made excellent hand and foot holds. The light at the top grew closer and closer after a few minutes of squeezing, twisting and reaching. Higher and higher I climbed; tighter and tighter the space became. Good thing we were all thin, small or both; Jack, Steve, Rob, and I. The final arm pull and leg push that propelled me to freedom came with a shout of victory and a big breath of clean air. I looked down into the dark depths to see a head of hair, hands, and fingers clawing for leverage. Rob? Not sure. Steve or Jack?—I didn't know for certain. Not until this fella emerged at the summit next to me did I recognize him. When he poked through the narrow opening enough to see me, Rob, caked in black soot and white ash ... laughed. I laughed at the sight of him as well. We looked like two dirty coal miners covered head to toe. Steve and Jack followed, and the four of us sat with our legs hanging over the side laughing hysterically, coughing and sneezing. We took a quick poll on how to get back down. The vote results were unanimous; climb down the outer wall. We climbed down the chimney sides to our bikes and headed for the next order of business ... the main water fountain between the second and third ponds for the clean up and ensuing water fight; priceless.

Gebhard Woods during winter transformed the fishing ponds, the creek, and the canal into an ice-skater's dream. My season of choice has always been winter. As much fun as I had swimming to keep cool in the heat, I preferred winter. It was easier to keep warm in the winter and have a blast doing so, than trying to keep cool on a hot, muggy summer day. Repressive heat and humidity never appealed to me. When the ponds froze over, the park became a true winter wonderland. My favorite, the first pond, froze into a huge round ring of ice with enough room to accommodate well over a hundred skaters with plenty of room to spare. For a more quaint setting, pond number two (which is now gone) provided a picturesque setting very much like a holiday card—small, kidney bean shaped, and bordered with maple and cottonwood trees. Longer, winding, skate journeys through the park took place on Nettle Creek. Even the canal's dirty water froze to a shiny glimmer. I often entertained a group expedition west along the canal to the five mile bridge, but we never got around to that one. A ten mile round trip on skates quite possibly could have been the end of any skating for the rest of that season. Maybe it was a good thing we avoided that idea.

One winter after a major rainstorm, just before the freeze, came the greatest most unusual skating circumstance of all time. The wild section of Gebhard Woods had a tendency to flood during substantial rainfall. It still happens today. But for the flood to come in winter was highly unusual. When it flooded that year and quickly froze virtually overnight, the results were outstanding, once in a lifetime ice-skating conditions. Steve Holbrook and I stumbled onto this winter bonanza while skating along the canal. We looked down into the lowlands on the north side of the canal near the stone aqueduct and noticed ice everywhere. A sheet of ice covered the entire wooded area. We quickly skated off of the canal ice. Still wearing our skates, we carefully chopped side steps down the slope from the canal tow path to the woods ten feet below. Upon reaching the ice, we got the surprise of our winter lives. The ice wasn't level! Everywhere, around each tree and bush, the water had receded from underneath the ice. This had created rolling mini hills of curved ice surfaces. Bent ice of all things! The mini hills were unbroken and only cracked in a few places. The wonderful scene looked very much like a series of white sagging bed sheets with huge trees poking through all around us. Some of the bumps resembled moguls on a ski slope.

We marveled at these spectacular conditions while gliding over the countless mounds, careful not to slam into any trees. We did glance off of a few trees now and then; minor fender benders. In order to slow down, smaller saplings served as poles to grab when passing them. The highly entertaining but exhausting skating session had to end however. I hated having to go home when it got too dark to stay any longer. Ice-skating on the mini hills only happened that one year. Wish I had a camera that day. Actually I did … my vivid memory.

17

Fourth Grade, 1961–1962

o o o o o o o o o o o o o o o o o o o o o o o o o o o o o o
"Oh, well I'm the type of guy who will never settle down ..."
Dion

"*B*onjour, Monsieur Zef." Aside from the *Pledge of Allegiance*, bidding hello to a television image of a French language instructor became a regular event in fourth grade. In that school year we students were given a choice to learn French or Spanish. I picked French. I already spoke a foreign language so French or Spanish didn't matter to me. The interesting thing was how I made the selection.

Fourth Grade, 1961–1962 125

About the time a choice had to be made between the two, I had gone to the show to see a movie called *Moon Pilot*. The story line is about an Air Force captain who volunteers to make the first manned flight around the moon. For that reason he is immediately placed under the watchful eye of various security agencies. Despite the security, a young woman makes contact with the captain. He eventually discovers she isn't a spy but a friend from another planet. She is played by a French actress named Dany Saval. In 1961, Ms. Saval was quite an attractive blonde and I began to have more pronounced feelings for females beyond the innocent little friendly kisses with Tina Rainwater. Ms. Saval's French accent worked as part of her alien character which appealed to me. As a result, I wanted to learn more about French. That is how French won over Spanish.

◆ ◆ ◆

My good friend John Halterman and his family moved away during the summer just before fourth grade started. I remember the day they rode in their car down Wauponsee Street alongside Chapin Park headed for Streator Illinois, about thirty miles away. For me, thirty miles might just as well have been three hundred because I couldn't ride my bike there. As Mr. Halterman drove his family away, I pedaled my bike next to the car for a few yards and waved good-bye to John who waved back. Unfortunately, we lost touch. I wouldn't see him again for a long time.

In fourth grade, I found myself sharing the same class with several classmates from first, second, and third grades along with some new faces. Jay Heap and I sat next to each other at the head of the class. The two of us exchanged papers and laughs quite often.

Young and attractive, are the words I like to use to describe Mrs. Schweikert, our fourth grade teacher. Given the fact that I already had an attraction to a beautiful French actress, nothing kept me from having those same feelings for a pretty teacher. The actress would never be in my presence, but my teacher showed up for class right there in front of me five days a week. My first crush happened to be my fourth grade teacher—an older married woman! There, I've admitted it in writing for the first time.

One day as we worked on an assignment, classmate, Nancy Norris, leaned over Mrs. Schweikert's desk listening to her go over one of Nancy's papers. Frail and shy, Nancy didn't seem to like class participation or attracting attention to herself. It seems this teacher/student session created a high anxiety level for Nancy, and she passed out. She fell to the floor next to the desk. I looked up to see my teacher dart past me in somewhat of a panic running for the door to get help. It happened so fast. Mrs. Schweikert had to slide her feet across the floor keeping a delicate balance as she ran in order not to slip and fall. That event shifted the day's focus rather abruptly. By the time Mrs. Schweikert returned with help, Nancy had regained consciousness and ultimately went to the nurse for rest and observation. She recovered without damage except for perhaps a bump on the head and a little embarrassment.

As fourth graders, we were the *seniors* of Franklin School which meant the boys qualified to become patrol boys. I became one of those patrol boys. The position afforded us an official looking white belt of authority. We wore it buckled over our shirts and jackets. Patrol boy responsibilities were to oversee recesses which took place in the closed off street directly in front of the school. Each day, long, yellow and black striped, wooden barricades were put into place by Mr. Johnson the custodian. If a ball rolled outside the barricades, only the patrol boy or a supervising teacher could go beyond the set up perimeter to retrieve it. I had to do that often. It made me feel important and respected by my peers. Thinking back on this, I am amazed. The school essentially blocked off a street with a minimum number of boards. A few teachers and ten year old patrol boys were placed to oversee dozens of little kids playing with balls, hula hoops, jump ropes, and marbles—unbelievable!

This same year, boys and girls began to take notice of each other in larger numbers. Valentine's Day proposed a little problem for me. Kay Oakland, a pretty girl in one of the other fourth grade classrooms—Mrs. Gleghorn's perhaps—caught my eye. Well, word got around to Kay that I was a little sweet on her. However, I wasn't the only one. A competitor existed. I remember our eyes (Kay's and mine) meeting as the classrooms emptied out into the hall toward each other at the end of Valentine's Day. Kay and her friends exited the school and walked in the same direction as I did with my friends. I wanted to talk to Kay about the attraction but had no clue as to how to begin. My appearance as a nervous wreck must have been quite obvious. Suddenly she turned to me and showed me a Valentine with a red heart-shaped sucker attached to it. Looped over the stem of the sucker, Kay pointed to a friendship ring. I heard her say to me …

"This is what you do for a girl if you're interested in her."

I stood there embarrassed. My competitor had outplayed me. Coming up with a response at that point didn't really matter. It actually got me off the hook, much to my relief. After that clumsy fourth grade attempt at romance, I reverted to adventures in make-believe where I felt safe and comfortable with my buddies … for a long time. Oh well, it seemed to me Kay had a larger interest in the other boy anyway so … se la vi. Merci, Monsieur Zef!

♦ ♦ ♦

My fourth grade report card is the first of the grade school report cards that I have managed to save. Beginning with my attendance record, it indicates only two days absent and never tardy. My grades for the six week long grading periods of the year include five As, twenty-five Bs, and twelve Cs. Those figures create my benchmark. I started the year at four feet five inches tall weighing in at sixty-four pounds—skinny. I grew one inch during the course of the year and gained only four pounds. My school habits and attitudes page indicates respecting authority, showing courtesy, accepting responsibility, and following directions well all year long. These grades and behaviors earned a promotion to fifth grade.

PART III
Center School Days

o o o o o o o o o o o o o o o o o o o o o o o o o o o o o o o
"Hey teacher—leave us kids alone." Roger Waters

Impressive rendering of my second school

18

The Brick

During the year 2003, the Center School building I knew built in 1923, bit the dust. It wasn't the first time Center School met with demolition. The original Center School building fell to the bulldozer many decades earlier making way for the modernized replacement. The building which held so many memories for thousands of us had to be torn down for reasons I didn't understand at first. Rumors spread to me in California about a bank outside of Morris purchasing the property in order to build a new banking facility. Since the Center School building had been sitting idle for several years due to newer schools having been built, it had deteriorated somewhat and fell out of code. Authorities decided it would be in the district's best interest to sell the property; hence the sale to the banking institution from out of town and the ultimate demise of an important landmark. Whether this edifice went down due to greed or asbestos contamination doesn't matter to me. It is gone and can never return. It is a shame.

Much to my dismay, the demolition went ahead as scheduled and my old school joined the original as a memory. From two thousand miles away, I heard the walls come crumbling down. With the crashing of those walls, any nostalgic hopes of ever revisiting the old place obviously disintegrated as well. My sentimental thoughts of Center School are all I have left to visit; aside from a few photographs and a brick. Yes, a *brick*.

Roughly three years prior to starting this book, I had expressed to a few friends my desire to have a piece of Center School. Exactly how I would accomplish this remained to be seen. Word of my ambition also got around to my nephew, Tony Kidonakis, Ann's oldest son, who still lived near Morris at the time. Tony had planned a trip to California and unbeknownst to me he crafted a surprise. He placed a call to my wife, Jan, informing her of his success in obtaining a brick from the rubble of what was once Center School. Tony, Jan, and our son Harrison, also in on the caper, were able to keep this secret until I drove Tony to our home from Los Angeles International Airport. After initial greetings and some unpacking, Tony casually and unceremoniously presented me the brick. Jan and Harrison watched, eagerly anticipating my reaction. At first I didn't get it. It took a moment to recognize what I held in my hand. As my brain finally deciphered the identity of the artifact, the look on my face must have been priceless. Everyone laughed and began to explain to me in a chorus of excitement, the whole plan. Totally surprised and grateful for the efforts put forth in acquiring this important piece of history, I thanked my nephew.

This particular brick is perfect because it's an external brick based upon the vertical texture lines visible on the one side. That side is perhaps one I may have leaned against on the playground, or hit with a ball made of rubber or snow one day long ago.

The brick represents much more than just four hard years of enduring class work and school in general. It holds within it the echoes of hopes and dreams from thousands of fellow Morris children who passed through the Center School doors. Like a conch shell, when I hold it up to my ear, I hear the lessons in English, math, science, music, art, and history; my history. I hear adolescent footsteps running on the playground amid the laughter and cries of the brilliant and not so brilliant; the handsome and not so handsome; the talented and not so talented; the athletic and not so athletic; the well to do and the not so well to do. Our collective philosophy at the time was (whether we knew it or not) to be the best youngsters we knew how to be and to have a great time doing so. I definitely did.

19

Pom Pom Pull Away!

This story begins on a cold winter Monday morning; not bone chilling but just enough below freezing for snow to pack well and not melt away. The snow appeared to be knee deep outside my frosted bedroom window above Liberty Street. Peering through this window, I waited impatiently for my friend, Frank Kahanek, to come into view. Dad still snored in the next room. His busy day wouldn't begin for another hour. Mom, on the other hand, rose with the sun and presided over breakfast service downstairs in The Basket.

Frank lived with his family in an apartment one block south of ours, so Frank and I walked to school together often. This day started like any other school day except for one important fact. The first big snowfall had covered the ground after Christmas vacation. I automatically knew the guys would be excited about … Pom Pom Pull Away!

Pressing my nose against the frozen window, I had become concerned.
Where are you Frank?
The First National Bank clock chimed, telling me I would be too late to get downstairs for a hot, healthy breakfast of oatmeal or Cream of Wheat. This time, breakfast had to be a grab and go. For late starts such as this, Mom momentarily left the restaurant and called up to me from the bottom of the apartment stairs.

"Mikey? You'll be late for school," she called out in Greek of course.
"Okay Ma. I'm waiting for Frank," I responded in English.
When Frank appeared in front of Roth's Bakery moments later, he looked up to see me anxiously peeking through my clouded window. Our eyes met in a moment of boyhood expectation. We both knew the seasonal event we had waited for had finally arrived.

I flew downstairs and out the door where we greeted each other as young boys do in fresh snow, with a quick shove, a laugh, and a few well thrown snowballs.

"What took you so long? I was about to go without you," I said.

"Sorry, it took awhile to find my ear muffs," Frank apologized.

We looked at each other for a moment, suspicious of one final body slam to the cushioned ground.

"That's okay. Come on, let's go. We're late," I said covering my next trick.

With a low sweep of my leg and a quick hand push, Frank ate snow.

"Hey! Aw ... I shoulda known." Frank gave in.

Our laughter echoed off the brick wall of our building, and we rushed into The Basket pulling the frosty air in with us. Morning customers near the front door warming up with hot coffee and breakfast felt a momentary wrap of sharp cold over their shoulders. My excited voice blurted out a crisp greeting.

"Good morning everyone," I announced.

"Yeah, me too," Frank added.

"Good morning boys," said my mother as she topped off Mr. Benner's coffee cup. Mr. Benner, a regular breakfast customer, ran the shoe repair shop half a block away.

I whisked past Mom and Mr. Benner and rushed behind the counter snatching two long johns from the dessert case.

"We gotta run Mom."

I handed one pastry to Frank.

"Grab and go. Cool. Thanks," Frank said.

"Just a minute mister—" Mom started to say, but was silenced when we bolted out the door.

Munching our pastries, Frank and I smashed our way through the eight inches of fresh, sparkling new snow along Liberty Street on our way to Center School. Some of the local merchants had dutifully shoveled their sections of the sidewalk. Others were in the process of huffing and puffing behind their red handled aluminum snow shovels. We trudged past Hecht's Ladies Wear shop complete with warmly dressed mannequins in the window and Marben's men and boy's clothing. The middle aged Bernstein brothers, Ben and Eddie, dressed their window display with the latest men's winter styles and waved to us. They seemed to know the reason for the enthusiasm that the two of us wore openly.

The next store fronts were Harry Benner's Shoe Repair, the Sears Catalogue outlet store managed by Mr. Varland, The Book and Gift Shop, and Matteson's Hardware. By the Jackson Street intersection, we had finished our grab and go breakfast and felt no cold whatsoever. Old man winter, our good friend, provided us with the wonderful gift of snow ... lots of soft, beautiful snow.

"Do you ... hear anything ... Frank?" I asked between breaths.

"No ... not yet, do you?" breathed Frank.

"Nope, we still have three and a ... half blocks to go," I puffed. The vapor from my breath hung in a cloud surrounding my flushed face.

At the Ford dealership we waved good morning to one of the salesmen, Mr. Barkley, Confederate General Barkley's Dad. He waved back.

"Hey Mikey, you think Mr. Barkley likes the snow?" asked Frank.

"Sure. Everybody does. It's great!" I said convincingly.

Frank gave me a look to the contrary.

"I think adults don't like the snow. They have to work in it."

"Yeah, and we love playing in it. Come on," I responded with a mischievous smile.

The trek continued up to the traffic signal at North Street. The journey so far lasted a full two blocks. Frank's cheeks shined bright red as he lifted his navy blue ear muffs to hear more clearly.

"Now ... can you hear anything Mikey?"

With two and a half blocks to go, I pulled back my heavy fur-lined hood and strained to listen. I could feel the steam rising from my thick, dark brown wavy hair. Off in the snow-muffled distance, I faintly heard the joyful sound; dozens of screaming classmates.

"Yeah, it's happening. Let's go Frank!"

We took off running.

The old public library building loomed tall against the clouded morning sky. Its pitched roof was thick with a new white coating. Thankfully, the library janitor had shoveled the sidewalk. Exhilarated, we ran the fifty foot dash in no time to the next property line.

"That was great!" I exclaimed.

"Yeah," Frank shouted in total agreement.

With each crunching step through the fresh snow we knew one thing for certain; the greatest winter game ever invented waited for us only moments away. I had no idea who invented the game. Even the name remained a mystery. *Pom Pom Pull Away*, what did that mean?

Next door to the library, a small storybook house stood almost cartoon-like with its light green color and thick swirling smoke rising from a red brick chimney. This neighbor didn't do any shoveling on this special morning. Even worse, the library's snow plow had pushed a wall of snow up to the little house's property line. Piled only three feet high, but to us anxious kids itching to get to the school playground rapidly, we stared at Mount Everest.

Who was this inconsiderate ... character? What rodent of a ... person wouldn't be happy to clear the way for *professional* Pom Pom Pull Away players?

Didn't this ... mortal know that every super kid taking this route harbored a mission? Didn't this ... moron know the most important event of the cold season had arrived? There couldn't have been a kid living in that cheesy little green house. No way. It must have been a little beady eyed ... creature who woke up in the morning scratching his portly little belly. He had to be a whiskered, long snouted ... fellow who yawned his way to a frosted window for a squinting look outside. The sight of all that snow probably made him tremble as he scurried back into his warm feathered rat's nest.

"Mikey, this ... this'll take ... forever. We're not ... we're not gonna make it in time," Frank worried slightly out of breath.

"Sure we will. Don't give up now. We're getting closer with ... with every step. Okay? Move out soldier!" I commanded. My brown corduroy pants were now frozen stiff to the knees.

"Over the wall men—take no prisoners!" Frank charged.

The motivating battle cry did its job. We breached the Himalayan snow wall—"*Ehaaa!*"

At the Chapin Street corner, patrol boy, Big Jim Waddell, worked with proud precision. I think being a patrol boy meant more to Big Jim than playing a playground game. His bright orange patrol belt made him look important. Seeing Big Jim meant Frank and I had almost reached the school. Jim waved us across Chapin Street to the next curb.

"Thanks, Jim."

"Okay you guys. See you later," Big Jim said in his best authoritative voice.

Frank and I moved on. The crunching, squeaky sound of passing car tires pressing against the snow-packed street competed with kids voices from the playground a mere block away.

We arrived at the used car lot near the Benton Street intersection. All the old beaters were blanketed in white giving an illusion of rolling hills—rows and rows of gently frosted hills.

"We're almost in the game now, Frank," I encouraged.

"Yeah, but ... we really have to hurry. I just know ... the buzzer is gonna sound off," Frank worried.

The *buzzer*, next to the noon siren/fire alarm, had to be the most recognizable sound in town. Most schools use a bell, but not Center School. It belched a loud, long, deep, and gutsy growl; a unique signature indeed.

With one block to go, a few more restless kids including Ralph Varland, Mike Tucker and Jim Hume joined us. We all waited to step off the Liberty Street curb for the final stretch. Denny Thorson, the patrol boy stationed on the other side, signaled us to wait for traffic; yet another frustrating delay. Frank and I nervously looked both ways up and down Liberty Street apprehensively stomping our feet. The line of cars seemed endless as we waited for a break in the traffic. We waited, and waited—rolling tires ... crunching snow ... rolling tires ... crunching snow.

"Come on. We're missing it," Frank called out in desperation.

"It's not safe. Wait," Denny barked.

"He's right Frank. Keep you pants on," Ralph blurted out.

Everyone started to laugh except for Frank when finally ... a break in the traffic. Our patrol boy carefully walked out into the snow packed street and held up his red canvas stop flag in one hand.

"Okay ... come on," he said with a gesture from his other free hand.

"Opa!" I sang out and the group darted across.

"Slow down," the patrol scolded.

We obeyed long enough to get to the other side holding back a few chuckles in the process.

"I bet he wishes he could be in the game," Frank whispered.

"No kidding," I added.

The muted playground noise filled the chilly air. Only three-quarters of a block remained! Great luck; the school custodian had plowed this entire length of the school block. Half a dozen wild and crazy kids flew past Mick's Quick Chick. The empty diner indicated all the students had put in their advance lunch orders and had long since left for the playground. Only the waitresses on break sat in a booth smoking cigarettes, drinking hot coffee, and looking relieved. The morning rush had come and gone. Mick himself relaxed behind the counter reading his morning paper. He looked over the newsprint at us running past his large plate glass window and gave the thumbs up gesture. He knew the score. Then, from only a hundred feet ahead, came the chorus of voices shouting out those beautiful, magical, words.

"Pom pom pull away!"

We charged ahead as fast as our snow booted feet could go. Reaching the playground perimeter, we had found the game already in progress. Ralph, Jim, and Mike didn't care one way or the other, so they barged right into the on-going game. They lost themselves in the crowd of about a hundred-something heavily breathing boys playing ... *Pom Pom Pull Away.*

In the game *Pom Pom Pull Away,* players bundled up in hats, ear muffs, gloves, heavy coats, scarves, and snow boots. Participants gathered at one end of the playground appearing ready for full contact football. The game began with one lonely boy in the middle of the playground calling out "Pom Pom Pull

Away!" Then the pounding stampede streaked toward him, and that boy tackled one of the sprinters onto a mattress of soft snow. The running crowd came to a stop at the other end of the playground. For the return pass, those two boys in the middle shouted out the magic words in unison. This next flight of youthful humanity screamed out a chorus of battle cries from Spartans, Romans, Vikings and other imaginary warriors. Aggressive tackling then yielded four souls in the center. This went on and on, back and forth until the last kid ran across unscathed or more likely got creamed by a host of bodies. He was declared the winner and got to stand alone facing the hoards to start the next game.

All the kids were caked with snow from head to toe while Frank and I stood frozen; not from the weather but from disappointment.

"We missed ... we missed the game Mikey," Frank lamented, breathing hard.

"Yeah ... but hey ... we should have enough time for one more game before the bu ..."

Buzzzzzzzzzzzzz!

"Oh, no!"

"It's okay, Frankie. So we missed the first round. No big deal," I gulped.

"No big deal? What are you, nuts?"

At that moment, the snowfall started again. It quickly increased in density filling the air with big, fat six pointers. They were the kind of snowflakes that stuck to each other in clumps as they floated lazily to the ground. I marveled at them when I looked up into the gray sky—beautiful. I brushed a few away that tickled my nose, and I realized what lay ahead on this gorgeous day.

"I mean, there's always recess," I said.

"Recess!"

We ran into the building and pulled off our boots. Frank and I threw them onto the huge steaming pile that formed every winter just inside the Center School doors. What a great time; one of my favorite memories.

20

Music

Music is the common poetic thread that opens people up to their own emotions and connects them to other people. Music inspires, warms, excites, provokes, and soothes. It generally gives us all a profound sense, of being in some place in time where we feel at home.

Music played throughout our home in many ways as I grew older. Mom sang to us the Greek tunes she knew as a child. We listened to old Greek 78 rpm records all the time. To this day I love listening to the clarinet played by a talented Greek musician. By many accounts, the clarinet is the instrument most associated with the music of the northwestern mountains of Greece; the area known as Epirus. Mom joyfully danced for me and my sisters in our apartment as the clarinet trills filled the room. She sang along so well, I often thought of her as a singing star. In many ways she was my star. Most of the lyrics were hard for me to understand, but it didn't matter because the music lifted our spirits. Mom projected fun and joy when she sang and danced, making it easy to love it all.

Other musical sources came from the 45s my sister collected and played whenever she had her friends over. Her collection began growing in about 1960, with these songs; *Cathy's Clown* by the Everly Brothers, *Personality*—Lloyd Price, *In My Little Corner of the World*—Anita Bryant, *It's Now or Never*—Elvis, *A Hundred Pounds of Clay*—Gene McDaniels, *Runaway*—Del Shannon, *Take Good Care of My Baby*—Bobby Vee, and *Why?* by Frankie Avalon. There were many others, because we had an excellent source. Every few weeks when the juke box representative came by to change the records in Mom's restaurant machine, he gave us each a record. Ann and I loved watching him open the machine and change out the 45s, hoping he would hand us one. He always did, and he also played several songs when he finished. He inserted the same quarter several times while the coin box remained open and allowed us to pick any of the dozens of songs we wanted—lots of free music.

The music coming from Britain beginning in 1963, took the teen idol pop tunes of the late fifties to early1963, and turned them into oldies in the blink of an eye. I enjoyed early rock and roll including Elvis, Chuck Berry, the Everly Brothers, Ricky Nelson, Fabian, Bobby Vee, and Frankie Avalon. But, when I heard the new British rock sound influenced by old American blues based pioneers—wow. I'd never heard of The Howlin' Wolf, Johnny Lee Hooker, Robert Johnson, Elmore James, Buddy Guy, Fats Domino, or Muddy Waters. This *new* British music, led by The Beatles and others such as The Dave Clark Five, Herman' Hermits, Jerry and the Pacemakers, The Zombies, and The Rolling Stones changed my life.

The Brits managed to infiltrate our very own backyards so to speak. They harvested guitar styles from our southern musicians who weren't fully promoted by the main stream modern music moguls of the time. That was the irony of the whole scene. All of a sudden American music lovers thought the music they were hearing was brand new. We had been tricked so to speak. In many ways we were listening to new music, but the roots came from the American Deep South—from those fellows mentioned above who weren't popular beyond a regional or even local status. Somehow, people like Eric Clapton, John Lennon, Jeff Beck, George Harrison, Jimmy Page, Keith Richards, and many others got wind of these old musician's styles and developed the music dubbed the *British Invasion*.

Music played a major role in my young life. Dad had an old arch top acoustic guitar in a closet at the top of the stairs to our apartment—not a great guitar but not a bad one either. It came from Montgomery Wards and was good enough for a beginner to shred his soft fingertips on the frets. Initially, I played (or attempted to play) that old guitar for so long my fingers developed blisters and even bled from just goofing around on it. The poor fingers of my left hand hurt so badly sometimes from playing only a few minutes that I wondered how anyone could ever play a guitar. After several days of forcing myself to suffer through the pain, the blisters, and the bloody cuts, I noticed calluses forming. My fingers hurt less and less. Later when I started listening to The Beatles, my abilities as a musician began to take off. Beatle records helped me improve greatly. One of the very first lead riffs I learned was the intro to *Day Tripper*.

Making the decision to quietly take this instrument out of storage daily and play it developed into an adventure in top secret operations. Dad never offered it for playing or even acknowledged it existed until I discovered it one day. Without telling anyone, I surreptitiously pulled the case from the closet when home alone. I played for hours and then returned it to its hiding place until the next session.

This pattern continued for weeks. I have no clue as to why I didn't simply ask Dad about the guitar so I could learn. I figured Dad wanted it kept off limits, so I feared bringing it up. In retrospect, I had more fun going through the furtive motions and risking detection followed by the possibility of some kind of punishment. The excitement and the adrenalin rush were an addictive thrill.

Eventually, my sisters noticed, Mom found out, and by then I figured what the heck, nobody cares. Even Dad somehow knew. I stopped the subterfuge and adopted the Montgomery Wards guitar, leaving it on my bed for all to see. After that, everyone knew I had a new hobby ... playing guitar. I bought a beginning, Mel Bay, how to play guitar book from Badino's music store on Liberty Street. I stopped in for an apple turnover at Roth's Bakery on the way back home. I hit upon a spending spree brought on by the excitement of my new found hobby. There has never been a better long john, glazed donut, or my favorite, the apple turnover, anywhere ... period. We bought our birthday cakes there as well. I was very fond of the double layer white cake with white frosting and blue, pink and green flowers decorating the top and sides. Mr. and Mrs. Roth were instrumental in satisfying my sweet tooth for years and years.

In time, I longed for a better guitar, especially when I saw them in the music store when purchasing new strings, picks, and other essentials. I needed to devise a plan to get my hands on a new one. In those days, when grocery shopping, the cashiers handed out King Corn, or S&H (Sperry Hutchinson) Green Stamps after customers paid for their groceries. Since Mom and Dad bought tons of fresh foods on a daily basis for the restaurant, we accumulated sheets and sheets of both kinds of stamps. Mom, my sisters, and I sat at the kitchen table often with a large pile of stamps, a bowl of water, and a couple dozen empty stamp books for stamping marathons. These books piled up quickly, and Mom redeemed them for a multitude of items we needed. Each stamp company had a catalogue showing pictures of merchandise available and the number of filled stamp books required to make the order. We wet and pasted thousands and thousands of stamps over the years. Each sitting created a new batch of fat books, wet with freshly moistened stamps adding to the already burgeoning brown, shopping bags. My excitement grew quickly knowing our labor led to acquiring neat stuff. It didn't take me very long to figure out the best way to get what I wanted. Mom agreed to apportion the necessary number of books it took for me to order a new acoustic guitar. I quickly put my fingers to use wetting and pasting until I finished the required number of books. With my plan in place, stamp books filled, and my selection made, I ordered the guitar, and it came within a matter of days. With a new acoustic guitar, I spent hours practicing and learning every day. I couldn't quite master the lead guitar riffs, though, especially on a Spanish style acoustic with nylon strings. Instead, I learned chords and developed a strong rhythmic ability. I became a rhythm guitar player.

21

Chapin Park

"Mom, I'm going to the park to play!" I must have made that statement several thousand times as my exit line from home on my way to Chapin Park only three blocks away. When Mom heard those words she knew I was gone for the better part of the day. I called out my intent and disappeared until dusk or even after dark—well, at least until I got hungry.

Many of Chapin Park's huge oak trees still exist as I knew them years ago. Two sidewalks once crossed in the exact center of the park in a pedestrian *round about*. Just to the northeast of this circle grew two large oak trees with a huge four foot diameter round boulder between them. The city had painted it bright silver. The rock made a good hiding place for us when we played *Hide and Seek* at dusk. We sat on it, stood upon it, and used it as a centerpiece during Flash Gordon outer space adventures. Sometimes we leaned against it licking Fudgecicles and orange flavored Pushups purchased from the ice cream boy on his rolling ice box. This unique landmark unfortunately met with the city removal service. Apparently someone in city hall at one time valued its presence there enough to paint it. Why then, would the city have it dug out and hauled away? Perhaps a slip and fall caused an injury?

The park had a swing set with a trapeze bar, a high bar, a slide, two swings, and two see-saws for playing *Farmer, Farmer Let Me down*. The swings and trapeze hung from a round metal frame whose top tube existed for more than just to hang a swing or two. The daring ones, myself included, climbed the slide ladder to the top and crossed over to the overhead tube and straddled it. We scooted all the way across to the high bar at the other end and swung back down to the ground. This stunt required good balance and no fear of heights since we were at least ten feet off the ground. Luckily, everyone survived that dangerous stunt. No one ever fell off. Chapin Park also had a jungle gym we called *the monkey bars* for climbing and playing King of the Jungle. Because of all these metal bars for little hands and fingers to grasp, my palms and fingers always sported calluses.

There were two old, unique merry-go-rounds in the park. The smaller one had been designed and built as a six sided, red, wooden box about eight feet in diameter and three feet high with thick metal poles for grasping. It had steps built into the sides for standing and pushing with your feet. Anyone standing around its perimeter intent upon adding more speed to this thing grabbed a pole as it went by and pulled as hard as they possibly could. This increased the speed to the point of becoming a vomit machine. It spun so fast at that point that the pullers had to quit for fear of losing an arm. The centrifugal force this contraption generated threw me overboard many times. The trick was to climb to the center hub and hold on as best you could. Would I ride this thing as an adult? Answering that question is easy enough; no way in the world. My digestive system couldn't handle it.

The bigger of the two, was a true relic. In fact, even back then I don't recall seeing another one of its kind in any park. Rumor had it another one existed in a park in Ottawa or Marseilles. I don't have a photograph of it but it begs description so, here is a sketch of it.

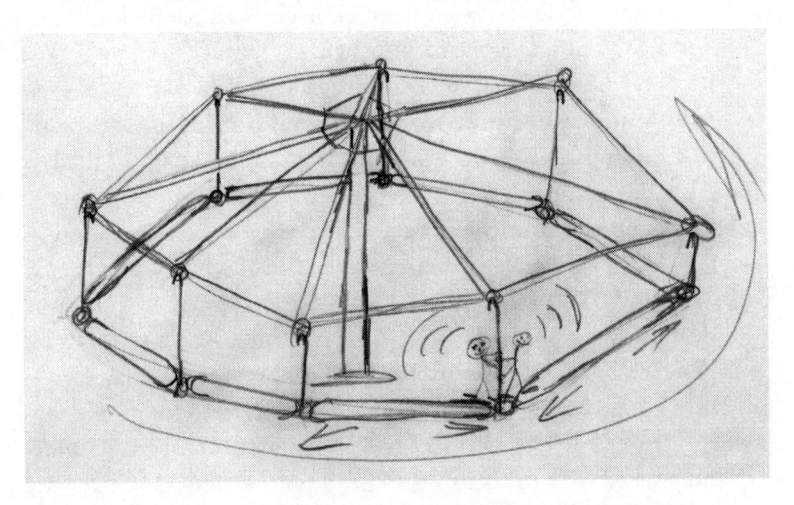

The craziest merry-go-round ever, I'm the one on the left

As you look at this drawing, the entire machine was made of steel except for the long narrow wooden platforms we sat or stood on to create the swinging motion for which it was known. The entire piece of equipment could be pushed around in a circle while we stood at each pole pushing and pulling with our hands, arms, feet, and legs. All that exertion created a wild carnival type gyration. Wild!

I'm sure my technical rendering is missing a few supports or trusses that held this thing together, but you get the idea. It basically looked like something built from an Erector Set.

Chapin Park also had a small sand box. Except for a few outer space club meetings where we used the sand to diagram the solar system, I think I spent a total of fifteen minutes in that sand box before it disappeared. Too many neighborhood cats made deposits I didn't care to find.

One lonely basketball hoop and backboard stood near the only drinking fountain in the park. Funny thing about that basketball area; workers installed it among the trees on a grass surface. Since I didn't excel in basketball, I exploited it about as much as the sand box—hardly ever.

Our gang made use of the drinking fountain as a popular hang out for filling water balloons and mixing mud to make bases for the baseball field. It also functioned well as a filling station for the variety of squirt guns we fired at each other on hot summer days. The fountain attracted bees, wasps, hornets, and yellow jackets. When approaching for a refreshing drink, fill a balloon or squirt gun, we had to respect the stinging insects. Bees were no big deal. The yellow jackets which looked like a cross between bees and hornets were the most unpredictable. At any moment they might buzz around your face and head, threatening to attack. The hornets; large and colorful with their black and golden yellow abdomens ruled the ever present mud puddles. They dipped into the water to drink and collected mud for their nests like they owned the place. For me, the most frightful of them all were the ominous, shiny, black, thinner wasps. They were so black they looked purple in the sunlight. Although fewer in numbers; these guys instilled a terrible fear in me. Fortunately, none of these aggressive creatures stung me at the Chapin Park water fountain. I hadn't forgotten the pain and suffering from the triple sting years earlier at Carlson's service station. I learned to respect their right to water, mud, and the pursuit of insect happiness.

By far, Chapin Park's best asset, in my opinion, had to be the dirt field where we played baseball in the summer months. We used two trees as first and third baselines and we made bases out of mud. No one worried about any thugs stealing our bases because they conveniently became part of the field at the end of the game. Playing baseball was the number one sport for us in those days. We talked baseball. We traded baseball cards and stuck duplicate cards in our bike wheels using clothes pins for that special hot engine sound. Continuous debates abounded, as to which pro team rated as the best, the White Sox, or the Cubs.

Player comparisons dominated sports related conversations in Chapin Park all the time. Who performed better at shortstop; Louie Aparicio for the Sox, or Don Kessinger for the Cubs? Rob Enger, a big Cub fan, and I, a devoted White Sox fan, argued around and around that subject for hours.

With all my neighborhood friends living in close proximity to Chapin Park, we had little difficulty gathering enough guys to play a ballgame on almost any given day. The ritual of choosing up sides usually happened by tossing a bat vertically through the air from one boy to another. The process, an exercise in spatial acuity, had us using a combination of holds and figuring out which ones worked best to get the last good grip. Our hand over fist procedure to claim first choice of players proved riveting for all who watched.

Should I use a full hand? Is it time for three fingers or two? Nuts, I should have called bottle caps.

If you wanted to use *bottle caps*, they had to be called before the start of the process. In order to win by *bottle caps*, you had to grip the rim of the bat handle using only the finger tips of one hand to hold the weight of the bat; capping the bat.

One particularly interesting episode took place between Denny Holbrook and Randy Meister. I have a vivid picture in my mind of Denny and Randy studying the bat intensely for which grip combinations to use and win the coveted first choice. The process turned into a shoving match between the two of them. They argued about the rules and started pushing at each other in a series of palm to palm hand presses. They pushed like wrestlers keeping each other at arms length. This went on for several minutes, each accusing the other of cheating. At first I really thought they were going to get into a gnarly fist fight but neither wanted to throw the first punch. They were the two biggest kids, and it could get ugly. Besides, we were all friends and no one really wanted to fight. Cooler heads prevailed and eventually they stopped.

You guys are such pansies.

I'm sure if they'd heard that thought, they would have pounded me. We picked sides for a game as if nothing happened.

When we first began playing baseball on the Chapin Park field, the home run marker was hitting the ball out into Fulton Street—on the fly of course—about ninety feet away from home plate. Denny Holbrook held the home run king title. Whenever he came up to bat his opponents prayed he would strike out. He rarely did, and on top of that, his intimidating ability to rip the cover off the ball caused the pitcher to duck with each swing of the bat. He lined one right into Jack's shin during one game knocking him to the ground. I stood at first base watching Denny pull his bat back behind his head. When Jack's pitch reached the plate Denny took a mighty swing ... and pow! Fortunately, it only bruised him. As we grew bigger and stronger, the home run marker moved to across the street. Later still, it became over the sidewalk across the street. After that, we reluctantly decided to quit. Once we started breaking windows in the houses beyond the sidewalk and losing baseballs to ... shall I say ... less than happy homeowners, we knew time had come for Chapin Park baseball games to end. One of the adults suggested reversing directions and playing toward the center of the park. We couldn't play in that direction; too many trees in the way. We simply stopped playing.

If we didn't engage in a game of baseball, we played the next best thing ... *Five Hundred*! *Five Hundred* in Chapin Park saw everyone in the neighborhood participate. We had occasional adults join in, but mostly older kids in their early to late-teens such as Paul Meister, John Bruder and Jerry Walker on down through my age group. The younger kids included Jack Enrietta, Phillip Meister, Frankie Halterman, and little David Cameron.

Five Hundred allowed all the kids to play together no matter what their size or ability level. The rules were simple. We picked someone to bat first by a variety of means; flipping a coin, picking a number from one to ten, bat toss (hand over fist), or my personal favorite ... "First dibs at batting!" If you were the first to call first dibs ... that ended it—no arguments. The chosen one stood with a bat at home plate alone, or with a catcher who received the return throws from the outfielders. With one hand, the batter tossed the ball up in front of him and swung mightily. A fly ball caught in the air commanded one hundred points. A ball that bounced on the ground once tallied seventy-five points upon being caught. Two bouncers were worth fifty and all others (basically ground balls) equaled twenty-five points. Dropped or missed balls meant the value of that play had to be subtracted from your running total. The first fielder to reach five hundred points won and started a new game as the batter.

When played with lots of kids in the field, fierce competition ensued. Fielders fought for position like dogs after a bone once the batter sent the ball high in the air. Bodies flew through the air, arms flailed wildly, and feet got tangled up. Bumps, bruises and minor bloodshed were common. Calling, "I got it. I got it!" meant nothing in this game, especially when a line drive came screaming at your face. At any time, another glove could pop up in front of you and steal the ball in an instant. Every man for himself; that's the best way to describe *Five Hundred*—scuffling, struggling, and maneuvering to claim five hundred points and next batter status.

♦ ♦ ♦

Chapin Park's dirt infield area transitioned into a bicycle race track many times. This is the activity I mentioned earlier which could very well have been the catalyst for my friendship with Steve Holbrook. Round and round we rode, kicking up dust and crashing onto the ground after locking up pedals in close side by side duels. Riding as fast as we possibly could in a relatively small circle led to spectacular crashes and wipe outs. No one wore gloves, helmets, or pads of any kind. We took our injuries in stride as part of the way of life in the park. Knees, elbows, hands, and sometimes chins and heads sustained huge scrapes from gritty sand pebbles in the dirt. Each of us certainly suffered his share of blood and scabs.

Bicycles and curbs sometimes didn't mix either, especially when riding double on a bike built for one person. Riding double, commonly practiced by just about everyone at one time or another, yielded interesting occurrences such as the swimming pool hill crash. Steve Holbrook sat on the front handlebars of my Monark as we rode along Fulton Street toward Chapin Park one pleasant afternoon. Normally, when approaching a curb while riding alone we made a simple maneuver—lifting up on the handlebars—to make the leap. Very few (if any) handicap ramps existed in those days, so getting from the street to the sidewalk without stopping required this jump move.

Well, as we approached the curb, I began to slow down a little for the upcoming jump maneuver. Steve held on tightly. I pulled up with my hands and arms as hard as I could—uh oh. What happened to the lift? *Crack!* That's what I heard when my wheel hit the curb and my bike frame snapped in two. The front end, with Steve still on it, rolled ahead a few yards and crashed. I tumbled to the ground in a heap with the larger portion of my now two piece bike. Dumbfounded and looking pretty stupid, we stood up; each holding a section of my Monark while rubbing out multiple pains. Fortunately, Steve came away with all of his toes intact, but my bike lay in pieces—destroyed. Tears welled up in my eyes.

"What do I do, Steve?"

"Boy, I don't know," Steve said.

Luckily we had no serious injuries. As I recall, Steve held onto the front end of my bike. I wrestled with the rest, and we started walking. Because of the trauma, I don't remember where we went; if we walked kitty corner through the park to his house, or back toward mine. Sometime later, Dad took my Monark to Sereno's welding shop on Division Street where they completely repaired it, much to my amazement and relief.

◆   ◆   ◆

In the fall, we played football in the grass along Fulton Street. Our field of play extended from Benton Street south almost the entire length of the park to Chapin Street. Most of the games we started eventually morphed into a game we called, *Smear the Queer*, which of course now sounds politically incorrect. Uniforms and equipment such as shoulder pads, helmets, kneepads, etc. were inconsistent. If we had a jersey over any shoulder pads, we were lucky. Everyone had a helmet—the most important item. The game, *Smear the Queer*, evolved from something called, *Dogs Pile on the Rabbit*, which we borrowed from an old Bugs Bunny/Elmer Fudd cartoon. One kid lined up across the line of scrimmage from a host of other guys. The one loner had to break through the line against everyone else. Doesn't that set up sound familiar?—sort of a reverse Pom Pom Pull Away. Instead of one going after many, it's many going after one. That loner, or *queer*, repeatedly got smeared! The pile ups became efforts of little forward advancement and lots of laughs as the *queer* continuously absorbed being pounded into the ground. One player who managed to get through without too much pounding was Rob Enger. Rob, as a smaller guy, seemed to always slip through as if he were a greased piglet. He used his smaller size to his advantage. His scheme; make everyone else laugh so hard we couldn't hang onto him, really worked. I swear Rob had a force field surrounding him sometimes.

We played on that section of grass for a few years and then one spring, *the man*, or in this case the city of Morris, decided to plant a row of trees along the length of our beloved field of play. Of course our way of objecting to the newly installed saplings was to continue playing right over them ... or through them as we often did. It didn't take much to launch into one of those tender saplings and bend it all the way over to the ground. In a way, they functioned as tackling dummies. The trees grew bigger and stronger by the next year. We avoided them altogether or suffered the consequences of a major injury. Eventually, the football games had to end as did the baseball games, and the trees declared victory.

◆   ◆   ◆

Morris, Illinois for years has held the honorable title of *The Largest Inland Grain Shipping Port in the World*. Huge grain elevators line the Illinois River in town. My friends and I visited these grain ports to watch scores of trucks arrive and unload their farmers gold for shipping worldwide. We rode our bikes to the river and gaped at the billions of soybeans and corn kernels falling into the loading pits to be conveyed up into the enormous silos. While there, we stocked up on a few small paper bags full of soybeans. Our intent wasn't to start our own food processing plant but to re-supply our bean shooters with ammunition.

A huge bean shooter battle took place one day that began in the yard of Jeri George's house one block from Chapin Park. These were the days of fruit flavored lipstick; the rage of the day. I remember Jeri and her girlfriends discussing the latest flavors at the swing set in the park, and how some of the guys got a taste. Soon after, the girls walked across the street to Jeri's house, and the boys tagged along for more taste testing. Instead of more fruit flavored delights, the subject of bean shooters came up and all those so armed (each boy) produced their weapons. The girls took cover inside. An impromptu battle started. Mouths full of freshly gathered soy beans soon shot through the air peppering anyone unfortunate enough to be in the line of fire. We ran all around the George residence firing beans by the hundreds. The usual suspects from the neighborhood were the ones involved in the battle, Cameron, Holbrook, Meister, Skopes and a few others. In a matter of seconds, the exchange of bean fire moved across the street to the park where the battle reached a new level of insanity. Guys dipped into their reserve bags of ammunition. Beans by the thousands missed intended targets falling harmlessly onto the ground. Others hit their marks first, and then fell into the dirt and grass. No place in the park was safe; the crazy big merry-go-round, the little wooden one, the large silver boulder, or behind the large first base oak tree. No one felt safe until everyone finally ran out of ammo. War over; time to go home or at least move on to something else.

About a week later, the entire grounds of Chapin Park had sprouted thousands of soybean plants. We had succeeded in planting a new field in Grundy County. We got back at *the man* for planting trees in our sports field. Unfortunately the other man, Mr. George, was puzzled, if not incensed, at the crop that sprouted all around his yard. Like most consequences from our *boys will be boys* actions, we somehow dodged this one too. The soybean plants eventually disappeared before they matured. Chapin Park survived, and over the next few years, contemporary improvements replaced outdated park equipment. A new generation of young visitors took control of the park. Quite possibly they restrained themselves ... maybe.

22

Fifth Grade, 1962–1963

o o o o o o o o o o o o o o o o o o o o o o o o o o o o o o o
"There are places I'll remember all my life ..." John Lennon

ooking back to my fifth grade teacher, Mrs. Elsie Langley, I see a true contradiction. At the time, she must have been about sixty five years old—probably older. To a ten year old boy, that was ancient. Retirement waited just around the corner for her. While Mrs. Windsor in second grade, and Mrs. Sykes in third, were grandmotherly in appearance, Mrs. Langley looked great grandmotherly. She seemed ... really ... old. Her dresses were mostly a flower print style associated with many senior citizens of that era. Shoes she wore had wider than taller heels giving them an orthopedic appearance. Her face had long deep wrinkles from her nose to either side of her lips.

Mrs. Langley's hands were her most obvious age indicators. Large, arthritically knuckled fingers angled toward the little fingers on each hand. This is where the contradiction lies. Observing her hands, one would presume it difficult and painful to write. If indeed she suffered any pain, she never showed it. Her hands didn't seem to affect the quality of her writing at all. She had excellent penmanship. Those gnarly hands had the uncanny ability to manipulate a pen, pencil, and even the white chalk sticks for the blackboard with ease. I remember watching closely, almost mesmerized by her deformed hand slowly gliding across a sheet of paper on my desk leaving in its wake perfectly crafted cursive letters. These letters formed a remarkable line of words which astounded me considering the condition of the hand that wrote them. Her sentences were like a line of well formed tire marks melted onto the pavement by the ugliest old dragster on the street.

We had just received our class pictures for the year, and Mrs. Langley walked up and down the rows getting a closer look at everyone's smiling face. She made polite comments about everybody; this handsome boy, this pretty girl, nice smile etc. When she got to me, she stood next to my desk and pointed her old arthritic finger at my picture. She said, "Now here's a handsome boy." At that point some of my classmates came over to my desk for a closer look. I can see in my mind's eye one of the girls, Cathy Drazy, craning in to get a better view at my supply of 8x10s, 3x5s, and wallet sized pictures. Cathy sat close to me in class, and we interacted quite a bit. She had a raspy little voice and a bubbly personality I found humorously attractive.

Mrs. Langley then dropped a big word on us as she described me. She referred to me as a *tactile* person. I can't recall what I had said or done which led Mrs. Langley to describe me to the class as a tactile person. We didn't know what that meant so a definition soon followed. The fact that she knew that about me mystifies me to this day. Did I offer that much insight for her to know that about me? Who told her I ran the sheets between my toes in bed because it helped me fall asleep? Did she also know how much I enjoyed the cool mud between my toes when wading in Nettle Creek? Mrs. Langley may have been a good teacher, but I don't think she was psychic. Anyway, I remain clueless.

I recall a short lecture one day on the "disgusting, repulsive behavior" as she described it, of nose picking—probably prompted by a wayward student finger during a grammar lesson. Who knows for sure? Whatever the reason for the admonishment of nose picking, she insisted we refrain from doing it. Then one day ...

My desk had the perfect sight line into the hall area before the entrance to the classroom. Nothing could go through that spot without my knowledge if I happened to be on the lookout. On this day, we troublemakers busied ourselves with usual turmoil when she left the room for a few minutes. I acted as the door guard ready to signal her return. When I spotted her, the room quickly settled down—little devils to sweet angels. She approached the door with one—old—gnarly—finger up one nostril digging for a golden nugget! I had observed my teacher picking her nose as she walked all the way to the door. I sat in disbelief recounting her previous lecture. Adults and especially teachers don't do that ... do they?

Please, I didn't just see that. How can I go through the rest of the day with a straight face? Mrs. Langley is picking her nose!

In fifth grade, the day's teaching responsibilities were shared by two teachers. They switched rooms as we students stayed put. Mr. Black taught the second half of our day. Overall, my memory of Mr. Black is limited. A man of average height and weight, he taught math and science and wore Hush Puppies shoes. I figured him to have been in his late thirties then, soft spoken, and the only teacher I knew with a stutter. The fact that Mr. Black suffered through this distracted me somewhat. When Mr. Black started to stutter, we respectfully waited in silence for it to pass. He had our sympathy and certainly our fifth grader's degree of compassion and understanding increased.

◆ ◆ ◆

My fifth grade report card indicated a good citizen student with an outstanding attendance record; one day absent at the very end of the year and never tardy—exemplary. There are five As, twenty three Bs, and two Cs—the benchmark. My body style continued on the skinny side at four feet, eight inches tall and seventy-two pounds of lean Greek. The year ended with one inch of added height and four more pounds; must have been from all the Fasano pies. I continued to have the same habits and attitudes with an additional; *does good work*. Mrs. Langley promoted me to sixth grade.

23

Combat

"Checkmate King Two, this is White Rook ... over. Checkmate King Two, this is White Rook ... over." That line, spoken often during the five seasons of the ABC program, *Combat*, brings back many memories. The WWII, TV series began its first season in October of 1962. Sergeant Saunders (Vic Morrow) and Lieutenant Hanley (Rick Jason) were the main characters, but the character of Paul "Caje" LeMay played by Pierre Jalbert interested me the most. Caje got his name coming from Louisiana Cajun country. Caje spoke French, and I had started learning French about the same time the series debuted. He had a lanky body frame, spoke two languages, fired his rifle left handed, and had dark features. That was a perfect description of me; a lanky, bilingual, left handed shooter with dark features. For those reasons, I naturally identified with him.

"Kirby, Caje, Little John ... cover me!" another command often spoken by Sergeant Saunders to his men. We repeated that one as well during our make believe war games. Our M1 rifles blazed at invisible Nazi soldiers while we jumped from the foxholes that we dug in strategic places in the woods of the *toe path*. Each of us had a unique sound we made with our mouths to imitate gun fire. My ability to roll the letter *r* made my automatic weapons fire sound pretty good actually. I hammered the tip of my tongue against the roof of my mouth behind my front teeth rapidly, while at the same time vocalizing a long *ddddd* sound ending with *dow. Dddddddddowww!* Imaginary Nazis dropped all over the battlefield.

The Holbrook yard provided our training ground for becoming battle ready neighborhood soldiers. In doing so, our exercises sometimes raised the wrath of Mr. Holbrook. *Combat* taught us the proper way to determine if a French farmer's open field contained land mines. We trained for such an eventuality by poking our bayonets (I used my pocket knife) gently into the ground at a low angle until the tip of the knife struck a solid object. With the object identified as a land mine, the first crawling soldier or point man, stuck a marker into the ground warning the others behind him.

Short of digging large holes in the yard and placing something in them posing as land mines, we developed a different technique. Mr. Holbrook could construct just about anything. He had an extensive tool cabinet filled with all kinds of tools and hardware. Denny, Steve, and I borrowed a few hammers and a bag of the largest nails we could find that were the size of pencils. In one section of the yard, we took turns designing our own mine fields. With our hammers, we pounded clumps of five or six nails in tight groupings into the grass. Each little group became a land mine hidden by the blades of grass. I didn't know where the Steve or Denny nails were located, and they didn't know mine. We crawled around the yard on our bellies cautiously poking our pocket knives into the ground searching for the improvised land mines.

"Careful Caje," Denny warned in his best Sergeant Saunders voice.

"Right, Sarg," I responded in my best Caje imitation as my old pocket knife prodded the ground.

When we struck nails, we identified each clump with a twig from our pockets. This continued until we located all or what we thought were all the clumps of the pencil-sized nails buried in Mr. Holbrook's lawn. We picked the warning twigs out of the ground along with the nails and retuned them to the tool cabinet.

Well, you guessed it. We missed a few mines. Sometime later Mr. Holbrook managed to find them. Steve, Denny, their cousin Rob, and I were playing an electric football game inside the Holbrook house—the game where the small players were placed onto a metal playing field that vibrated wildly at the flip of a switch. This caused all the players to scatter until the one with the magnetic ball attached to him got lucky. He either scored or became surrounded in a corner and the play ended—high tech toys back then you know. Suddenly, we heard a loud booming voice coming from outside.

"Mona!" (Mrs. Holbrook). "Where are those kids?" Mr. Holbrook shouted.

The football game came to an abrupt halt, and we gave each other the, *oh crap we're in trouble now*, look. Apparently after the passing of time, rather than staying hidden deep within the ground, the nails sprouted their way up into view like growing weeds from the under world. Mr. Holbrook had found them. He stormed into the house holding a fistful of nails thrust in our general direction.

"Explain this," he commanded.

We did, and the consequences were pretty much the same as past indiscretions by his two sons ... they were grounded for a week. I rode my bike home for something to eat from The Basket.

When it came to toy guns, Steve and Denny had the coolest M1 rifles made with a wooden stock and a bolt action that opened for loading and ejecting fake cartridges. I saw them in the Ace Hardware toy room. Our plastic helmets, covered in string netting were made for inserting extra leaves and twigs, and we rubbed mud on our faces; all as camouflage. From Hornsby's, we purchased packaged WWII weapons sets. They included a plastic hand grenade that could be filled with water through a hole that had a little rubber stopper like a squirt gun. The advertised idea was—when thrown, the rubber stopper disengaged releasing water shrapnel everywhere. Actual performance didn't quite live up to what the packaging illustrated. That is until the life of the toy reached its limit in what ultimately became … the final throw. At that point the molded plastic shattered at the seams, and an explosion of water gave the packaging illustration its justification. Good-bye grenade. What a great marketing scheme, get all the little soldiers in town to break the toys in order to go buy some more—brilliant.

We played army year round just as they did on TV. When Caje strapped on a pair of skis to get away from Nazis we had to go out in the snow and try it out too. We didn't ski, but we still rolled around in the cold snow in our helmets, guns, and newly acquired Christmas gifts; the Sears TransTalk 600 walkie talkies.

These radios had a range of one mile according to the specifications inside the box. In reality, soldier boys were lucky to get reception beyond five blocks. Opening this gift excited me because up to then, the only communicators I had ever played with were the homemade cup and string kind from room to room—which by the way, worked pretty well. The science behind the cup and string communication fascinated me in an old world science sort of way, but having an actual radio to use outside during war games really registered as cool. I had opened up my gift and installed the nine volt battery, eager to begin transmitting and receiving. I called Steve from the phone in the restaurant (we didn't have one at home yet) telling him to turn on his radio. He did, and so began this extra dimension to our war games. We each had our own TransTalk 600 that created new excitement in our version of *Combat*. However, we had a problem. We were all on the same channel, and the opposing armies could hear each other. The TransTalk 600 had limitations in that respect. As a result, we started speaking in code as a necessary tactic. Deciding on exactly what the codes would be became a challenge. Who got to use the call signs *Checkmate King Two* and *White Rook* also became a source for argument. Somehow we worked it all out for our neighborhood battle purposes.

Even today, the child in me still gets excited about *Combat*. Recently I've collected several DVD sets of the series and have learned some interesting facts about my favorite WWII drama. Many of the exterior location shots were filmed in areas near my home in Southern California. On a daily basis I drive through the very property where Caje, Saunders, and the rest created the illusions of WWII France. My son, Harrison, and I watch episodes together late at night searching the screen for familiar landmarks. We've positively identified ridge lines and mountains we see from our backyard hill. His middle school sits exactly on land utilized in several episodes. Sharing this bit of my childhood with my son is a special treat for me. I get a huge kick out of re-discovering my childhood memories and sharing them with him in this unique way. We live in the *Combat* zone! How cool is that? The child in me wants to jump on my current twenty seven year old bicycle and ride off into the local hills. I close my eyes and my two wheeled time machine takes me back to the *Combat* sets where I'm right beside my heroes firing their weapons. Saunders takes aim at the Nazis with his Thompson sub-machine gun; Kirby blasts his BAR (Browning automatic rifle), and Caje, giving me a wink, empties a clip from his M1 rifle. I'm one of the weekly guest stars; a son of a Greek mountain man who is assigned to the squad. Together we work tirelessly creating make believe history in the dry, dusty hills of California.

Combat had it all. When we played army as kids we emulated only the characters from *Combat*; Sergeant Saunders, Lieutenant Hanley, Caje, Kirby, Little John, and Doc. The program, arguably the best WWII drama ever on television, had its detractors. Some kids claimed that *The Gallant Men* or even *The Rat Patrol* were better shows during that era, but my favorite remained ... *Combat*. The show had gun battles of course, but much more effort in storytelling went into the series than that. It had intrigue, history, passion, and human interest stories. Some teleplays included children as the main characters. In hindsight, it's interesting to know I could get engrossed in the episodes with little battle action. I did because the young characters about my age were given such realistic dramatic situations. One episode had a little French boy who longed to join the squad to fight the Nazis. I was a little Greek boy who immediately empathized with him. My favorite hour of television became live make believe for us in Morris when we recreated it at a place we called ... *The Toe Path*.

24

The "Toe" Path

An undeveloped section of Goold Park at the end of Benton Street functioned as a favorite place to stage our tributes to the TV series, *Combat*. We called this two hundred yard long, by forty yard wide piece of property, the *toe path*. I'm spelling it t-o-e instead of t-o-w because mule drawn barges weren't towed along it like the traditional towpath along the Illinois & Michigan Canal. This trail served as a footpath used to access the west side of town from the end of Benton Street. Half-way along the path, a narrow steel bridge about fifty feet in length still spans Nettle Creek today. Beneath that bridge and the immediate vicinity of Nettle Creek was a popular location where my friends and I celebrated our young lives. We exploited the toe path in spring, summer, fall and winter.

Looking west down the *toe path* toward the bridge spanning Nettle Creek

The main toe path trail lay higher than the floor of the woods on either side. Through those woods secondary trails led to Nettle Creek alive with crayfish, minnows, and water striders. We called the crayfish, crawdads, and the water striders we mistakenly referred to as water spiders. These insects were not spiders. Figuring out how the striders were able to walk on water wasn't as much fun as trying to catch them by sneaking up on them with open cupped hands. The striders always escaped. My friends and I picked delicious wild strawberries, blackberries, and mulberries that grew everywhere, often returning home with dark red and purple stains on our fingers and clothes. I can imagine what our mothers might have said during laundry day.

On any given day when school wasn't in session, that magical strip of real estate came alive with the voices of young adventurers doing what we did best ... having good old fashioned outdoor fun. We took advantage of this natural treasure during the summer heat by wading in the creek and searching for crawdads under the rocks. Running water, flat rocks, and little boys inevitably led to splashing, throwing, slipping on green moss, and falling in. On hot summer days it felt great to get wet in Nettle Creek. Upstream from the metal footbridge about a hundred feet, the creek flowed under the railroad tracks. This large tunnel was lined with a steel sleeve held together with large bolts and one inch nuts. The sleeve arched all the way up one side, over the water to the other side. Only inches above the water level, a concrete curb at the base of the steel walls ran the entire length of the tunnel on each side. Facing the wall and using the nuts as hand holds, we shuffled atop the curb to reach the other side of the tracks above. This posture created a problem because the curve of the steel sleeve pushed us away from the wall causing our body weight to pull against our gripping fingers. Muscle fatigue set in quickly on the journey across which was also littered with another problematic obstacle ... spiders, real spiders!

Each potential grip nut had to be carefully scrutinized before grabbing it. We could have found ourselves knuckle deep in a revolting, sticky spider web. Shouts echoed off the tunnel walls when our fingers came in contact with webs. The loudest shouts came when an actual spider crawled onto one of our hands. The grip would be lost and ... *splash!* Those who didn't fall started with the playful insults immediately.

"Ha ha, Mikey fell in! What's the matter Mikey ... afraid of a little spider? You big chicken," Jack shouted.

"Shut up! You're a chicken," I said back.

"Chicken, chicken, chicken! Cluck, cluck, cluck ... Ahhh!"

Jack, so caught up in his insults lost his grip and fell in. I laughed real hard.

"That's what you get stupid!" I laughed.

With that happening, Steve had to deliberately let go and he landed on a little sand bar saving himself from a drenching. The steel tunnel filled with loud, strange, metallic echoes of splashing water, name calling, and fits of laughter.

High over this same spot, for some reason, the railroad had placed a layer of charcoal along the tracks. We climbed up the slanted edge of the huge concrete structure to the tracks above. At some point, we got the idea to make piles of this charcoal at the very edge of the railroad bridge. Shoving it all off into the water and turning the stream into a flowing black cloud sounded like fun, but dangerous as well. The bridge had no safety railing. To this day, I'm thankful not one of us fell from the top of the railroad tunnel into the shallow creek below. We avoided disaster more times than I care to admit. Had anyone become careless, slipped on a rock or charcoal dust, it would have been a free fall to certain death thirty feet down.

Another outstanding toe path activity was climbing my favorite tree which grew just a few yards from the water. At the top, a good forty feet high, we saw all the way to Liberty Street and Mick's Quick Chick restaurant. John Halterman, Steve and Denny Holbrook, Jack Cameron, Randy and Steve Meister, Rob Enger, and I took residence high above the toe path many times in that tree. With warm summer breezes in our hair, my friends and I skillfully climbed around in our tall tree holding on tightly while reciting knock-knock jokes—there's a great combination—a sort of group tree hug.

The toe path during winter provided us with just as much fun. Winter meant a magical transformation of familiar territory. In the snow, we sledded down the sides of the trail into the hollows below. Skating along frozen Nettle Creek for hundreds of yards in each direction or just walking on the ice presented an imaginary tale like setting. Nettle Creek looked and felt remarkably different from this frosty perspective.

Often during these skating excursions we broke through some of the thinner ice because after all, it was a running stream. We really didn't mind it much. We knew the depth of almost the entire waterway. Our primary problem remained only a matter of how long we endured the cold until our feet started aching. At that point we simply walked home and warmed up with hot chocolate and dry socks.

Again, as you can see, my adventures included plenty of danger and risk of injury. There have been half a dozen injuries in my life I categorize as the type I would never ever want to experience again. In the Carlson's Service Station chapter, I mentioned there would be worse pain in my future. It happened here, on Nettle Creek at the age of about ten.

On a typical Midwest winter day; overcast, cold and perfect for skating; Steve, Denny, Jack, Rob, and I had been skating on the creek about three hundred yards southwest of the toe path bridge. The ice had formed a small rounded hump the size of a pitcher's mound over a rippling rapids section. I heard the water running underneath. I wore a pair of hockey skates given to me by my cousin, Johnny, in Chicago. Over the hump, I started pushing short quick strokes like a cartoon character's legs spinning a hundred miles an hour while standing still. The pointed back end of the right skate blade smashed into my left shin bone. Initially, the cold dulled the pain but it soon shot through my leg with a vengeance. Oh, did it hurt. Falling to the ice, I rubbed it and rubbed it wishing with all my might the pain would subside, but it didn't. I prayed and crossed myself, hoping I hadn't been seriously injured. After some consoling from my friends we skated back to the toe path where we changed back into our shoes and snow boots. Limping noticeably, I groaned through the pain along the toe path to the Holbrook house.

When we got to the Holbrook residence, the pain became much worse. I needed to take my first look at the injury, so I pulled up my pant leg revealing my long underwear. My long white cotton underwear had a partially frozen blood stain the size of a half dollar stuck to my skin; time to go home. Without making a fuss about anything to Mrs. Holbrook, I started walking the four blocks home.

I must have been quite a sight to passersby. My skates were thrown around my neck, and my face flushed red from the cold. I had a running nose and watering eyes from sobbing most of the trip. The more warmth generated by walking through the snow, the more unbearable pain I felt. Half way home I could barely walk. No one stopped to help me because whenever a car passed me I hid my anguish by stopping and turning away or looking down. I didn't want others to see me in pain and in such an un-composed state. For all I knew, my leg could have been fractured.

I finally made it home after several minutes, as late afternoon turned to dusk. I limped upstairs to our apartment with much assistance from the wall hand rail. Mom and Dad were downstairs working. I didn't immediately seek them out. Instead I went directly to my room for closer examination of my wound. After rocking and rolling on my bed, I removed my pants. The sight of the bloodstain having grown larger frightened me. My leg burned with pain. Ann must have heard me and rushed downstairs for help because the next thing I recall—Mom had entered my room asking what had happened. My explanation didn't come easily. I didn't want her to touch my leg at all. No one could touch it because of the intense pain. Mom left the room and I sat on the edge of my bed rocking back and forth crying until Uncle Nick entered. He offered his help. I have no idea why I allowed him and not Mom to take a look. Together, Uncle Nick and I slowly peeled the cotton fabric off of the scabbing wound. I winced the entire time. Uncle Nick, sans cigar, attended to my problem gently and quietly during the entire procedure. That had a calming effect on me. He succeeded in touching the leg and taking a good look at a pretty gross wound. It's weird—because Uncle Nick gave hair cuts and shaves not prescriptions and stitches. But he conducted himself very much like a doctor examining for a broken bone. The leg wasn't broken. Gallons of calcium laden milk I had consumed must have contributed to the strength of my skinny Greek bones. However, a good sized piece of skin had been torn away leaving a hole the size of a dime. I watched fluid mixed with a little blood flow out of it quickly filling in the hole. The bone must have been deeply bruised by the skate blade causing the severe pain. I took aspirin for the pain, sprayed Bactine on the area and covered it with a Band Aid. That hurt like crazy. That's it—I didn't even go across the street to see Dr. Roth. Uncle Nick left shortly afterwards.

I nursed myself through several days of pain with Mom's help. And where had my dad been through all this? In hindsight, I think he should have at least come up for a look that day. He didn't until a day or so later, curious to know about the injury. He did show some concern but didn't fuss about it. A huge green and brown, puss oozing scab developed. It slowly went away after a few weeks leaving a hole in my skin that has been with me ever since. Like my dad and his leg scars, I have mine. Like his old shepherd boy story from the rugged mountains of Northern Greece, I have mine to tell from the frozen waters of Nettle Creek.

25

Gorilla Balls

Hot and humid; the most common adjectives used to describe summers in Morris, Illinois. Not even the wind in my face while riding my bike could cool a day such as the one in this story. I had made the trip up and down Wauponsee Street from home to the Holbrook residence four blocks away hundreds of times. I knew the route and its pavement's textures very well. The tar filled cracks in the concrete made discernible patterns in the street. They became a visual roadmap leading me along. While riding, the slapping of car tires crossing those same cracks sounded a warning of cars approaching from the rear. Within my first block of travel, I heard the slapping. I turned back to check only to suddenly find myself flying through the air as I slammed into the rear of a parallel parked white, 1962, Buick. I catapulted onto the trunk lid of the car, and my red Coast King lay in the street with the front wheel spinning. Luckily I wasn't hurt; only embarrassed because a lady living in the house on the corner saw the crash from her porch.

"Are you alright young man?" she called.

She had to know me. We lived on the same block, and I traveled back and forth hundreds of times—a highly visible *young man*. I could only muster a quick "yes" and a face saving wave to the woman. I scrambled off the car and back onto my bike which luckily didn't receive any damage, and I rushed off trying to hide my red face.

Crashing into the rear of a parked car is enough to make any boy feel stupid. I knew that much. Alas, eleven year old boys have short memories about such things and the three blocks remaining to the Holbrook house comprised enough distance to forget all about it. I kept the accident to myself for obvious reasons.

Most days spent with my pals Steve and Denny had unplanned, improvised activities. Did we want to go fishing at Gebhard Woods, or ride to the strip mines for some hill climbing? Should we hang out in Chapin Park for a game of baseball or Five Hundred? Many of these decisions depended upon whom and how many of, *the whom*, were available. This day found me alone with Steve.

What would we do on this stifling day? Hmm; well, boys with lots of time on their hands and wild imaginations can and do come up with creative answers to that question. We ran the hose in his backyard to cool off. Puddles had formed, and we churned up the rich Midwest soil with our hands. The mixture felt cool and refreshing to the touch. Much of the Midwest soil is a dark, black dirt; the Lexus of loam that when mixed with water becomes the Mercedes of mud—a superbly thick, sticky mix of alluvium which we scooped up in our hands to form what we called … *gorilla balls*. I guess because they were large, black, and round we thought of gorilla gonads but it sounded better to use *balls* instead. These perfectly engineered spheres the size of grapefruit made awesome organic hand grenades.

The backyard of the Holbrook house had a neatly trimmed hedge bordering the northwest corner. Wauponsee Street ran along the west flank of this hedge. Distance from curb to bush—ten feet—an ideal hiding place for young boy soldiers to initiate operations. This story is so crazy now that I think about it. What in the world were we thinking? As I write, my inner child is laughing, but at the same time the responsible adult in me cringes at the thought of what I'm about to tell.

Steve and I lay on the grass behind the hedge playing army make believe with our pile of homemade organic grenades ready to go. The enemy approached in a light colored car, but we saw a German Tiger Tank and we let our gorilla balls fly over the hedge.

Normally, when the balls landed, we heard a splat or thud sound. This time, we only heard the loud screeching tires of the car braking hard. Steve and I looked at each other wide eyed like a pair of terrified deer. We high tailed it around the other side of the house and—the perfect hideout—the old style, double storm cellar type doors to his basement. You know, like the ones Dorothy and Toto tried to enter as the twister came barreling toward them. We lifted the heavy wooden doors and ran down the concrete steps to a regular door leading into the basement. My friend and I quickly moved to the opposite side near the wooden stairs and door to the kitchen. The side entrance to the house just above our heads soon welcomed a visitor. We heard a loud knock followed by Mrs. Holbrook's footsteps headed toward the door. My heart pounded and our breathing pumped in oxygen at a rapid pace. Can you say … big trouble?

The woman's muffled voice made it difficult to understand most of her words as we craned to listen in. Obviously upset, she stated her case involving among other things, a ruined dress and redecorated car interior. Mrs. Holbrook listened respectfully and denied any knowledge of the incident. She promised to investigate followed by a sincere apology, and the poor perturbed woman left. The door closed and we heard ...

"Steven!"

I said good-bye and headed back to the other exit where we entered the basement. I took off for home on my bike. I found out later that Steve's parents grounded him ... again. I escaped any repercussions ... again. *Whew!* I don't think throwing gorilla balls (at cars anyway) found a place on our list of things to do any time soon after that encounter. I wonder ... could that light colored car have been the same one I had run into earlier?

26

Sixth Grade, 1963–1964

o o o o o o o o o o o o o o o o o o o o o o o o o o o o o o
"There's a place where I can go and tell my secrets to ..." Brian Wilson

$\mathcal{M}$ention the year 1963 and most people, mainly the baby boomer generation, will think of two historically significant events; The Beatles coming to America and the assassination of President John F. Kennedy. Those two historic events helped define sixth grade for me.

We had barely begun the school year, and someone murdered our young president. For a period of time, we endured a level of sorrow at school and at home.

During the televised funeral for President Kennedy I saw my dad shed tears for the first time. We watched the broadcast from my favorite booth in the bar. I looked up at Dad's face as he stood behind me leaning his elbow on the booth. Tears ran down his cheek and the depth of the tragedy really hit me. My dad never cried. He always presented himself as an example of rock solid masculinity to me. To see him express his sadness during this tremendously tragic time revealed a side of my father I had never contemplated. He had it within him to show deep sorrow.

Sixth grade also saw the beginning of a transitional period regarding my circle of friends. Slowly, over the course of the next three years, my time spent with friends surrounding Chapin Park gradually shortened. Most of them were members of another class year in school, both younger and older. As a result, I had two completely different groups of buddies who didn't really know much about each other. I found strong relationships developing with classmates Lee Randall, Bill Fruland, and Tom Clayton all of whom lived on the east side of town.

Lee's interests included fishing, taking photographs with his new Polaroid Swinger camera, and listening to music. He and I spent a good amount of time at all three activities. I can easily say Lee's taste in music greatly influenced mine. My affinity toward The Beach Boys music (*Little Deuce Coupe, In My Room, Surfer Girl*, etc.), and other top forty hits I'd heard at Carlson's gas station and the juke box in Mom's restaurant, were quite a contrast to Lee's favorites. He introduced me to folk music; specifically Peter, Paul, and Mary.

Struggling through adolescent trials, I had found a soothing sensibility in this calm style—folk music. When Lee turned my attention to Bob Dylan's, *Don't Think Twice, It's Alright*, performed by Peter, Paul, and Mary, it instantly made me aware of how this music could help me through personal tribulations. Sure there were ballads by the Stones, Beatles and other rockers we both enjoyed, but folk music turned my thoughts to a more settling place—optimistic musical poetry in easy keys and chord changes I could play on my guitar. I have Lee to thank for his musical recommendations and inspirations.

♦   ♦   ♦

Mr. Mike Fry and Miss Shirley Hanson led my sixth grade experience. Mr. Fry, a friendly, likable teacher had a reassuring, fair, and inspiring style of teaching. He taught math, science, and geography. Every sixth grader should have the good fortune of learning from someone like him.

We had two major projects in science that year; one in geology where each student gathered and assembled an impressive looking rock collection, and the other in entomology, creating an elaborate insect collection. Both projects were presented on large, white sheets of cardboard divided into a number of marked squares. The rock collection came first.

In order to gather the assortment of sedimentary, igneous, and metamorphic samples, we embarked on two field trips—one locally in Chapin Park that yielded only a few samples of stones and the other, south of town. Several students excitedly pick up stones in the park. Kids flocked around Mr. Fry. One after another they presented their samples to him for identification.

"What's this Mr. Fry?" asked Jill Bergstrom.

"Well, let's see, Jill. That is ... chert."

"What about this one Mr. Fry?" inquired Cheryl Larson and Barb Mitchell almost in unison.

"Those are also chert. It's a common type of silica rock. Okay everybody ... you're going to have to search a little harder—no more chert please."

His expert diagnosis identified several stones as ... chert. Chapin Park overflowed with chert and necessitated a second field trip requiring more planning and resources.

On another day, we loaded up in several cars provided and driven by some of the parents. This second geology field trip took us south of the Illinois River to a remote location near the river itself at the base of where the original river bridge was built at Calhoun Street. How in the world did Mr. Fry ever know about that place? Hidden among trees and bushes, the spot looked about the size of a baseball diamond—literally a pile of rocks ranging in size from walnuts to basketballs.

In it, we found just about every type of rock needed to make our collections complete. We discovered quartz, feldspar, granite, conglomerate, sandstone, limestone, shale, and slate; a geological potpourri surprise.

During the rock hunt, I vividly recall Tom Enger finding a snake crawling among the assorted orbs. Suddenly, Tom grabbed the serpent by the tail and flung it away—the story of the day! Of course, the girls nearby let out the usual shrieks, and the guys thought they witnessed the neatest thing ever. The field trip to the rock pile turned out to be a memorable one. I learned about the location, observed some reptile wrangling which helped solidify the day in my memory, and I earned an *A* on my rock project. Pretty good I'd say.

Our second major science project was the insect collection. I wasn't kidding earlier in the gas station chapter about why I might have missed the rear end rebuilds of Bob Chally's hot Chevy. I really did include a common house fly in my project, among many other more exotic insects.

For this gruesome school project, we set out on a bug hunt to the toe path just four blocks from school. We had our nets, jars, cotton, and nail polish remover; necessary weapons for battle. This mission to the toe path would be for real, not make-believe like the *Combat* war games we played there. This time students did some real stalking, stealthy advance, dynamic capture, and inflicted ... real death. Our cause was scholastic achievement, and our efforts were focused on the top prize ... an *A* for excellence.

The west end of the toe path woods opened into a flat meadow along the railroad tracks. Classmates, intent upon capturing every species living in the toe path woods, had spread all over the meadow chasing butterflies, grasshoppers, moths, and beetles. There, Darlene Zeman let her quest for an elusive butterfly raise the hairs on the necks of Mr. Fry and his other young troops. A freight train approached from the west at close to fifty miles per hour. I heard the train engineer blow his warning blast for the approaching Union Street crossing. Traffic lined up waiting at the lowered gates. Bells clanged and red lights flashed. Darlene held her large white net high in the air and ran after a fleeing butterfly headed directly up the gentle slope to the tracks. Didn't she hear the train horn? Didn't she hear the loud clanging of the crossing gate bells? Didn't she hear Mr. Fry shout at the top of his lungs?

"Darlene! Darlene!"

By the time Mr. Fry trampled every piece of vegetation between himself and Darlene, the train had rushed past them in a vortex of swirling dust and hot air. Darlene landed safely in the arms of Mr. Fry only a few yards away from the tracks. He led her away from the thundering freight train toward the main path, the toe path—and safety. What became of the butterfly is left to Darlene's memory, not mine. The delicate creature may well have wound up on her specimen board, or the windshield of the diesel engine. Maybe it was rudely flushed away in the powerful gust of rushing, smelly, railroad air. Intent upon catching the fluttering life form, Darlene almost became a squashed bug on the Rock Island engineer's windshield. I hope she got an *A* for her effort.

Incapacitating the bugs was an exercise for the stouthearted. Specimens had to be collected and placed one by one in a jar containing a cotton ball dipped in nail polish remover. After tightly sealing the lid, the little creatures met their demise in the name of sixth grade science. Many of these executions were conducted in the field. For those who couldn't bring themselves to perform the deed out in the wild, Mr. Fry obliged in the classroom. Specialist, Mike Fry, quickly and without ceremony finished the procedure with a resolute twist of the lid. He then moved on to the next student's desk.

◆ ◆ ◆

Miss Hanson's homeroom was next door to Mr. Fry's classroom. She arrived after lunch for the second half of the day. She had brown hair in a beehive; attractive, in her early thirties probably. She walked slowly in high heels with a statuesque posture as I recall. I also remember she had thick ankles—not much definition between the ankles and calves. I preferred shapely legs in my female teachers or there could be no crush! She was more like an aunt.

Miss Hanson, I'm sorry but you're not my type. How about a real girlfriend?

One project assigned to us by Miss Hanson that I distinctly remember was a diorama. I chose an ancient Greek temple (what else?) as it may have appeared high in the clouds of Mount Olympus. I used a shoe box, aluminum foil, cotton, and several white cardboard insert spacers from Dutch Masters, and other cigar boxes from Dad's bar. Those rectangular inserts made excellent columns when standing upright. Round would have been more authentic, but the cigar box rectangles sufficed.

Charlie Doss discovered he had a hearing problem while we were in sixth grade. At the same time, I began to realize my vision deteriorated somewhat. For a while Charlie and I were placed in front of the class by Miss Hanson. This seating arrangement lasted until I started wearing glasses prescribed by my new optometrist, Dr. Kayle. His office was above Riz's Foodliner, kitty-corner from our apartment. Old Dr. Kayle reminded me of the Scottish actor, Alastair Sim who played Ebenezer Scrooge in the 1951 movie classic, *A Christmas Carol.* They had similar facial features and even walked alike—kind of bent over with a little hunch back. With my new black framed eye glasses from Dr. Ebenezer, I returned to the main body of the room. This time, I sat next to Terry Nelson.

Terry, a music enthusiast as most of us were, played the cornet in the school band. He flashed a secretive look at me one day as if to show me a new Beatles record, but pulled out this teeny tiny pencil he had in his desk instead. Bummer, I would have preferred the record album. The pencil had been ground down to about a half an inch long. For some reason he got a kick out of sharpening his pencils as short as he could get them. He had tons of them in his desk. Now, we all know what a nice break it was to get up out of your seat for a trip to the pencil sharpener. It felt good to stretch your legs and crank the sharpener's handle a few extra turns to prolong the break ... but man—an entire pencil?—bunches of them ground down to next to nothing? Terry had lots of nervous energy to burn and took it out on the pencils I guess. Some guys, myself included, collected marbles. Terry collected his mini pencils. Out of curiosity, I gave it a whirl and made one of my own, but I didn't get a big thrill out of it. Also, I didn't care to waste a perfectly good pencil—frugality being a family trait.

I don't have time for this pencil baloney. There are more important things to worry about ... like girls for example.

My buddy, Lee, during this time had an interest in a girl in our class named Vicky Castanier. Vicky, a pretty young lady, had honey blonde hair and sultry, sleepy, eyes that easily pulled you into her world. They worked on Lee and eventually worked on me as well. Being shy however, I had trouble actively pursuing, developing, and mastering the skills needed in obtaining the sixth grade boyfriend/girlfriend relationship ... whatever that entailed. As a result of this burdening shyness, I resigned myself to observe how other guys operated in the game of social skills. Lee reacted favorably to the sleepy eyed Vicky, and they had a few—I guess you could call them dates. For me, though, getting out of my comfort zone of adventures with my pals and into the twilight zone of girls kept haunting me.

West Side Story played at the Morris Theatre sometime that year and I went with my sister, Ann, to experience my first movie musical. Not knowing what to expect, I soon witnessed cinematic diversity unfamiliar to me due to my preferences for Jerry Lewis movies, and the B movie horror/outer space adventures I loved. What was this musical all about? I already knew about *The Wizard of Oz*, (humor yourselves and sing along. You can do it.) *Because, because, because, because, because, it played every spring around Easter time.* But what about this idea of a New York City love story trapped between gangs called Jets and Sharks fighting with switchblades and dancing in the streets? How in the world could I get that? It turned out that I really dug it. A Greek played the lead Shark role of Bernardo! George Chakiris; his last name resembled my original one—Skopis. I thought ...

Chakiris ... Skopis; hmmm, could he be a compatriot from Epirus perhaps? This is good. He is dark, I'm dark. Caje from Combat resembles me. There might be something to this ethnicity angle. I could be a popular guy with the ladies if I just play my baseball cards right.

I discovered people with rolling *r* accents had admirers. This could easily carry over into my little skinny world. Alright! Singing, dancing, winning the love of a pretty girl, hanging with your pals planning strategies in a candy store, rumbling under a bridge at night; hey, this is my kind of movie! But then tragedy struck as Riff died at the hand of Bernardo, who died from Tony's thrusting switchblade, who died from a bullet fired by Shark Chino, who ended up riddled with guilt thanks to the angry and mournful Maria ... aye aye aye!

All I want is a girlfriend for cryin' out loud! Flash ... can you hear me Flash? This is Dr. Skopis calling Flash Gordon ... Dr. Skopis ... from the planet Morris. Come in ... do you read me? I want a girlfriend Flash ... a girlfriend ... do you read me? Can you help me ... Flash?

The audience sat in silent shock except for the sniffling I heard from various seats around me. I turned around to the row behind me and there she sat, illuminated by the light reflecting off the screen ahead, Vicky Castanier. Her sultry, sleepy eyes had become sad, teary ones. Tears streamed down her cheeks. Her hanky absorbed her sadness like a sponge. I wanted to jump over the back of my seat and hold her hand, console her, tell her everything would be okay. Her Bernardo (me) had arrived willing and able to comfort her through the tragedy that had unfolded before her sorrowful, sultry eyes.

I'm here Vicky. Your skinny, Greek, gang leader, hero is here to soothe your aching heart with a song from the mountains of Epirus. Who's got my clarinet? Give it to me or I'll cut you!

But I didn't do it. As much as my improvised thoughts may or may not have been a good idea, I had pride in my chest for at least beginning to develop a sense of style.

Out blasted shyness ... out! Go away and never come back. Can't you see the time is now? I have to act now when the moment is right. My lady needs me.

I would have had to displace her female companion next to her—younger sister, Janet. That could have created a problem. Besides ... I sat with my older sister so my fantasy remained just that ... a fantasy.

Crap!

Music started to become, more and more, a vehicle to lead me into the world of girls. When I listened to songs from The Beatles especially, I began associating the lyrics written by McCartney, Lennon, and Harrison with my innermost feelings. For example, the song *I Call Your Name* from *The Beatles' Second Album* has the line; *I call your name, but you're not there.* Well, I called (to myself anyway) Vicky's name but she didn't appear there in the way I had hoped she would. We talked in class and I even went to her house on Armstrong Street a few times for casual visits with other friends present, but the blossoming relationship I had longed for never happened. I couldn't quite make the next step. I was a social ... invalid ... chicken!

◆ ◆ ◆

This next sixth grade story is really, I mean really stupid behavior. Kids, please do not attempt this at home or anywhere else for that matter. Before exiting our classroom for recess one day, a group of about five boys, myself included, lingered behind for an unsupervised demonstration in scientific experimentation. We'd heard a rumor about the procedure used to make a person black out. Curiosity got the best of us that day. We needed a volunteer, and I raised my hand. Dumb. We were the only ones left in the room, and one of the guys had explained the instructions as he knew them. I took several deep breaths while low to the floor. I quickly stood up and another kid applied a squeeze from behind. I found myself alone on the floor. The room lights had been switched off. I had passed out cold for I don't know how long. It may have been only a few seconds to as many as twenty or thirty seconds. I don't know. I jumped up and ran out of the room scared out of my mind, and angry that I had been left alone on the floor. Not one of those punks stayed with me to snap me out of my stupor. Either they ran way afraid of getting caught, or they simply found humor in it and took off. My guess, I would hope, is that they freaked and didn't want to get caught—not that they thought it was funny. Either way ... thanks a lot guys. You know who you are. I could have been brain damaged.

My frustrations from everything sixth grade, ultimately manifested themselves by way of venting in written form. I sat toward the back of the class goofing around with Tom Enger when in a stroke of grotesquely poor judgment; I lashed out at a textbook by scrawling two choice obscenities in the margin. The words were noticed by a few students and one of them (a girl) decided to take the book to the front of the class and Mr. Fry. There were nineteen girls in my sixth grade class. One of them at the time didn't know who she was potentially about to incriminate. If she's reading this ... now she knows. I watched in horror as my female classmate carried the book forward along the row of desks and handed it to Mr. Fry. He started reading what some disrespectful student in his class had blazed across the page. His face became seriously disturbed. He looked up and out into the sea of faces before him. He paused as he scanned the room. He sent the girl back to her seat. Then he spoke in a calm but angry tone. I shrunk down at my desk hoping my actions wouldn't reveal my guilt. His words are lost to me now but the message—clear. He gave a quick expression of displeasure in both face and words admonishing the guilty party. He attempted to get that person to admit his guilt without success. I sat there like a coward not taking the heat which put others undeservedly in jeopardy. I should have stood and taken it—I didn't. So what if these other guys were suspected of writing a couple nasty words in a book. Hey, a few of those fellas were guilty of deserting me passed out on the floor. Each of those events scared me for different reasons.

◆ ◆ ◆

My report card from sixth grade reflects a number of good grades. My trend continues with three As, twenty five Bs, seven Cs and oops ... a D shows up in arithmetic (my problematic subject) at the end of the year. Attendance follows the norm with only three absences and no times tardy. I avoided missing school unless I was really, really sick. The habits and attitudes page reflects the same outstanding behavior and citizenship patterns. Apparently Mr. Fry and Miss Hanson thought of me as; *capable of doing better,* so the corresponding boxes were checked across the page that year. However, the truth is flawed by the lack of any reference to that written profane outburst. How could there be any reference to that? No one found me out to be the guilty one. I'd like to amend the card in one of those boxes with a check mark next to the words ... *Lacks responsibility,* and adding ... *for being an idiot one day in class.* Mr. Fry and Miss Hanson promoted me to seventh grade.

27

Backyard Camping

Backyard camping, a popular summer activity for Morris youths, occurred regularly. Every neighborhood group had their favorite spot and ours was surely not the grassy patch near Carlson's gas station. We camped in the enclosed patio of the Holbrook backyard. Along with his brother-in-law, Chuck Enger, (Rob's dad), Mr. Holbrook built this great garage/summer activities building. On many summer days, the Holbrooks and Engers got together to spend time inside the completely screened in patio section celebrating Independence Day, drinking beer, enjoying barbeque, and playing cards. Other times, people gathered together to watch Cubs and White Sox games, proclaiming adnauseam the better of the two teams. On warm summer nights, the facility turned into a campground for us a few times each summer.

A spotlight night in my backyard camping memory included the usual players; Steve and Denny Holbrook, Todd Johnson, Roger Roth, Rob Enger, and me. This night also included my friend Ted Trenter. Shortly before midnight, we had our blankets and sleeping bags set up in our select spots for the night. While playing *Five Card Stud* with deuces or one eyed jacks wild, the group stumbled upon a conversation about things we claimed absolutely impossible to do. Not a bad conversation topic for bunch of kids on a backyard camp out.

"Deuces and one eyes," Steve called as he dealt the cards.

"What?" Ted objected.

"He said deuces and one eyed jacks are wild," I repeated.

"Well, that's stupid … you can't do that … not possible," Ted complained again.

"Shut up and deal the cards," Roger snapped.

"I am, I am … and its deuces and one eyed jacks. I called it, okay?" said Steve defending himself.

"Yeah … come on, come on, let's just play." I said backing up Roger.

"Wait a minute ... you can't have both deuces and one eyed jacks wild in the same game. No way man, it's impossible," Ted insisted.

"No, it's not. Who cares anyway? This isn't Las Vegas you know, so it is *possible* for Steve to make up his own rules," I fired back.

Denny sat there quietly observing the banter back and forth between the younger guys. He seemed to be waiting for the best time to chime in. Everyone watched and listened as Ted and I kept going at it.

"Impossible, you dummies!" Ted said.

"Possible; you dim wit! Why don't you think of something that's really impossible?

The dimly lit patio suddenly got quiet. A late night breeze blew through the trees in the Holbrook backyard—ahh, summer nights. The gentle rustling of leaves gave a sense of calm before the storm. Everyone waited for Ted to respond to the gauntlet I had thrown down at his feet. Serenity and silence were broken by ...

"Oh, yeah? Okay, alright ... well ... I'd like to see you try to sew a button on a fart!" he finally blurted out.

For a nanosecond only silence filled the patio. The thought sunk in and we burst out laughing at the visual. Finding my breath, I quickly offered the solution to the problem between screams of laughter.

"Oh, yeah? That's easy. All you have to do is fart into a tube, condense it into water, store it in a container, freeze it, drill holes in it, get a needle and thread and sew a button on it!"

Pillows and laughter flew through the air. Cards went all over the place.

"Aw crap! I had two deuces and a one eyed!" Rob screamed.

"No way!" came from everyone toward me and Rob.

"No way! No way!"

"Aw come on. How the heck are you supposed to do that?" Ted shouted.

I quickly resorted to my science abilities since science had been my best and favorite school subject.

"It's easy," I said defending my solution. "All you're doing is changing a gas into a liquid and freezing it. Piece o' cake. Scientists do that every day."

"How do you know what scientists do all day?" Ted countered.

"I don't know. Just shut up you morons," I shot back at all of them.

"Oh yeah? Well that's stupid," Ted quipped.

"You're the one that's stupid," I laughed back.

Denny finally chimed in.

"I think you're all nuts ... sew a button on a fart ... that's crazy."

"Ted brought it up. And I don't think it's impossible that's all," I said.

Denny's repeating of those words; *sew a button on a fart*, kept us in stitches. I thought Rob was going to piss his pants as he grabbed himself to hold it in. That created more laughter. We were losing it. Now all of us had to go. We ran the path through the hedge around the back of the building and watered the blacktop on Depot Street.

◆ ◆ ◆

Another common camp out adventure saw us weaving in and out of the shadows in the very early morning. At about two or three o'clock, we silently snuck out onto Wauponsee Street for the hushed trip downtown for fresh baked donuts. We always visited the Morris Bakery on Liberty Street instead of Roth's because Roger's parents usually worked the ovens in those wee hours. We also had to watch out for the Morris police cars patrolling the streets. We had violated curfew by slithering silently along the quiet streets and alleys. Even the alleys were risky because the cops patrolled them as well. If a squad car entered one, we had no trees to hide behind. One alley crossed through my block. It gave me an uneasy feeling sneaking around knowing my family slept nearby. The police station itself occupied a building only half a block from the Morris Bakery. In fact the alley at the bakery back door was the same alley that opened out to City Hall and the third shift officers. One route to the bakery meant taking Liberty Street, and the other ran directly across the street from the cops. We always chose that final half block along Liberty Street. We decided to risk Liberty Street's night lights rather than dash the forty feet on the sidewalk across the street from the police station ... duh.

The bakery's alley entrance had dual swinging doors. We politely knocked before entering so we wouldn't frighten the baker. We dug into our pockets to pay for the awesome fry cake donuts and made a quick getaway back to base camp. Eventually we fell asleep. The harmless juvenile delinquents never got caught running the shadowy nights during backyard camping.

28

Free Goose Day

In later grade school years, or junior high, Friday meant boys could take a whack at hitting another boy in the crotch for the fun of it—Free Goose Day—how creative. If you had a large hard cover notebook, and we all did, it became defensive armor placed directly in front of your groin for the entire day at school. Walking out of home room—the notebook found its place. Bending over for a drink from the drinking fountains ... the shield held its groin ground. The notebook shield had more value than any nut cup. If the schools in those days had security cameras, it would have been very interesting to view a few minutes of any Friday in the halls between classes. Every boy on camera would be holding his testicle shield in a defensive posture to ward off any attack from some nutty kid taking advantage of Free Goose Day.

What genius invented Free Goose Day anyway? How did it start? What whacko decided to assign such an invasion of private property on any day, let alone Friday just before the weekend?—weekends—when we had to be healthy for important sporting activities. This mystery will never be solved. I don't expect anyone to call me and say ...

"Hello, Mike? Hi, this is your older pal ... so and so. I invented Free Goose Day on September 18, 1962, after getting out of Mr. Hankins' science class. That day we discussed the male anatomy which made me curious to know the effects of random phalangeal, testicular contact and, well ... you know ... things kind of got out of hand ... so to speak."

Free Goose Day wouldn't be that interesting unless I had a personal account to use as an example. But, do I really want to go there? I mean it's only a subject involving the injured private parts of a school boy ... nah ... I can't do it—too painful.

If you remember the film *Stand by Me* from 1986, you'll probably recall the *two for flinching* bit. We really did that. *Two for flinching* worked because the target had no idea when it would be launched. If you feigned hitting another kid on his arm and he flinched you were allowed to really hit him twice because of the flinch. Many times the two hits were wiped off by the hitter after connecting. I never understood the meaning of the wipe off. How that ever got started I don't know. Hey, old friend from 1962—do you know?

Guys came up with strange reasons to hit each other during those times. One fella even encouraged assaults upon himself—Tom Bednarik, (Beth's brother). Tom took pride in the fact that he could take a punch directly into his breadbasket and not feel a thing. That fascinated me. Try as I might, I could never hurt him. Tom flexed his stomach muscles tight, held his breath and gave a go ahead nod. I pulled my arm back and punched with whatever strength I could muster. My fist simply bounced back like a baseball off a brick wall.

"Once more Tom, come on," I begged.

"Go ahead," he grinned.

I tried again; this time thinking of a way to get more leverage. What leverage? He laughed it off—amazing. I couldn't hurt him. No one could hurt him—unreal. I watched other guys go for the belly bashing with the same results. Tom Bednarik had a steel belly—a belly that wouldn't budge.

We did a lot of hitting for one reason or another—mostly innocuous except for this one time ... on Free Goose Day. Did you really think I wouldn't tell you? I'm writing this chapter on a Friday! Feeling momentarily safe one Friday morning, I let my guard down while walking in the hall between classes. Suddenly, Jim Schaible nailed me.

"Free Goose Day!" Jim proclaimed.

He smugly walked away as if the emancipating proclamation really justified the act. What a strange thing. I mean really. Boys actually walked around school on Fridays boldly and proudly announcing "Free Goose Day!" every time they connected. How crazy is that?

Man oh man. In a way I lucked out ... he missed the testicles. In another way—not, he hit me directly on the head of my—well, without getting too graphic, it created a tiny cut or tear that hurt like wild fire for a few days until it healed. I kept my pain to myself out of embarrassment and didn't retaliate. No hard feelings Jim. I hope our next class reunion is on a Friday.

I wonder what the girls thought of the whole thing. They no doubt witnessed the loony boys taking advantage of Free Goose Day. There certainly were plenty of Fridays during the school year. Did they coyly walk the halls of Center School observing the boys and their stupid Friday game hoping to catch the next act of gonad grabbing?

And what about the girls? Can you imagine them inventing a similar game of Free Jab a Boob Day—say ... every Monday? Hey, maybe that's why they held their books close to their chests?

I hated Free Goose Day.

29

Seventh Grade, 1964–1965

o o o o o o o o o o o o o o o o o o o o o o o o o o o o o o o o
"Got a good reason, for taking the easy way out ..." Lennon/McCartney

*S*omething happened half way into seventh grade—some fundamental change within me I can't quite define. No, it had nothing to do with Free Goose Day. I continued with my pattern of average math grades, good spelling, good in language/English class, and best grades in science and geography. French began well, but by the third six week grading period the decline started. Perhaps hormones deserved the blame, or rebellion, or a little of both laced with a mild dislike for one of my teachers.

Mr. Phillips, a nice enough man, had a gentle and good natured personality—in his middle thirties I'd say. We nicknamed this thin, six foot tall man, *Eagle Beak*, because of his large hooked nose. Mr. Phillips lived in a Benton Street house on the same block as Center School with his wife and children (*Eaglet Beaks*). Mr. Phillips had a southern accent which I found to be disconcerting whenever he spoke French. He taught my French and geography/social studies classes. Having him for two classes a day grew to be too much for me. It was such an odd thing, because he always seemed to be smiling and easy going, so I have to attribute the miss-meeting of minds to myself. Maybe I lost interest in French, or French with a southern accent. I really can't say.

I can remember sitting in French class with Mike Tucker. Having two of us named Mike in the same class, Mr. Phillips gave the French equivalent, Michelle, to Mike and Henry to me. I didn't like that and wanted it changed, but he denied the request. Eagle Beak may have been confused because both Mike T. and I had a mole on the right side of our upper lip just below the nostril. Mike eventually had his removed, probably out of fear of chopping it off while shaving. Me? I still have mine—nicked it countless times but wouldn't part with it for all the French books in South China.

Things were going south (no pun intended) on an almost daily basis in French class, and I began having zero interest in participating. As a naturally bilingual person, I used that as my justification to simply drop out of class, so to speak. Seventh grade would be my final year of taking any foreign language in school.

One day's events were enough for Mr. Phillips to contact my parents regarding my behavior. Dad walked the entire way to the school still wearing his white bar apron. He never took it off if he had to go out for a brief time. It only took my dad two or three minutes to walk four blocks to the school for a spur of the moment, mini, parent/teacher conference out in the hall. Dad climbed up the south stairwell to the hallway near French class where the two men spoke briefly. Mr. Phillips asked me to join them in the hall where I witnessed my father tell Mr. Phillips …

"You do what you have to do to keep him in line, that's all."

"Thank you Mr. Skopes," Phillips said.

Dad would not tolerate disrespecting authority. With those few words, I could sense the disappointment in my father's voice regarding my behavior. He turned away barely looking at me, and he walked downstairs returning to work. I think I may have embarrassed him.

My disinterest in French class caused an uncomfortable vibe between Mr. Phillips and me. It carried over into his social studies class where it all came to a head. I think most of us, at one time or another, were guilty of inappropriate talking in class. Whether it was only a simple thank you to a classmate for returning a dropped pencil, or a brief invitation for an event after school didn't seem to matter to some teachers. No talking meant ... no talking. My specific infraction in Mr. Phillips' class escapes me. Given my relationship with him in French class, it may only have had something to do with talking out of turn, or worse, an unsolicited, disparaging remark directed at him. I had been frustrated with our relationship. Mr. Phillips stopped the lesson and called out to me to see him after class. The hour continued. At the end of class I walked apprehensively to his desk. In a calm, authoritative, southern voice, he dictated an assignment for me to complete by the next day of school. This happened on a Friday, Free Goose Day, so I had to be extra careful not to get injured which might impede my assignment efforts over the weekend. Boy, I hated Free Goose Day with a passion. Anyway, I had the weekend to complete the work. He spoke as he began writing on a sheet of paper.

"I want you to write the following sentence five hundred times and turn it in to me by Monday," he said.

I looked at the sentence he wrote. It read ... *I will not talk out of turn during social studies class*. I made a sigh of *woe is me*. He continued to explain.

"If you do not complete this assignment on time, this is the alternative."

And you know where you can stick your sentence Eagle Beak.

At that time, he made an attempt at drawing something on the paper. The attempt lacked any artistic talent because I had no clue what he tried to draw.

"Do you know what this is?" he asked.

"No, not really," I said quietly. Inside I wanted to laugh at his art and let him have a piece of my mind.

Where'd you learn to draw?

"It's a paddle. It will be your punishment if you fail to complete this assignment."

"Five hundred times?" I asked hoping for a reduction.

"That's right. Five hundred times," he reiterated.

I hate you. Take your five hundred times and shove them up your eagle beak.

I left the room fearful I wouldn't fulfill the order. My head started spinning.

Five hundred sentences ... I might as well write a novel. I'm going to get the paddle. I've never gotten the paddle before. How in the world will I be able to write five hundred sentences? It's impossible. I'd rather sew a button on a fart. What am I gonna do? Ahhhh! It's Free Goose Day too. Eagle Beak!

I made it safely through the rest of Free Goose Day. What a relief. Later that night, as I sat at the little desk in my room, I started to write. A standard sheet of paper has twenty five lines. That meant I had to fill twenty sheets of paper with that stupid sentence.

Okay, no problem.

I started writing. I worked fast thinking this would be easy as pie. By the bottom of page one, my hand got a cramp. Rubbing it out helped alleviate only some soreness. I wrote a little more and had to stop again because of the annoying pain from only having written two pages.

This isn't good.

A simple task, or at least it seemed simple enough, became a major challenge. What could I do?

Eureka! Three pencils at once!

After trying the three pencil technique I failed again. I started talking to myself.

"There is no way anyone can possibly do this ... get three lines written at the same time to look right ... no way," I muttered to myself.

Out of twenty pages due, four or five were completed properly. A few others had written lines that resembled mass production by cheating. I quit for the night.

The next day, Saturday, I felt somewhat defeated, so I went looking for a boy who had gotten the wood earlier that week. Ricky Cain lived north of the railroad tracks near Goold Park. By bicycle from my apartment downtown, it took all of two minutes to get there. Good fortune smiled upon me because I spotted Rick right away riding his bike and playing in an open field near the park just over the tracks. I can still smell that railroad odor—the acrid bleeding creosote and tar aroma of the railroad ties. Rick saw me coming and waited for me to get alongside him.

"Rick, you gotta help me," I said.

"With what?" Rick asked.

"I'm gonna get the wood Monday if I don't finish writing a stupid sentence five hundred times for Eagle Beak.

"No kiddin'?"

"Yeah. No kiddin'."

"Well, whadaya want?" Rick asked.

I felt a little strange with this whole conversation thinking Rick must have thought of me as a chicken or something. Forcing myself...

"Um ... what does it feel like?" I asked him.

"What, the wood?"

"Yeah, the wood."

Rick smiled a little smirk of a smile going along with my problem.

"Well ... it hurts ... a lot."

"No kidding," I said nervously not as a question but as a confirmation. "Does the pain last a long time?"

"Pretty long."

"How long?"

"I don't know ... a few minutes I guess." Rick added.

My line of questioning didn't help ease my fears of getting the wood on Monday. A neighbor friend called Rick away, and he took off leaving me on my own.

Resolved to finish what I had started no matter what, I rode back home. I picked up where I had left off and decided to keep the mass produced lines as they were. I finished the rest of the lines and pages one by one. Monday morning, and paddle or no paddle, my twenty pages would be done one way or the other.

Monday, Monday. Time had come and with twenty sheets of—*I will not blah blah blah* in my notebook, I handed them over to Eagle B—uh ... Mr. Phillips. He perused my work as I stood anxiously awaiting my fate. After only a few seconds, he looked up at me from his chair behind his desk. His hand picked up a pencil and he once again attempted to create art. The squiggly thing supposedly resembling a paddle appeared a second time on paper before me.

Dang it! Give me a break you hillbilly.

A desk drawer opened and out it came ... a foot long paddle made of brown wood—no holes, just a small flat board with rounded edges and a handle cut out at one end. It didn't look anything like the drawing. He called out for another boy scheduled to get the wood; I don't remember him because of my own deep seated fears at the time.

The three of us walked out of the classroom, around the corner a few steps, and into the boy's restroom. At least punishment would be administered privately and not in front of the entire class. Mr. Phillips selected me first. In the bent over position, facing away from Mr. Phillips, he wound up for the pitch. Then it came, but hey—I didn't feel anything other than a skimming over the top of my butt and lower back. He missed!

Oh lucky me. Man, you're such a jerk.

From my perspective, the punishment phase failed, and I had the freedom to leave. So, I stood up and headed for the exit—wrong! He stopped me before I got very far and instructed me to assume the position once again; just my luck. This time he connected. I could tell by the force of the swing that he didn't intend to be cruel or hurt me. It wasn't his nature. I actually took the slight pain quite well. When I turned to face him he looked a little sad. I think he really didn't want to do it, but felt a responsibility to follow through with the punishment. I rubbed it out while the other kid got his swat. We exited the restroom and went back to class.

◆ ◆ ◆

There is very little I can I can say about Mrs. Bealor. That is strange because she was my homeroom teacher—a pleasant young woman in her early thirties who couldn't quite pronounce the word *further*. She said the *ur* like the *oo* in book, *foother*. I never understood that one, and I thought it best not to ask. Oh well.

I do remember the day a new kid in town first entered Mrs. Bealor's class—his name—Sherman Workman. Mrs. Bealor introduced Sherman to us when he walked in, and he made his way to the row closest to the windows. He shuffled along to his empty desk where he took up residence for the rest of the year. Sherman, a sturdy boy with an awesome personality, became one of the most popular kids in our class. I'm pretty sure Sherman coined my new nickname. It made perfect sense. After all ... I was the only Greek boy in town, so I became known as ... *Greek*. It fit.

In seventh grade, I met and befriended another new kid in town from Florida; Eddie Johnson. Eddie also had an interest in music. He played guitar well, and I learned a few guitar licks from him. Later, we thought we could form a band with singer Lee Randall, Jack Cameron on drums, Bill Fruland, Eddie, and me on guitars. As cool as it could have been, it never happened; aw shucks!

One thing I couldn't learn from Eddie was how to swallow air and belch on cue—another of his talents. One of my family's distant cousins from Chicago, Tony Fotos, a man in his forties, worked as a painter (he is pictured in the chapter on farms). Mom and Dad invited him and his family to Morris for family visits and also to paint our apartment. Eddie and I walked out of my room and passed by Uncle Tony napping on the living room couch. Well, what do you think two seventh grade boys, one a born belcher and the other a born laugher might do to a sleeping man? Belch and laugh of course. Eddie leaned over just inches from Tony's ear and belched out *Thhonneeeee* a few choice times while I choked out a few belly laughs. Uncle Tony pretended to stay asleep.

Eddie and I ran out before we fell deeper into trouble.

"This stuff is too funny. There's no way he didn't wake up," I said laughing.

"He must have been born without a sense of humor." Eddie added.

How could he, or anybody for that matter, keep a straight face under those circumstances? I couldn't believe what I saw. He stayed the great stone face with eyes closed. Not one crack of a smile which made things even funnier. What a gas.

◆　　◆　　◆

At this point I must explain why I include the attention to report card details. Up until seventh grade, the pattern remained consistent with the number of As, Bs, and Cs, and the same with the habits and attitudes sections. In seventh grade, as I mentioned, something happened that caused the grades to noticeably drop, and good behavior patterns went out the window so to speak. All the check marks I received for *respecting authority, working well with others, does good work, accepts responsibility,* and *follows direction well* disappeared. In place of those admirable qualities came; *capable of doing better, wastes time, work carelessly done, inattentive,* and *discourteous.* I find it interesting that for the first four, six-week grading periods, not one of the spaces for good qualities received check marks by any of my several teachers for the year. Then, in the column for the fifth six week session, Mr. Phillips labeled each of the negative boxes I just mentioned. No other teacher entered anything at all. This is the exact opposite of teachers' marks received in prior years. I had been a well behaved student for each past year. For the last six week session, after the Phillips fifth session onslaught, the boxes are all blank again. What does this mean? Hormones? Does it mean anything at all? Did Heidi's broken collar bone and my responsibility for the accident (which happened about the same time) have any bearing? What about, the associated guilt I felt?

Mr. Phillips actually was a good hearted family man. He performed his teaching duties well I suppose, and I actually did get good grades in geography and the first half year of French class. But, I couldn't quite connect with him. This is well documented in the fifth column of my report card that year. I admit; I was capable of doing better. Did I waste time? Yes. Was I careless in my work habits? You bet; inattentive and discourteous? Yes, again. How did I come to be that way?

Why did I do those things? I can't answer for sure. Getting along with others had always been my way of relating with people.

Regardless of the problems I had that year, good attendance meant a lot to me for two reasons; I detested making up the missed work, and feared being left out of something cool happening in class—something that I'd remember forever. I only missed a half day that year and true to form—never late; Mom certainly contributed to my punctuality. The two *Ds* and the one *F* in Phillips' French class are ugly to be sure, but I earned my promotion to eighth grade.

30

The Gebhard Brewery

For years, my friends and I referred to the large unoccupied building at the end of Washington Street as the flour mill, or Brown Milling Co. We were partly wrong. Originally named The Gebhard Brewery built in 1900, it became the flour mill after prohibition when the Brewery shut down. The structure still stands abandoned and boarded up.

Gaining access to the inside of the brewery/flour mill back in the 1960s came to us by simple observation of its exterior—specifically—the backside facing Gebhard Woods. We were destined, as curious, adventurous, young boys, to discover an overlooked, obscure, portal into the mysterious bowels of the decrepit building.

During one of our daily bicycle rides around Morris, Steve and Denny Holbrook, Rob Enger, Jack Cameron, and I rode toward Gebhard Woods. We decided to use the back entrance. To enter the park from this direction, our bicycle cavalry had to pass between two flour mill buildings. Something piqued our curiosity as we rode between the buildings. We stopped short of the park entrance thinking it might be possible to find a way into the foreboding place—a great idea. We had heard rumors of kids getting inside, but not about how they did it. The best kept flour mill secret was about to be uncovered.

We dismounted our trusty two wheeled steeds and leaned them against a brick wall. Finding this portal didn't take long at all. It glared at us; beckoning us to come closer … we did. There … protruding from the brick wall—a stainless steel chute at the top of a wooden frame. The chute itself resembled a large plumbing pipe with a ninety degree angle pointing down toward the ground. It may have been a product delivery system from the mill to a waiting railroad car. We climbed up on the wooden frame and stuck our heads one at a time into the metal chute for a look. This gave us an unobstructed view into a large room. We were in!

Without second thoughts we crawled through the chute into a large, naturally lit, ghostly chamber. Weathered windows from all around the second floor, provided a gossamer-like daylight. The room had an acrid odor; probably from fermented grain remnants sprinkled with years worth of rat urine. After a minute of wide eyed observations panning the majestic room, our mischievous group fanned out toward various places of interest. I found a stairwell to the next floor above. Every step added to an exciting adventure in unfamiliar territory. A rusted door led to a small office filled with dusty desks and file cabinets. I fully expected to see the Ghost of Gebhard Past at his desk entering numbers in his company ledger. If ghosts existed anywhere in town, this room had *ghost* written all over it. Rifling through the drawers, I discovered hundreds of unused business forms and various operations papers. I didn't take any. I drew the line at trespassing. Burglarizing the place didn't seem like a good idea.

I exited the office and climbed to the next floor where turning a corner, I found myself at the precipice of disaster—staring at a huge hole cut in the floor ahead of me. One room filled the entire floor. The opening took up almost the whole room. The edges were roughly cut and unfinished as if it were part of a demolition phase. Peering into the giant hole I saw the floor below. Obligated, I called out to my friends. They came running. We stood beside the hole looking into an accident waiting to happen. Some unsuspecting adventurer could fall through to the level below and certain death.

"This place is so cool," I said.

"Yeah, just watch your step," Denny warned.

"What's this hole all about anyway?" asked Steve.

None of us knew the answer to that question. Perhaps a large milling machine or brewer's vat passed through the cut out during some kind of demolition. Who knows? The brewery/flour mill mystery grew larger and more compelling. What were the last living hours of the place like? Better still ... what would we discover next?

We moved on to another area through a narrow corridor leading to what looked like a hatch or trap door to who knows where. Rob opened the hatch and peered into total darkness and an even stronger nose full of rancid grain and urine.

"Hello, hello down there," Rob called out into the blackness. Only his echo came back. Any other response would have sent us scrambling over each other to get out of there fast.

"Hey!" I shouted into the abyss, "Anybody down there?"

"Yeah right ... who do you think is down there?" Jack said wryly.

"There's nobody down there you morons," said Denny.

Of course there wasn't, but what else would a kid shout into a creepy dark hole? We put two and two together and surmised the black place was a large indoor grain silo. At this time we weren't prepared to explore any further. We had no ropes, no flashlights, gloves, or a harness ... but next time ... we'd bring it all.

We also brought along reinforcements for the next visit. Needing more muscle power for our intentions, we let the Meister brothers, Steve and Randy, in on the caper. If one of us had to be lowered into the unknown, we needed to be sure he could get back out ... safely.

Okay ... if this wasn't the most reckless, ill thought out adventure we ever did, it ranked somewhere up there in the top three for sure. Half a dozen kids on a secret mission, improvised climbing gear, and a deep dark storage silo, all in an abandoned sixty-something year old, seven story tall factory building; *eeeha!*

When we showed up at the ancient brewery some days later for the rappel into the unknown, two other kids exited the chute. I recognized them instantly as fellow classmates Mike Tucker and Jim Hume. It seems a lot of guys knew about the secret entrance to the brewery. Mike and Jim had finished the first shift at the mill. Second shift was clocking in with ropes, a harness, flashlights, and an adventurous itch to be scratched.

Standing at the door to the deep dark silo, we determined the person to enter. First, we needed to have the strongest of us holding the rope. Second, someone had to volunteer. No one spoke up right away prompting Denny to say …

"Come on Dukey … you chicken?" Denny prodded his younger brother.

Steve had no intention of volunteering, and no one else jumped to the front of the line either. Rob would have been the perfect weight being the smallest. As leader of the pack, Denny bravely offered to go. That meant the most physically strong of the lot and the heaviest, would not be holding the line. This worried the rest of us who had chickened out. Our rig had no pulley system to ease the effort of lowering Denny down into the black hole. After a few minutes of discussion, we decided the group could hold Denny's weight by wrapping the rope around a pole and slowly letting it out. Without so much as a practice run with a grain bin dummy to determine good positioning for a lowering procedure, we started.

Everyone gathered to look into the deep pit through the small hatch using a flashlight. I saw very little. The light wasn't powerful enough to show much from the top hatch. With Denny in the harness, and the rope looped around the pole, he pulled himself up to the level of the hatch and stuck his feet and legs through to begin the process. Our collective strength slowly let out the rope. Friction from the rope against the pole made a tight, grinding, squeaky sound as we lowered him into the unknown. He trusted the rest of us to keep him from falling.

"What do you see?" Randy called out.

"Not much … just an empty silo. Stop … hold it, that's far enough," Denny responded.

The rope ground to a halt, and we looped the remainder around the pole to lock it in. Secured, Denny hung in the darkness of a large, smelly, old grain bin with only a small flashlight as his light source and no gas mask to filter the rancid air. He hung there for a few seconds and said …

"Pull me out! It smells pretty bad."

After two minutes at best and with nothing to really see in there, Denny decided he'd had enough. We tugged, pulled, grunted, and groaned in an uncoordinated effort. Struggling with the pole/rope system in the reverse direction presented a new problem—one we failed to anticipate. How do we manipulate a taut rope with 150 or more pounds at the end of it dangling in mid-air?

"What are you waiting for up there? Get me out."

It's a good thing Randy and Steve Meister joined us. They had the strength necessary to hoist Denny back out.

"We're working on it, Den," Randy called into the cavern assuming a leadership role. He quickly assessed the small space we were in and assigned positions for the group. Randy and Steve, being the strongest, took up positions at the front of the line followed by the rest of us. The last in line stood by the pole.

"Okay ... when we pull and slack forms in the line, you guys in the back pull it tight around the pole to hold his weight. We'll keep doing that until he gets to the top," Randy ordered. "Got it?"

We got it. After several repetitions of pulling and slack tightening around the anchor pole, Denny appeared at the opening unscathed and with a *no big deal* look on his face. One short spelunk by a courageous kid brought the highly anticipated adventure to a close.

No treasure came out of this expedition. No reward gained, other than going through the process of gathering the meager equipment, discussing the simple, reckless plan, and flying by the seat of our pants in its execution. We relished in the journey.

Back then, we created our own daring activities to keep ourselves occupied. Our choices were highly influenced by viewing movies that dramatized great adventures like those in *Journey to the Center of the Earth*, or *The Time Machine*, for example. The Gebhard Brewery caper turned out to be pretty cool even without a big payoff. On the other hand, there is a payoff—telling the story.

To my best recollection, that was my last day spent in the flour mill. Not long afterwards, the authorities got wind of a group of curious trespassers in the building and they sealed it off for good. Rightly so, because when I think about the immense hole on the third floor, some unsuspecting person could have made gory headlines in the Morris Daily Herald.

31

Goold Park

*O*pportunities for adventures in Morris existed everywhere. If we didn't find something to do at Chapin Park, the toe path, Gebhard woods, or Stratton Park and the Illinois River, we could be found in Goold Park, one of the largest parks in town. The swimming pool was in the park's center and there were two separate play areas with swing sets. One, at the top of swimming pool hill, had a big set of monkey bars and a tennis court nearby. I didn't play tennis at all, but still got a lot of use out of that court in the winter. Each year, the city flooded it with water for ice-skating day and night. I loved skating at night up on that hill. Skating under the flood lights, shining from one corner and barely illuminating the frozen court created an ethereal glow.

The Rock Island railroad tracks ran along the south border high up on a ridge. At the foot of this ridge, was a ditch lined with huge elm and oak trees. Strong vines hung down from these trees in several places, absolutely perfect for swinging. We stepped off a small dirt rise and flew twenty feet across the dry ditch to the base of the railroad ridge. This vine swing rivaled the one over Nettle Creek in Gebhard Woods with a different payoff. Instead of landing in cool water, we made one long dramatic Tarzan swing—outstanding fun!

Another vine just to the east set us sailing through the air over a section of the ditch that had a tendency to collect water run off. Some of the guys thought it would be fun to see how many could vine swing at the same time. I stood by and watched Denny, Randy and Steve Meister, and Phillip, their seven or eight year old little brother. The boys pulled the vine close and took their positions, laughing the whole time in anticipation of the group launch. They shuffled around for the best configuration of body placement and grip strategy.

"Five, four, three, two, one blast off!" little Phillip counted down.

"Yahoo!" they shouted.

"Hang on tight Phillip!" I called out.

Three big kids and one little one, like a string of lead weights on a fishing line, flew across the ditch and back, holding on tightly for dear life. They knew if they fell off at the wrong time ... mud would be in their immediate future.

The vine and its high anchoring tree branches let out a deep ... slow ... groan. Suddenly, at just the right second, the vine broke away from the high branches above with a sharp *snap*. The entire string of weights and vine fell directly into the center of the muck. The mix wasn't like quick sand. It wasn't like a pool of dirty water. The consistency of extra thick chocolate pudding comes to mind—foul smelling, stagnant, slop, deep enough to completely cover every one of them from head to toe. My friends falling into this concoction of naturally accumulated stench ranks as one of the funniest things I'd ever seen. Watching them crawl out from that disgusting trough of putrid, muck, had me rolling. They spat and groaned revulsion, just short of puking. Everyone had concern for little Phillip who looked as if he were about to cry. Humorous reactions from the others distracted Phillip, and kept him from sliding into a funk. I am thankful to have evaded the group vine swing.

The Meisters lived in a trailer about twenty five yards away. For them a garden hose was only seconds away. They took advantage of that short jog home immediately. But for Denny, his walk home extended a full two blocks. I guess he didn't want to wait in line at Meister's hose. Instead he and I walked together (I actually kept my distance) to his yard where Mr. Holbrook laughingly sprayed him off in the street. I remember watching him getting such a kick out of seeing his oldest son caked with this awful smelling crap; a priceless mental picture from beginning to end.

On another day in that same general area between the slop ditch and the Meister's trailer we found a manhole cover that we could remove. There is no way we weren't going to go down there. Are you kidding? Come on ... we were the vine swinging, brewery exploring, strip mine hill climbing, Illinois Michigan Canal swimming, adventurers of Morris, Illinois! We'll explore anything. The cover lifted easily.

Into the ground we went about three feet down. Steve, Jack, and I had no gas masks, no miner's hats, or canaries in a cage; just a small flashlight. We crawled along the concrete conduit listening to our echoes as we each ruined yet another pair of pants at the knees. We came to an intersection. This cross tube was too narrow for exploration and the sewer smell intensified tremendously. The great adventurers threw it in reverse and got out of there in a big hurry. One trip into that underground catacomb did it for me; just stinky and not very exciting. Had we used matches for a candle instead of a flashlight, I can only imagine what would have transpired. Some time later, while walking through that area of Goold Park, I looked at the very same manhole cover ... it had been welded shut. It appeared our group stayed one step ahead of the city authorities more than once.

◆ ◆ ◆

Treasure turned up on occasion in Goold Park. I mentioned earlier about often finding change in the gravel driveway of Mrs. Neal's Bughouse. One sunny day along the main pea gravel path through the park's east side, Denny, Steve, John Halterman, and I rode our bikes like the wind. We were only yards away from the vine ridge; riding parallel to it when John slowed down around one of the large oak trees. He looked down at the base of the grand old tree and spotted green paper—a small pile of bills.

"Holy cow!" he exclaimed as he slammed on his brakes.

The rest of us approached, skidding to a stop and sprayed gravel. John bent over, picked up the cash and counted out three dollars. Three dollars in 1963 was a lot of money for a little kid. We rode to the Holbrook house and were advised by Mr. Holbrook to divide the money equally. Since John found the money, he wanted to keep one dollar for himself and divide the rest equally three ways. Two bucks can't be divided equally three ways, so a neighbor boy, Jim Lanier, generously offered a quarter to give the rest of us seventy five cents each. We ran off on a candy bender to Mick's Quick Chick, followed by a visit to Richards' Diner one block away to drop dimes into our favorite baseball game machine.

The pin-ball-like game had a long box type base with a glass cover. The playing surface was laid out like a bird's eye view of a baseball field. It had a trap door in the center where the pitcher's mound would be. A metal lid opened up and released a steel ball that rolled toward home plate and the flipper, a small bat. By pressing a button you could tell the machine what type of pitch you wanted to hit; a curve ball, a fast ball, or a knuckle ball. The curve really curved, and the fast rolled fast. Even the knuckle ball did a little jig. After hitting the ball with a well timed swing of the bat flipper, the ball landed in a single, double, triple, home run, or out space on the field. Between bites of Bonimo's Turkish Taffy washed down with cherry Cokes, we played the game until our money ran out.

32

The Union Street Drag Strip

𝒰nion Street stretched from the end of the toe path at the Rock Island crossing, past Morris Community High School and ended at the intersection of U.S. Route 6. That stretch of road, about a half mile in length during the 1960s, gave every gear head who dared, a perfect place for a quick hot rod road test.

Dr. Roth's son, Richard, drove one of the coolest hot rods I ever saw, a 1930 Ford Coupe, and a work in progress. It may have had an unfinished body in gray primer, but it could go fast and seriously disturb the peace. When Richard pulled into Carlson's service station we drooled at its fender-less body, huge rear slicks, and low riding chassis. Even without a flashy paint job, this car turned heads.

While on a bike ride along Union Street, I heard Richard's coupe grumbling. I had just ridden my bike over the tracks and felt the roadster's vibrations behind me. It crawled over the steel rails at a snail's pace. Richard revved the engine breaking a peaceful silence and I pulled my Monark to the curb to look over my shoulder. The Ford looked like an Ed *Big Daddy* Roth (no relation ... I think) creation poised to set Union Street on fire. Richard came to a full stop. I waved hello. I couldn't see his eyes behind his shades. His fingers lifted from the tiny steering wheel in a James Dean type cool response. They returned to a tight grip preparing for blast off. Then, one hand dropped out of sight, no doubt resting on the gear shifter. Richard punched it! The engine roared. Rubber and blacktop melted together in a pool on the street. White blue smoke billowed behind the vibrating machine. My nose contorted from the smell of gas exhaust and liquid rubber as the gray ghost screamed past me, disappearing down The Union Street Drag Strip. Wow! All that remained were the two jet black parallel lines on the street surface, a lot of smoke and the odor of burned slicks invading my nostrils. Cool! Real cool!

During the summer of 1965 the Bednarik family, Mrs. Bednarik, Beth, and her brothers went on a vacation to Louisiana. Mrs. Bednarik left the yard work responsibilities of their Union Street home to my, *sew a button on a fart* friend Ted. The homes on Union Street had massive backyards needing riding mowers to do the job efficiently. I visited Ted's house on a hot mowing day and I offered to assist. Ted kept Bednarik's small riding mower at his house a few doors away. We cranked it up and started the short trip down the street. Ted drove and I stood on the back end holding Ted's shoulders. We quickly realized my extra weight on the back made it easy to pop a wheelie when gunning the engine. The little mower didn't look or perform like a supercharged 1930s Ford hot rod, but Ted couldn't resist pretending it could. He rolled to a stop on the baking blacktop. His fingers gripped the swiveling handle bar (the mower didn't have a little steering wheel). Up ahead, the steaming heat rising off the hot roadway created a distant rippling illusion.

"Hold on," Ted said to me embroiled in his James Dean moment.

"Don't worry about me. Let 'er rip!" I encouraged.

I held on tightly. Ted floored it. The engine chugged. Instantly the little mower jumped its front wheels off the sticky blacktop into an aggressive vertical position nearly flipping over. I fell off the back landing on my feet. Ted fell off too, but he held onto the handle bar laughing his insane laugh while running behind the perpendicular machine. He ran for a few steps then let up on the gas, and the mower's front end landed back on the street in a jerk. I caught up and jumped back on. We repeated the act again until we realized ... the blades! Idiots! The blades had continued to spin furiously, exposed with each wheelie! *Oops.* I quickly decided this activity stretched the boundaries of good judgment and stayed off. Ted finished the ride to Bednarik's house ... alone, and he eventually cut the grass. I decided to watch; taking it easy in the shade. Later, Ted and I went back to his house and hopped on our bikes. We rode to the end of Union Street and into Benny's Tap for a few minutes of air conditioning and a round of O'Henry candy bars.

Well, it turns out that Judge Windsor got an eyeful that day when we wheelied past his house. Shortly thereafter, he, the Justice of Union Street's Peace confiscated the mower before we had a chance to do it again. I think I might have thought twice the next time and not participated in the sequel, but ... who knows? Maybe we could have disengaged the blades.

33

Eighth Grade, 1965–1966

o o o o o o o o o o o o o o o o o o o o o o o o o o o o o o
"Yesterday, all my troubles seemed so far away ..."
Paul McCartney

*M*y eighth year of formal education was the fourth and final year spent within the red brick walls of Center School. From September of 1965, to graduation on June 10, 1966, our class ruled the upper floor of that magnificent building. The floor itself had a disconcerting quality about it. If you paid attention to your weight striking the floor while walking, the floor seemed to give a little as if it were suspended—or at least sagging. It definitely creaked. We reigned as the kings and queens of that beige, locker-lined top floor.

Eighth grade did not come with a group or home room class photograph. I still began each day with a homeroom and corresponding teacher; Mr. Max Lindsay, a math aficionado. Keep in mind the fact that young boys of this age group tend to be prone to mischief from time to time. What else is new? Because of this reality, teachers invented creative counter offensives to sustain discipline in class. Mr. Lindsay had ... *the rap.*

Mr. Lindsay, a stern looking man at 170 pounds, and maybe five feet ten inches tall in his flat top hair cut, insisted on his students paying attention in class as much as any other teacher. That hair cut gave him all the authority he needed. As a point of reference, pay attention to the character, General Bogan, played by actor Frank Overton in the film, *Fail Safe,* starring Henry Fonda. You'll get a good idea of Mr. Lindsay's appearance and vocal tone. I think it is remarkable.

So, define the *rap* you say? *The Lindsay Rap* was neither a dance tune nor a precursor to the late twentieth century rap phenomenon. The *rap* was a sharp concentrated pain delivered like lightning. It came at you from your blind side as Mr. Lindsay walked silently in his Hush Puppies up and down the rows of desks. When a student's (they were always boys of course) eyes wandered instead of concentrating on a lesson; when he should have kept his eyes on his own paper during a quiz and didn't, the *rap* would fly. *The Lindsay Rap* could have been described as a modified knuckle sandwich. Instead of a punch in the mouth, one protruding knuckle landed with precision against the top of the head. One swift, silent, attack quickly got the wandering student's attention.

Okay, back in those days, as previously indicated, the usual weapon of choice was the wooden paddle. Paddles provided a level of classroom deterrence and worked much like sending an aircraft carrier overseas as a show of force. But the invisible *rap* ... functioned like a stealth bomber. Although painful, Mr. Lindsay never administered this punishment (to my knowledge) with malice. He may have been strict or dictatorial in how he conducted his class, but not vindictively spiteful. I think the idea behind the *rap* was more of a motivator than a sadistic act of violence.

I wonder if any of the parents ever knew about the *rap*. The paddle, or *getting the wood*, seemed like common knowledge as a disciplinary tool, but the *rap* ... I'm not so sure. The only possible evidence would be a red and/or sore knuckle on Mr. Lindsay (depending on how many sorties he flew) which could have been explained away as a plumbing wrench mishap. Paddles could be found everywhere. *The Lindsay Rap* lurked out of sight before your very eyes. You know ... as an afterthought, I didn't see any girls get either the wood or the *rap*. I really have to wonder what local conversations would have been like if the girls ever got it—must have been a guy thing I suppose.

On one occasion Ted saw the *rap* coming. He opened his mouth just at the right second sending a loud knocking sound across the room. I sat behind Ted and saw the whole thing play out—an example of the unexpected classroom fun I always enjoyed. First, a beat of silence as if everyone waited for a hint of how to react. After a second or two, the whole room erupted in laughter including Mr. Lindsay. Our flat topped math teacher recognized the humor of the event. How often would a smart ass kid attempt to take down a stealth bomber?

Mr. Lindsay had a habit of avoiding eye contact with us when he stood at the head of the class explaining a math problem. He gazed off to one side over our heads toward the back of the room or even out the window, almost as if he envisioned the problem in some sort of private virtual reality. I can't help but wonder what would have happened if Ted blurted out something like, "What are you looking at Mr. Lindsay?" I can only guess his response. Too bad; I could use another comical story from the Lindsay math class.

◆ ◆ ◆

New teachers came and went as with every school district. For our final year at Center School we had one new guy, who in my opinion, goes down as the most vicious, ill tempered, spiteful, teachers I've ever encountered. Manley Gilliam was a small, wiry, reddish brown haired, late twenty something with a ruddy complexion. He spoke with a thick southern drawl and walked erect almost like a little soldier marching in a parade. Thankfully, I didn't have a formal class with him; only study hall. My interaction with him had been limited to that one long room filled with about fifty kids.

Classrooms up on the top floor housed the seventh and eighth graders—Jr. High. The only class that combined both seventh and eighth graders was study hall. We all know how study halls can become breeding grounds for letting off a little bottled up steam. This man would not have any of it ... period. The study hall's back wall shared a common wall with the library. Part of this wall included a large window which allowed viewing from the study hall to the library and vice versa. One fateful day shortly after the class started, Gilliam left the study hall without any fanfare. One of my seventh grade friends and backyard camper, Roger Roth, decided to let off some of that pressurized steam. He checked through the classroom door making sure the coast was clear, and then took a seat in front at the teacher's desk.

When a teacher responsible for a study hall full of seventh and eighth graders leaves without a word, it is quite possibly a set up. I got that suspicion along with a few others. Meanwhile, Roger, full of himself, twirled a pen between his fingers pretending to be "little Gilliam" heading the class. In a short amount of time the room pretty much got out of control with nervous laughter and palpable anticipation for the inevitable return of you know who. Roger appeared to have no concern for any consequences if he were to get caught. Sure enough, in probably less than one minute from the time he left the room to the time he returned, Manley Gilliam let loose. To the complete shock of everyone in the room, and mostly poor Roger, Gilliam stormed in like a freight train from the nearby Rock Island Railroad. His already normally red skin caught on fire. I never saw an adult shoot so much venom out of his eyes toward any child. Roger, completely off guard, didn't see it coming. I felt so sorry for him. I can still see his round cherubic face contorted in horror as Manley Gilliam pounced on him like a mountain lion on a defenseless fawn.

You see, Gilliam, in my opinion, had it all planned as a setup for an ambush. He must have thought that someone might ... just might let off some steam, or in his mind, *misbehave* if he were to slip away for a moment. Remember the large window in the back of the room? By now you must have surmised Gilliam left the study hall, walked to the library, positioned himself behind a bookshelf, and spied through the window into his study hall. Boy, did he get an eyeful.

Meanwhile, we were so busy watching Roger mime his way into Center School history, no one thought to check the window. Even if we had, we would have seen nothing because the sneaky little weasel most likely secreted himself in his sniper's nest of encyclopedias. Anyone in the library must have witnessed smoke pouring out of his ears as he boiled over in the initial stages of re-entry burn up.

Upon seeing this next frightening scene unfold, my mouth dropped wide open. Gilliam had literally thrown little Roger onto the top of the desk stomach down and held him there with one hand. His other hand pulled a small fourteen inch, brown, paddle from the desk drawer. With a wicked series of hits in rapid fire succession to Roger's backside, Gilliam shouted out verbal swats as well. I don't recall verbatim, but his southern accented words went something like ...

"Boy, what makes you think you can disrespect me while I'm out of the room? This oughta teach you. Stay down boy!"

I couldn't believe my eyes and ears. Everyone in the room fell into a silent shock seeing Roger humiliated, in tears, and lots of pain. Gilliam sent Roger back to his seat in total anguish. This *teacher* went on to admonish the rest of us with his dire warnings of more of the same to anyone who hadn't learned from the event. I never saw anything like it before or since. By today's standards, such behavior from a teacher would certainly warrant a law suit and permanent termination of employment as an educator.

Manley Gilliam is not excused just yet. There is more. I believe he enjoyed wielding his pathetic power trips on children; especially during this next incident. Time had passed, days, weeks—who knows? In the back of the same study hall, a group of us sat together as we usually did. Ted Trenter, Mike Tucker, Jim Hume, and I, went about our normal study hall business. Behind me, Mike and Ted exchanged sotto voce jokes of some kind that made me and a few others laugh a little. That little bit of laughter sent him over the edge. Suddenly from the front of the room, the southern voice from hell spewed across the desks.

"Alright boy ... you've been askin' for it for a long time now."

He pointed in our general direction. I looked around thinking he had to be referring to Mike or Ted.

"You," he said with calm, sadistic, anticipation in his voice.

I wasn't completely sure, but it looked like he spoke directly at me. I feebly pointed to myself hoping to be ignored. The issue had to have been with someone else. No such luck.

"Yes, you," he drawled while aiming his finger at me.

Oh no, not the wood again. This can't be happening. I didn't do anything.

My mind flashed back to the Roger incident, and I trembled in my seat. My heart jumped into my throat—the wood. This paddling I feared most of all because of him; a real mean spirited egotist. Perhaps you think I'm unfairly judgmental. No, not really. I'm not alone in recalling Manley Gilliam. Tom, *punch me in the stomach*, Bednarik, confirms my assessment of Gilliam describing him as; "A younger man from the deep south with a mean streak in him." Tom is too kind.

Gilliam walked down the side of the room towards me and stopped.

"Git up here boy," he commanded.

I believe he wanted me to humiliate myself by making me take the perpetrator walk as he waited. I saw right through him. I saw the perverted pleasure he got watching me make the walk while everyone in the room witnessed me heading for the inevitable. I saw the brown paddle in his hand.

Crap. I'm in for it now.

With a quiver in my voice, I made an attempt for my own defense.

"I was only laughing," I pleaded.

"I don't care what you were doing. Turn around and grab your ankles ... boy," he ordered. Clearly, he dripped with self importance knowing what he intended to do.

You love saying that ... don't you? 'Grab your ankles ... boy' ... I can tell you love saying that phrase. You little creep. I hate you because I'm innocent of any crime. Why don't you grab your own ankles ... boy.

I bent over in the aisle about to be stung by that little brown paddle. I felt powerless to defend myself any further from this poor excuse for a teacher.

Take your best shot you short creep.

Whack! I took my shot and stood upright immediately so I wouldn't take another. He didn't stop me (how kind of him), and I gingerly walked back to my seat. My butt started hurting during the walk back to my desk. The pain took about two or three seconds to make the complete connection between the hit, the travel time through my nervous system to my brain and back to the seat of my pants. To say it stung is an understatement. I considered myself lucky to have received only one hit. Sitting down felt strange indeed. My butt tingled through my pants and almost vibrated the wooden seat of the desk. It felt fat as well; and that's saying something because of my skinniness.

That is how it went down that day; my second paddling in my history of grade school. Ted and Mike breathed a sigh of relief, and I took it like a man. As for Gilliam, I wonder what his philosophy could have been at that time. It must have gone something like; "I'm gonna get these kids. I'm a self absorbed tyrant and everything I do is right no matter who I hurt." I wonder if he ever changed ... nah, probably not.

◆ ◆ ◆

Miss Narrigon was an attractive, young woman in her early twenties with a southern drawl that gave her an irresistible charm. She had medium length brown hair, brown eyes, full lips, about five feet six inches tall weighing roughly 115 pounds; a babe. Unfortunately, I don't have a picture of her. It would be nice to have one since I had a crush on her ... big time.

Miss Narrigon, my English teacher, usually tolerated our immaturity and basic gentle humor. However, she reached her limit when we stepped over the line and rudely assaulted her name. My friends, Tom Clayton, Vince Hodgson, Jack Cameron, and I got our cheap thrills in that class by finding humor in Miss

Narrigon's nickname, which we so creatively invented. We called her, *Narr* (rhymes with *car*). Another student, John Gordon, also played along on occasion. He had a reputation as a tough kid in town; a loner who didn't necessarily involve himself with school activities or socialize in general. I remember him to be much like the character of John Bender played by Judd Nelson in the 1985 film *The Breakfast Club*. My perception of him was that he must have had a less than loving home life which preyed upon his hidden good side. I usually steered clear of him as did most of my classmates.

Knowing John and his proclivity for fighting made his presence in our class interesting to me. He hardly ever smiled, but I did see another side of his personality on those rare occasions when he did. I think sharing this class with us gave him reason to relax a bit and enjoy a few laughs. Tom, Vince, Jack, and I had a way to get John Gordon out from behind his tough guy persona. We used *the nickname*. During class we held our heads low just above our desktops, behind an opened book and uttered softly in a provocative growl … *Narr*! Needless to say, those calls created a generous amount of laughter from other classmates and nasal snorts from Tom, Vince, Jack, and me; the guilty ones. It was a futile effort on our part to suppress the guffaws that followed. You know … the sloppy sounds of fluids exiting your face from every orifice. Tears poured from my eyes, snot ran out of my nose, even a small amount of spit ran down my beet red face; very attractive. Indeed a rude thing to have done … the Narr thing, but simply impossible for a group of thirteen year old boys to resist. Thinking back, we entertained John Gordon about as much as we jabbed at our teacher. Ah … the propensities of careless youths.

Giving us what we deserved, Miss Narrigon folded her arms and fired a look of annoyed disappointment while leaning back against her desk. Even then, I couldn't ignore what a babe she was. So, here I am reminiscing about foibles of an adolescent twentieth-century Greek boy and his knowledge, *I have a crush on my teacher*, his being, *I'm thirteen*, his conduct *I'm disrespecting my teacher's name*. Socrates would be so proud.

There was a difference of opinion one morning between Miss Narrigon and one of the more argumentative students in the class. It may have begun with a class discussion of some literary piece by Shakespeare or another of the great writers. Ultimately, the exchange escalated and someone tagged the moment with a well timed muttering of the nickname, "*Narr.*" It may have been an attempt to lighten the situation because I heard a few laughs, but to Miss Narrigon the line had been crossed. She'd had enough of the nickname. She had been holding her wooden yardstick as a pointer during the discussion and by the time the *Narr* came out, she had placed herself in front of John Gordon's desk. Oh boy ... the yardstick came crashing down on top of John's desk splintering into several projectile pieces, some of which actually grazed John's forearms and zinged past his ear. An intense look of anger filled his face as he held himself back. John's muscled arms rippled as his fingers gripped and dug into the desktop. He looked like a volcano ready to erupt. He appeared ready to jump at Miss Narrigon which would have been a very ugly scene indeed. I plainly saw how John's reaction frightened Miss Narrigon. He contained himself though, and she backed away regaining some control. Luckily for everyone, the tension diffused after a few seconds. If John had attacked, I guess I would have intervened to protect her. That would have guaranteed an after school showdown with John Gordon. I lucked out.

One day I began to wonder where she lived, so I produced a plan—a very simple plan—follow her home. Ingenious—my *Combat* mission for the day—to complete the top secret operation and return to base with valuable information—"Checkmate king two!"

The final school buzzer sounded off at day's end. All along the top floor hall, lockers slammed shut. Students raced to catch buses, ride their bikes, or walk home. Rather than go home, I waited outside on the playground that crisp fall afternoon. A few minutes passed as I watched the guys playing a quick game of *Horse*. I kept one eye on the exit doors and waited nervously. When Miss Narrigon appeared she had a load of books and notebooks clasped in front of her breasts. I wanted to be one of those books. She wore a white blouse under a beige buttoned sweater and a tight, brown, knee length skirt—gorgeous. Coming back to Earth, I focused on my mission—be invisible.

She walked along the silver painted stanchions with their heavy draped iron chain that separated the playground from the sidewalk along Benton Street. Her route took her one block west to Liberty Street where she turned right (north). I stayed half a block behind—just enough to keep her in my sight and hopefully out of hers. I had become as invisible as could be among dozens of other kids walking home.

Maybe I should speed up and offer to help carry her books.

That idea died in a hurry. I chickened out and stayed with my original plan ... following carefully. I had no problem keeping an eye on her. My eyes stayed glued to her figure; her hips shifted as she walked. Hormones ruled. Breasts, figure, hips ...

What am I, crazy? If she spots me I'm a dead duck.

Okay, by then, we were in the middle of the long block beyond the tracks. All had gone well by the time I got to Valerio's Bait Shop. The bait shop sat off the street by about thirty feet to my left nestled between Valerio's house and their neighbor's. The bait shop momentarily distracted me. Boys love fishing, so I looked away to see who might be buying some fat, juicy, night crawlers. When I looked back to my mission's lovely subject ... she had vanished!

Oh no. Where did you go you gorgeous woman?

I ran ahead to a small apartment complex driveway another hundred feet away. She had turned into that very driveway. In the nick of time, I spotted her entering a front lobby doorway. Mission accomplished.

Aha! That's where you live. Now I know.

I promptly turned around, full of myself for having succeeded. I ran back the way I came, south on Liberty Street. I jumped the tracks and tore through five downtown city blocks to Jefferson Street and Mom's restaurant. With an after school hello hug, I asked for and received a favorite snack of lemon meringue pie and a big glass of milk. I finished my treat and ran upstairs to watch the Three Stooges.

Nothing could have prepared me for the following day in English class. The class began as usual. A pop spelling quiz earned the usual hums and haws from the class. Miss Narrigon had us fold our notebook paper in half length wise and cut the paper into two separate pieces. She sat at her desk pronouncing each word once and using it in a sentence. Pretty basic as spelling tests go. When the test ended, we traded papers with a neighbor for correcting. Everything proceeded as usual when out of nowhere, absolutely nowhere, Vince blurted out ...

"Miss Narrigon. Where do you live?"

Oh no! Vince, what in the world are you doing?

My mouth must have opened wide enough for the world's largest jaw breaker. I watched her as she slowly moved from behind her desk. She wore a little grin and assumed her familiar position, leaning back on the front of her sturdy teacher's desk. Our eyes met. I sank into my seat as I heard her say in her southern accent ...

"Well Vince, why don't you ask Mike Skopes that question. He knows where I live."

No, no, no, no, no!

She was having fun now.

What the heck just happened? How did she know? Who found out and spilled the beans? Vince, why would you suddenly ask that question—now of all times? Where did I make a mistake?

The feeling in the room could only be described as surreal. The answers to some of those questions would come to me soon enough, but at the time, I felt devastated, crushed, and highly embarrassed. She got me good. For all the times my sense of humor may have amused or irritated her; after all the outbursts of disrespectful laughter—her moment had come. In her eyes I could plainly see the; *I gotcha look*. My recall of what happened next is gone. Everything up to that point is clear to me; the plan, the mission, what she wore; all else ... gone.

Later, I pieced together what went wrong. I made my mistake while momentarily daydreaming about fishing at Gebhard Woods. I remembered one little detail which at the time seemed unimportant. She turned her head back in my direction when she walked into her driveway. While still in my little fishing daydream, I recall catching a fleeting glimpse of her. She had spotted me.

Babe factor aside, Miss Narrigon was one of my favorite teachers. One afternoon early in my freshman year of high school, I went back to Center School with friends Jack Cameron and Tom Clayton to visit Miss Narrigon. We surprised her when we entered her classroom. It was a short cordial reunion before she gathered her books and other things to go home for the day. Although I don't recall exact words from that meeting, I'd like to think we were kind enough to have apologized for our past behavior. She looked beautiful. We said good-bye after a few minutes and left the school. I never saw her again.

◆ ◆ ◆

During eighth grade, outstanding athletic abilities developed in many of my friends. We had a pretty good basketball team. My friends honed their skills out on the Center School playground every day in good weather. In the winter, if enough snow hadn't accumulated on the ground for Pom Pom Pull Away, the guys still chose up sides for basketball games in the cold. There were cousins Ken and Tom Enger, Ralph Varland, Vince Hodgson, Jim Olson, Jim Smith, Bill Fruland and others. Basketball skills always eluded me. They rarely chose me on the playground during recess or before school. Outside on the playground we had two backboards and baskets. The baskets were far enough apart to accommodate two different levels of playing ability. The *A team* always played at the east end near the main entrance to the school from the boy's playground. Center School separated the boys from the girls with the gymnasium portion of the school building. Girls had the south playground and the boys had the north. Whatever the girls were up to out on their side of the building remained a mystery to us boys then. We never witnessed their activities. I will, however, bet they didn't play Pom Pom Pull Away. Anyway, everyone considered the basket at the boy's east end as hallowed ground, and the *B team* boys and less talented played at the west end. That's where I almost always played. A team, B team; Red Birds, Blue Birds, Yellow Birds; systematic grouping of one kind or another based on ability appeared to be the way of the world. It hurt my feelings a little when my pals didn't pick me for the *A team* games, but I knew I didn't have very good skills at basketball. I got over it and moved on to something else.

Basketball may not have been a strong sport for me, but I still loved gym class and the variety of other sports and activities associated with it. We engaged in things like relay races on these scooter boards with wheels, volleyball, square dancing, and ... dodge ball, perhaps the game I enjoyed the most in gym class. We played this action packed game frequently. Nothing could come close to the satisfaction I felt when running toward an opponent clutching two or three air filled rubber balls and unleashing a barrage of full force overhand bombs. Awesome power!

During one particular gym class near the end of a game, only a handful of players remained ... including me. I anticipated an exhilarating victory for someone only moments away. Could it be mine? Or ... will the spoils and bragging rights go to an *A team* kid. Soon the number dropped—two guys left. I was the last player on my team, and *A teamer*, Ralph Varland, survived to be the last player on his team. We each had two balls at the ready. A quick moment of cat and mouse ensued as we jockeyed for the best position twenty feet apart. All eyes of the recently departed losers and Mr. Varner were focused on Ralph and me. Ralph's eyes and mine had locked onto each other. I faced the south side of the gym where Ralph had the sun at his back. The light advantage belonged to him. I remember thinking ...

This is it, Mikey.

Before I could make a move, Ralph let loose with a wickedly thrown ball headed directly for my knees. I could only watch wide eyed as the rocket ball came streaking at me in the sunlight. I was about to go down in a pool of sweat when to my extreme delight the ball came to a sudden halt right between my knees! I caught it with my legs. I looked down at the ball ... stunned beyond belief. It took a second to realize what had just transpired. I threw my dodge balls up in the air and grabbed the one between my knees. I held it high in triumph.

"Ahh!" I screamed elated jumping up and down. "I win! I win!

"Oh no! How did you do that?" Ralph shouted in frustrated shock.

The gymnasium crowd went nuts. Coach Varner's whistle screeched wildly.

"Game over, game over ... Skopes wins!" he announced with a big smile. "Okay boys, hit the showers."

We hustled toward the wooden shower room door and the few steps down into the locker room bench area. The room filled with voices recounting my unbelievable victory. Much to my pleasure, I repeated that story for weeks. I defeated an *A teamer*.

In the spring we formed a line on the playground and walked to Chapin Park for softball games. One of those trips turned into a nightmare for Charlie Doss. After a few minutes of warming up, playing catch, and swinging bats, somebody took a mighty swing at the wrong time. The bat landed squarely in Charlie's midsection. Down he went—real hard—gasping for air with the wind knocked out of him. Mr. Varner raced over in no time and turned Charlie onto his back. We all gathered around to watch the drama unfold. Mr. Varner began pulling up on Charlie's belt several times lifting him off the ground a few inches each time. Poor Charlie in such distress, tried to breathe but couldn't. It scared the daylights out of me. I'd never seen such an extreme case of wind knock out. The awful scene continued for a while. We heard the sickening moans and groans—frantic gasping for air coming from Charlie's contorted face. A face locked in a pitiful red grimace. I'm sure to Charlie it must have seemed like an eternity until he regained his composure and the ability to breathe normally again. In reality, it ended in about thirty agonizing seconds, and Charlie recovered to play ball thanks to Mr. Varner. He recognized the problem; he had the knowledge; he acted swiftly—a good man.

◆ ◆ ◆

Our eighth grade history teacher, Mr. Steve Benz, AKA "Spot" is at the core of this next story. Mr. Benz was short, sported a crew cut hair style and like many other teachers and students, wore Hush Puppies shoes. Man those shoes were popular. Personally, I never owned a pair. Mr. Benz rated highly among many students at Center School. He had a great sense of humor and often shared a good laugh with us. He even understood the humor we undoubtedly found in the way he pronounced the word—*hydrogen*. Mrs. Bealor, in seventh grade, had problems with *further*, and Mr. Benz slurred through ... *hyjhajhen*. Bealor's—*foother* (odd as it was), couldn't come close to the response elicited by *hyjhajhen*. The word sounded like a sneeze, or a combination sneeze and a six pack of beer slur. After I'd heard it the first time and discovered the great humor in it, I hoped the subject of *nookyoular* energy would come up in every class with Spot.

Spot got his nickname from the little bald spot on the back of his head. If you had the courage to do so, you could mime a shirtsleeve polishing of the spot. Mr. Benz often stood in the hall outside of his classroom door saying hello and chatting before the bell. I used to be fond those sessions in the hall especially when a perfect opportunity came for a spot polish.

Big John Maddox was one of the very few able to get away with a spot polish. Perhaps because of John's size (large) or his talent for coaxing the Benz sense of humor out into the open. Several of us gathered around Mr. Benz while John snuck up from behind. He exhaled onto the bald spot and shined it with his sleeve. The entire group roared with laughter including Spot himself in one of those student/teacher snapshot moments of camaraderie. The playful smile on Mr. Benz taking a good joke in stride, and the, *I got away with it again* attitude from John Maddox made another special memory.

I got the wood from Mr. Benz once, but I don't remember why. It didn't matter that much to me, though, because when Mr. Benz dished out the wood (in most cases); he did it almost like a lesson in comedy school. He didn't, in any way, have the mean streak that Gilliam had. The Benz paddle sessions had high comedic production value. He produced his weapon with a bit of melodramatic flair. After a student warranted getting the wood, Mr. Benz presented to the class his three foot long, white oar. Yes, a row boat oar with about three hundred holes drilled through it. The holes made it easy for the oar to pass through the air—less wind resistance. Over the white paint were dozens of signatures belonging to the formerly punished. There were so many names, the paddle barely looked white. The entire Benz paddling process incorporated a classic Benz blend of humor, formality, and pseudo-punishment. Mr. Benz didn't mix anger with the paddling. He had a gentle swing after he wound up like a pitcher about to hurl a slow ball toward home plate. The force of the blow registered somewhere between a tap and a whack.

Mr. Benz taught history. During one class, we discussed a lesson on textiles and agriculture. In the very back row of the long classroom, Gary Matteson sat alone leaning back against tall, lightly varnished, closet doors. This was the same Gary Matteson who wiped out on his bike in the strip mines. He had red hair and freckles; a quiet kind of a guy. Gary raised his hand and Mr. Benz called on him.

"Yes, Matteson?"

We all turned our heads to Gary.

"Mr. Benz ... what's hemp?"

"I don't know Matteson. What *is* hemp?" Mr. Benz retorted.

"Well if I knew that, I wouldn't be asking you, you big dummy!"

Okay ... now Steve Benz had a unique way of responding to a comment when it surprised him. His eyes opened wide and his lower jaw dropped slightly in a—*what did you just say?*—expression. Sometimes he did it in an exaggerated fashion for comedic effect which succeeded in getting us to laugh. But this time ... this time it wasn't funny. His eyes practically bugged out of their sockets and his jaw just about hit the floor. No one laughed because we knew this one really made him angry. If we had vocalized what we were thinking at that moment, I bet it would have been a vocal collage of things like; *Oh no, here we go, Oh boy, Uh oh,* and *Whoa*! This is because we saw Mr. Benz start plowing through the desks from the front to the back of this long room like a raging, little, half bald bull in a lamp shop. He pushed the chairs to the side in a cacophony of metal desk frames slamming into each other. He reached Matteson in that very last row against the closet doors. Gary just sat there not even attempting to get up. He must have been frozen with fear watching this little bull in Hush Puppies zeroing in on him.

Mr. Benz grabbed Gary by the red hair and began to bang his face into the desktop all the while saying ...

"Hemp? You want to know what hemp is Matteson, huh? I'll tell you what it is. Get up."

Gary got up as Mr. Benz had him by the sleeve and pushed him into what remained of the open aisle along the side of the room. He even gave Gary a swift kick to his rear on the way to the large classroom dictionary.

"There ... look it up ... hemp. Can you spell it? Find it," spat Mr. Benz. I never saw him so angry. He held Gary's head close to the pages of the book as Gary leafed through in a frightened effort to locate the word. His face turned as red as his hair. I saw his embarrassment through the layers of straight red hair that fell on either side of his eyes.

"You got it?"

"Yes."

"Read it. Go ahead ... read it out loud.

He began to read to us the definitions of hemp while Spot held him in place. Gary hovered over the huge book and read aloud phrases about hemp being a tough fiber, used to make rope, sailcloth, etc. I also heard the words marijuana and hashish as part of the labored reading. Upon finishing the reading, Mr. Benz let Gary go and gave him a little shove back toward his seat.

"There ... now you know what hemp is wise guy. Go back and sit down."

Everyone felt for Gary as we saw a tear form on his cheek. He sat there quietly for the rest of the class. Mr. Benz, having shown us another side of him, reacquainted himself with his desk and cooled off.

During that entire scene, no one said a word. No one made a sound. We all sat there shocked, watching this uncharacteristic display of temper loss. At the time it wasn't funny, but ever since then, the story has been a source of amusement for me when I replay it in my mind. It's the innocent opening question that gets me started; "Mr. Benz ... what's hemp?" Then, it's the look on Spot's face after the flashpoint; "... you big dummy ..." that kills me.

◆   ◆   ◆

For the boys, getting the wood in grade school represented a right of passage in a sense. Of the three times I got it, I can honestly say I only deserved the one from Mr. Phillips. I didn't satisfy the required assignment. As for the Gilliam fiasco, let me just say I sat in the wrong row at the right time. The final blow from Mr. Benz doesn't count because I viewed it as more of a symbolic act than punishment. Besides, I don't remember why I got it in the first place. With all the writing five hundred times, rapping, and paddling going on in Center School, I never saw or heard of a girl getting punished with any of these methods. The girls must have been immune; inoculated by femininity—a double standard? Hmm.

This brings me to a test paper that I have from Miss Narrigon's English class. We were reading *The Legend of Sleepy Hollow* at the time. I gave two wrong answers on the first page of that test. One of the wrong answers is very interesting to me. The seventh of the *True or False* section stated; *Ichabod Crane never paddled his pupils.* I answered *True* because after having been paddled three times, I must have thought in my perfect world fantasy that Mr. Crane would never dream of applying corporal punishment to children. It is not something a teacher should do. But I got the answer wrong. He did paddle his students; the boys, I mean.

◆   ◆   ◆

I grew two inches and gained nine pounds by the end of eighth grade. That equates to five feet three inches tall and one hundred nine pounds; still skinny after all those French fries and pies. Grades returned to normal numbers without a D or an F anywhere. My best subject continued to be science; all As and Bs. Mr. Benz gave me a *capable of doing better*. Miss Narrigon didn't pull any punches with two, *wastes time* entries, an *inclined to mischief*, one *capable of doing better*, and a personally hand written—*unnecessary talking*. Narr! There are no indications of being tardy and only one day absent. I wonder if I missed anything good that day; so much happened that year to be forever remembered. As my final year in grade school came to an end, it became evident to me that my world was about to change in a big way. High school loomed ahead of me like some kind of threatening giant. Orientation to this huge new school appeared on the horizon shortly after I earned a promotion to ninth grade and Morris Community High School.

34

Summer; 1966

Four events stand out that took place during the summer of 1966. First, our graduating Center School class party held in the Franklin School Gym. I remember changing out of my suit and tie in my room after the graduation ceremony. I swapped out my fancy threads for jeans and a sport shirt. New black leather shoes and black socks were replaced by my regular black PF Flyers, and white crew socks with the blue decorative rings around the elastic tops. I splashed a little Brut on my neck, ready for action. The skinny Greek boy faced young manhood. Grade school, in the blink of an eye became a place of the past; a memory for the future. Challenging, exciting, and frightening new times lay ahead.

Am I going to like high school? How will I do scholastically, athletically? Is it time to seriously start thinking about a career? Will I go to college? No wait, I'm still a kid. Where's my bike? I'll call the guys and we'll go fishing at Gebhard Woods tomorrow. Oh shut up and get your butt to the party.

I hugged Mom and Dad, thanking them for the card with the one hundred dollar cash gift and left for the party. They looked proud of me. I walked along the familiar route I took as a little guy to get to Franklin School. I thought about rainy days and Popsicle sticks floating away to distant shores. The clicking sound of glass marbles hitting each other along the playground curb and American Civil War battle cries filled my head. I remembered snapping my white patrol belt buckle into place. I recalled watching over the barricaded Franklin Street playground and chasing after runaway balls for the younger kids. I wondered …

What is this party gonna be like? Will Kay be there? Vicki Martinez? Vicky Castanier? Will I ask any of them to dance? And how about Beth, will she be there with Ted? Will I just hang around with Lee, Bill and Tom?

I also thought ahead about high school.

When will football practice start? Uh oh, I'm going to be a freshman! Some big upperclassman is gonna take me out.

Now the phrase ... *take me out,* or *take you out* ... brought chills to every eighth grade graduating boy—it meant the initiation into high school—hazing. It could happen at any time, anywhere. Once the upper class goons got wind of you about to become a freshman, you were ripe fruit. I had to be careful that night and every day and night for the whole summer, not to mention the entire freshman year itself—a whole year? Maybe it would be better to get it over with right away and not have to spend the better part of an entire year losing sleep. I couldn't help but wonder about the girls ... what happened to them as new high school fodder? Hazing rumors were everywhere about boys.

"Did you hear about so and so two years ago?"

"What about him?"

"The creeps took him out to the Catholic Cemetery and tied him to a headstone and left him there all night."

"No way!"

"Yeah. And did you hear what they did to so and so last year?"

"No, what?"

"Some scumbags taped his mouth shut; strapped him to the hood of a car and drove him up and down Liberty Street for half an hour ... *naked!*"

"That's messed up!"

"No kidding."

I worried that a few marauding junior or senior creep scumbags might jump out from behind a parked car—gag me, take my clothes off, strap me to the hood of their car and drive me all over town. For a night cap they'd take me out to the Catholic Cemetery on Old Stage Road, tie me up against a cold stone, and place a Playboy centerfold on the ground in front of me. My head was reeling from all the thoughts invading my mind during that short walk.

Ahhh! I'm just going to a party for cryin' out loud!

Once I got to the school I saw lots of classmates walking toward the doors. I felt safety in numbers.

Let the goons try something now ha ha!

Party music grew louder as I entered the side door on North Street and passed by my first grade classroom. How could eight years have gone by so quickly since Mrs. Coop's class? Now I'm a big guy preparing to do manly things. The dance waits.

The master of ceremonies, bathed in colored lights, had festivities under control. His sport coat reflected sparkling show lights throughout the darkened room. He played *Listen People* by Herman's Hermits on the stereo. Boys, girls, and chaperones filled the room typically decorated with a congratulations banner, balloons, crepe paper, chairs, and a table with cookies and punch. No sooner did I get there, than an announcement sounded over the music calling for a contest ... a singing contest. For the life of me, I can't imagine what prompted me to volunteer. I was the only boy competing against three female classmates attempting to recreate an opera type vocal. The emcee played the sample to which the guys whooped and laughed when they heard the female soprano voice; so much for doing manly things. I wanted to run and hide. My newly discovered self image of becoming a young man bit the dust. How am I supposed to get away with singing like a girl? Well, quitting would have been a worse option, so as petrified as I must have looked, I stood my ground. When my turn came, I belted out the best falsetto voice I could and nailed it. The room exploded in cheers. The skinny Greek boy sang like a fat Italian lady of the opera and won the contest. Unbelievable! My prize; a 45 RPM record by The Swingin' Medallions; *Double Shot (Of My Baby's Love)* is stacked with the rest of my record collection. I've had it all these years along with many other items including my rocking horse, Franklin School bag, marbles, baseball glove, pocket knife for locating land mines, homework, test papers, and the Sears TransTalk Walkie Talkie. I only wish I could add my baseball cards to that list. They, most unfortunately, disappeared.

I don't remember much else from the party. Everything had been overshadowed by the singing contest. Did I see or dance with Kay, Vicki or Vicky? I don't recall. Were Beth and Ted there? I think so. Did I hang with Tom, Bill and Lee? Yes.

◆ ◆ ◆

Stand out event number two in the summer of 1966 was a vacation I took to my Cousin Martha's home on the north side of Chicago. For years her son Johnny, three years my senior, and I spent dozens of fun filled days together. This would be my last visit with Johnny before they moved to Syracuse, New York. And what a visit it turned out to be.

The song I associate with this visit is by The Lovin' Spoonful, *Summer in the City*. Johnny worked at this new fast food place called *Colonel Sanders Kentucky Fried Chicken*. We stopped by on his day off for deep fried chicken, cole slaw, mashed potatoes and gravy, biscuits, and honey. I stuffed myself. The song played on his car radio as we headed to the shores of Lake Michigan for a day at the beach. We swam for most of the afternoon off a rock wall away from the sandy beach. Waves weren't unmanageable, but I did swallow a little water diving into one.

Later that evening, back at Johnny's house, I began to feel sick. Martha looked concerned after taking my temperature. My temperature had shot up to 104 degrees, and she called my mother back in Morris seventy miles away. I heard the worry in Martha's voice when she told Mom she'd take care of me. The next thing I know, I'm hearing the words, *enema* and *warm soapy water*, in the same sentence; oh no. I felt terrible. The song played again on Johnny's bedroom radio.

Hot town summer in the city back of my neck feelin' dirty and gritty.

Singing wasn't on my mind.

Inevitably ... warm soapy water would enter my lower gastro-intestinal area. The fever had to come down fast. Who would administer this invasive procedure? I recall Martha, Johnny, and me in the bathroom.

"If you're feeling shy, Mikey, I'll have Johnny do it for you," Martha offered.

"Okay," I managed to slowly respond, feeling weak and very shy indeed. Inside I wanted to hide. I had heard of enemas before and after getting a good look at the long black plastic tube with a big red squeezy ball at the other end, I became uneasy. I looked at Johnny who had a funny expression on his face. It appeared to me he was about to enjoy playing doctor by ramming this thing up my butt, laughing the whole time. Oh boy.

Martha gave Johnny a few last minute instructions and left the bathroom.

Hot town summer in the city warm soapy water goin'...

I leaned over the bathtub and ...

"Eeehaa!"

That felt pretty weird. Results came immediately.

It seems to me now, that a regular course of action would be to swallow a few aspirin and apply some ice packs. But what did I know back then? It must have been an old world Greek remedy.

With bed rest it ended in a day or two. I survived. After that vacation I wouldn't set foot in a Kentucky Fried Chicken joint for a long, long time. The cause of my illness could have been the food, but the best bet was the gulp of lake water I swallowed.

◆ ◆ ◆

Special event number three during the summer of 1966 involves my fourteenth birthday. Ann and her best friend, Maureen Radcliff, hosted a party for me in our apartment. I always liked Maureen—a good friend and much like another older sister who seemed to enjoy my sense of humor. Many of my friends attended this party. In fact I could name most of them because I still have the birthday cards in my collection of old letters, cards, and general stuff.

Well, my party certainly entertained everybody. Music played on the stereo, and kids danced and ran all over. This party incorporated many of the same characteristics as the living room sock hop Beth's mom put together at her house awhile earlier, and also the basement party Jay's mother had hosted. Each had music, dancing, and great food. I remember the Sloppy Joe sandwiches at Jay's house very well; I devoured about five of them. We held soirees in buildings, top to bottom. At my party everyone got a kick out of running up and down the long stairwell, dividing their time between the sidewalk outside and the activities inside the apartment. All the heavy foot stomping up and down the stairs might have been enough to make my dad and anyone else in the bar below wonder what all the elephants were doing. Without success, I tried to get everyone to step lightly, since I feared Dad might not appreciate the ruckus. It turned out my concern about *the other fella* didn't matter and I could have saved myself some grief. Dad didn't mind.

A fourteenth birthday party wouldn't be complete without the traditional, *Spin the Bottle* game. I had no problem being around girls, but the whole boyfriend/girlfriend thing continued to be numbing. The idea of kissing and dating petrified me. The boys gathered in one circle, and the girls formed another in our small living room. Each group had a Coke bottle to spin, and when the boy and girl were selected, they had to enter my sisters' room and … kiss. I really hoped the bottle would never land on me because of my fear of kissing girls. Older people and movie stars kissed in mushy love stories, not kids like me; at least not yet. I hadn't given up my version of the boy, Packy, from *My Friend Flicka*—too busy with marbles, wading in the creek, and stuffing things into my pockets for use at a later date.

The Coke bottles eventually pointed at me and Barb Mitchell whom I'd known since fourth grade. Barb, a real sweetheart and popular cheerleader for the Center School Papooses basketball team had a strange look on her face for some reason. My first thought hit me like a ton of Center School bricks. She had to be thinking; *oh no, not him*. The expression on her face plainly indicated to me that she felt annoyed by the whole thing. Then it hit me why, like half a ton of Franklin School bricks. Though my first, this was her third time being selected by that clever little bottle. She'd already had enough.

Okay then … self confidence don't you worry. I'm not a dork after all.

When we entered the bedroom, I quickly figured out a solution to both our problems. Barb's was a third round of kissing and mine simply being uncomfortable about having to kiss a girl because a stupid bottle said I had to. A solution to the problem needed to be found ... fast. Oh, what to do, what to do? She stood there with her arms folded, almost rolling her eyes waiting for me to make the first move.

Boy, girls and women sure do fold their arms a lot.

It was an awkward moment. I looked Barb in the eyes and said ...

"Barb, we don't have to do this you know."

"What do you mean?"

"Well," I nervously continued. "No one will know if we just ... fake it and pretend like we did it."

Barb thought for a few seconds. I waited.

"Okay, I guess," she said.

Okay, I guess? She agreed ... crap!

Something inside my hormonal skinniness hoped she'd follow with a ...

"Fake it? No way. Plant one on me Greek boy!"

Still, it seemed to me I did the right thing given Barb's initial reaction upon entering the room. However, re-entering the living room I felt conflicted knowing I chickened out. I thought to myself ...

I should have taken her into my arms and kissed her ... passionately ... like Flash Gordon planting one on Dale Arden after rescuing her from Ming the Merciless or one of his Planet Mongo monsters. After all, this is the same apartment where at the bottom of the stairs, I kissed little Tina Rainwater. You scrawny, little, yellow-bellied, chicken!

How would the Barb Mitchell kiss have changed my relationship with Barb? What would that act have done to eliminate my fear of future romance? Would she have hated me for it? Would she have realized Greek boys make good boyfriends? Maybe we would have exchanged friendship rings and gone to the show to hold hands in the back row like the older couples did. Who knows? Perhaps she would have just slapped me and I would never have been able to face her again. And what about facing the other kids with a big red mark on my cheek? What about that? I did the right thing. We continued through school as friends.

♦ ♦ ♦

This brings me to item number four in the summer of 1966. Summer vacation didn't last very long. Do they ever? So far, I had managed to elude the marauding goons for almost the entire hot, humid, summer. Steve, Rob, and I decided to ride our bikes to Gebhard Woods. We approached the main entrance to Gebhard Woods on Ottawa Street down a long gentle slope into a hollow along a corn field. At the bottom of this hollow, we slowed down when we heard a van coming up behind us. It squealed to an abrupt halt. We stopped. The side door of the van slid open to our left and out jumped two of the most feared upper classmen of Morris Community High School. Juniors, Mike Dummitt and Bill Wilson were two tough football players with fighting reputations off the field. My heart, already pumping from the bike ride, started racing even faster knowing my time had finally come—to get *taken out*.

"Hey, Mike Skopes, you're a freshman this year, right?" Dummit snarled.

"Yeah he is," Wilson played along with an evil looking grin.

I froze, straddling my red Coast King. Images of naked hood rides, grave stones, ropes, and mouth gags flashed before my eyes.

Oh no ... no, not Dummitt and Wilson of all people ... I am dead meat. Aw man.

I freaked and couldn't speak. I looked at Steve and Rob who had pity in their eyes for me. They were safe for now going into eighth grade.

"You two ... Enger and Holbrook ... you're next year," threatened Wilson.

I could only say to Steve and Rob ...

"Watch my bike will ya?" I guess I knew I'd be back sometime soon; after all ... it was daytime.

"Get in, Skopes," Wilson ordered.

Dummitt had already jumped into the driver's seat. I looked inside the van to see guys they had already snatched from the baking summer time streets. I remember Bob Feeney, Sherman Workman, and Terry Hiles. There may have been as many as two or three others. The van took off in the direction of Gebhard Woods, but rather than turning left into the park after crossing Shaky Bridge, Dummitt veered right onto Seneca Road (Old Stage Road) that ran parallel to the Illinois & Michigan Canal.

During this delightful little ride I exchanged silent nervous greetings with my classmates Bob and Sherman. Terry should have been entering high school with us, but he had been held back a year in grade school. I guess Dummitt and Wilson felt that didn't matter. We rode for a short while passing the Catholic Cemetery on the right. I saw it through the windshield and the right side passenger window.

Whew ... no gravestone action for me ... that's a relief. Where the heck are you goons taking me?

We continued to a place almost two miles out of town. Dummitt and Wilson pointed, searching for their next turn off. I heard them talking low in agreement as the van turned left off the main road and onto a dirt and gravel turnout sheltered by plenty of large shade trees. The van stopped in a cloud of dust. My hazing moment had arrived; but in broad daylight? What would it be? I'd never heard of daylight hazing time. All that stuff usually went down at night.

Dummitt and Wilson got out and opened the sliding door from the outside.

"Skopes ... Hiles, get out!" barked Dummitt.

Yeah, yeah, yeah ... you scumbags, I'll be right out.

The others stayed in the van. Turns out they had already been initiated but were still along for the ride. What their hazing consisted of I don't remember. Who knows, this could have been the second or third trip of the day to this location for the busy goons. Terry and I stepped out of the cramped van into the hot August sunshine.

"Over there ... now," Wilson commanded with a sneer pointing to the canal.

"Strip," Wilson said.

"What?" I stupidly asked.

"Shut up! Shut up and strip," Dummitt snapped back.

"Just do what they say, Greek," Terry said in a whisper.

We started taking our clothes off.

So this is what you want to do to me ... see me naked in the middle of the day? What a couple of ... of ... perverted goons. Yeah, that's it ... you perverts. Kiss my naked Greek butt.

"Now ... swim to the other side and back," Wilson piped out with a laugh. He and Dummitt were having a good old time.

I looked over to the water a few feet away. Dead branches stuck up out of the muddy water in several places. To my left, a gravel bridge had been poured into the canal over a large round culvert. It created a dam/bridge for the property owner to access a field on the other side. The thirty foot wide canal, with a depth unknown at this point, looked uninviting to say the least.

Hey buttheads ... I've got news for you ... I've done this before a few years ago. Ha ha!

Terry and I were down to our whitey tighties. I thought about my prior rafting experience wearing cut offs.

I'm not about to swim in the canal naked.

I found the courage to ask a question of the goons. Like my Orthodox baptism about thirteen years earlier, I wore another white outfit; my whitey tighties.

I couldn't really object too much to this upcoming immersion either. However, I once again elected to insist on establishing the terms to this agreement as well.

"Is it okay if I leave my shorts on? Snapping turtles you know ... and my shoes?"

My concerned interest lay in keeping my privates in tact. I made the shoe request because I didn't want to step on any broken glass or nails. I'd just gotten over a 104 degree fever in Chicago and had to do something to protect myself from any more up close and personal enema affairs.

Dummitt and Wilson looked at each other, not barking back at me to shut up or anything. They thought for a few seconds.

Well now, this is interesting.

"Yeah sure, go ahead," Wilson finally said.

Hey thanks. You're a couple of nice butthead goons.

The uncharacteristic good will on their part shocked me somewhat. The tough guy act must have been a show. Deep down inside they were Teddy Bears. Ha! That'll be the day.

Terry kept quiet in amazement that I managed to make actual requests of these tough guys. Wearing our shoes and white shorts we stepped into the water and made extremely shallow dives which took us across in no time. After only a few quick strokes we reached the other shore. Again, I didn't allow my legs to go vertical for fear of what might be submerged; just as I did about four years prior and three miles east. In just seconds, we were back on the starting side of the swim. Terry and I climbed out of the dirty canal, got dressed and jumped back into the van. The fear of hazing ended before high school even started. I liked that.

"Way to go, Greek," I heard Feeney say.

"Yeah, Greek, that was alright," agreed Sherman.

"Thanks. No big deal." I wiped the remaining canal droplets off my face with my sleeve.

Everyone started to laugh ... including Mike Dummitt and Bill Wilson. There would be no naked hood ride for me; no cemetery caper either. The fears I had harbored for almost a year disappeared in an instant. My initiation into high school didn't live up to the stories spread around town intending to scare the life out of me. My new goon friends drove me back to my Coast King. Steve and Rob, my honorable old friends, hadn't moved. They had found a cool spot in the shade and guarded my bike the whole time while waiting for me to return; commendable. I had officially become a bonafide freshman at Morris Community High School.

Conclusion

○ ○

"We were talking about the love we all could share ..." George Harrison

Dear Harrison,

In elementary school, shyness and stage fright inhibited my development in ways I wished they hadn't. When my friends Jim Smith, Lee Randall, and Bill Fruland performed onstage for the operetta *H.M.S. Pinafore* at Center School, I preferred the comfort of sitting in the audience watching. Instead of school plays or playing an instrument in the school band, I played neighborhood sports and bicycled all over town. In general, I kept relatively low key by engaging in goofball adventures with my friends. Those adventures gave me great pleasure at the very age you are now.

I began writing this book while you were twelve years old and in seventh grade. Now it is finished and you're thirteen years old in eighth grade. I've chosen to end my stories with the end of my eighth grade and age fourteen; the gateway to young adulthood. Our young lives at this age are so different. Mine, mainly filled with small town outdoor adventures, and yours dominated by indoor adventures of computer virtual reality. Sure, you have outdoor activities; some with me such as fishing off the pier in Santa Barbara and short bike rides together. Some favorite outdoor activities we share are backyard camping of course and going to the beach. In my childhood, we didn't have computers and video games on line. My indoor electronic activities were limited to broadcast television, radio, and playing records.

I believe this book is an excellent reference source for you. Leaf through it while you think about my life as a young boy. It is important to me that you understand what I went through. I want you to draw from my past and learn from my victories and my mistakes while at the same time knowing how much fun I had at that wonderful age. One of those victories I'm proud of was saving the life of my friend John Halterman. As far as mistakes are concerned, the gorilla balls caper comes to mind. It is a good idea to consider the consequences of certain actions. I learned as time went on.

I also want you to remember and think about what your grandfather (papou) taught me. Be considerate. If someone is sleeping, step lightly. Think about the other fella. Be generous and kind. Be strong and know the difference between right and wrong. I have always held dear; his wisdom, and his special way of communicating to us. That is why I always say to you as you leave home in the morning …

"Luck, and love, and skills—do great. Be careful. Be aware—peripheral vision. Be kind and have fun."

◆ ◆ ◆

It is interesting and satisfying to know how the timeless body of work by the Beatles carried over into your Cousin Tony's life. With passion, I introduced him to their music. He easily recognized the value of their contribution to musical history and took my passion to another level. Tony teaches, enjoys, studies, and performs their music with so much conviction and intensity. Now you have come to know and appreciate the very same songs of love, and peace—such superb listening pleasure. Three generations of Beatlemaniacs. I love it.

George Harrison expressed himself eloquently shortly before he passed away. I paraphrase: "To change the world for the better, it must begin with each individual." He enlightened us all. Goodness spreads from within each of us, outward to those with whom we intimately share life.

My son, I can't paint the world with one broad brush stroke of peace and harmony. Who can? Instead, I've listened to George's words and as a caring individual, shared my family, the childhood that I loved, the friends I played with, and the adults I tried to understand. In doing so, I hope I've done my small part to help make the world a better place. I've spoken about my sometimes reckless, youthful world of adventure and wonder. I've done this partly to remind myself of the countless events in my life and to continue to learn from them. Personal history is tangible. Remember it, share it with others, and repeat it … often. Life is too short not to.

◆ ◆ ◆

Your papou, Harry C. Skopes, was born on April 23, 1903 in Glena, Greece and he died on a Saturday afternoon the seventeenth day of May, 1997 in Morris, Illinois. You were almost three years old. This is the last minute of the final long distance conversation we shared shortly before he died.

"Dad? I love you Dad."

"I love you too, Mike," he said in a labored voice.

"I'm coming home Dad to take care of you. I'll make arrangements to fly home and be with you Dad," I struggled hard to say without breaking down.

I heard his breathing getting louder.

"I'll be home to take care of you," I said.

I couldn't hold back my tears and cried into the phone the tears I always dreaded from an early age when I realized that one day my parents would be taken from me.

"I'm dying, Mike," he struggled to say.

I wept louder and I could hear him laboring to communicate with me.

"Dad, I love you and I'm coming home to take care of you."

"No, Mike. I'll take care of you."

"Good-bye Dad. I love you."

His breathing became more labored and I heard some scuffling sounds when a nurse picked up the phone to inform me that Dad couldn't talk anymore. They had to put him on an oxygen mask to help make him comfortable.

With the last seven precious words my father said, he told me he would be my guardian angel. He knew I would understand him perfectly in our final short conversation. He was a man of few words in every conversation I ever had with him.

About an hour later that afternoon I called your mom at home to discuss my travel plans. She had already learned from your Auntie Ann that Papou had died shortly after he and I spoke. Yia Yia (your grandmother) sat at his side holding his hand when he took his last breath. They made peace with each other. They apologized for unrealized dreams and for the long hours of hard work they endured during life on Liberty Street.

I almost didn't have that last conversation with Dad. I tried to call the nursing home earlier, only to be told he didn't have a phone in his room. I didn't ask the nurse to get a phone to him, not knowing how bad his condition had become. Shortly after that I called home to your mom, and she convinced me to call again and this time insist a phone be taken into his room so I could speak with him. That's when I had the above final intimate moment with Dad that I can never forget for as long as I live. I'm so thankful I got to have it.

Harrison, we all have influences, ancestry, places, and people in our past who have played a role in shaping who we are. The events I participated in that took place on the streets and sidewalks, in the parks and yards, the hills and farms, the homes and schools of Morris, Illinois between 1952 and 1966 helped shape who I am today. In some ways, the person I am now is just a larger version of that skinny little kid described in this book; only with something extra ... wisdom. Wisdom I acquired in part by respecting and learning from individuals who were older and far more experienced than I.

For every spin of my bicycle wheels, head winds were intent on pushing me back. For every frozen pond or creek I skated, I learned to avoid thin ice or crash through it. Head winds and thin ice come in infinite disguises. As a boy, I plowed into them; parked cars and poor judgment. As an adult, I pay attention to what lies ahead, never forgetting where and how I started.

In my life, I've loved, cherished, enjoyed, and respected many people who have shared with me the treasures of themselves before leaving this world. I've written about some of them in this book. Their memories are the treasures locked in my soul forever. It isn't the red Coast King that warms my heart. It is the gift of having known Bernie Hanson and his kindness. It's not the Monark from Uncle Bill either. It is remembering the overwhelming emotion I felt the moment I awoke that Saturday morning when he returned from Greece with his new bride. The hair cuts from Uncle Nick are long gone, but his unselfish concern and desire to help me through my skating accident remains. The toys from Joe Farrell are also gone, but his friendly smiles during Sunday dinners with our family, I'll never forget. And how could I forget the piano playing, singing, and kindness from Happy or the frequent, friendly, company of Uncle George Tolias?

It took my Mom twenty six years of hard work, but she finally got her first house, something she always dreamed about. She and Dad retired in that house. The large backyard bordered a corn field just north of Interstate 80. The countryside setting afforded my parents contentment—peaceful and quiet. Ann lived in her house across the street with her family, so grandchildren Tony, Jimmy, and Elaine were only a shout away, evoking memories of her mountain village in Greece. Together, Mom and Dad transformed a large portion of their backyard into a prolific garden. Dad's favorite work; turning the soil, and growing fantastic fresh vegetables kept him and Mom active and healthy.

Harrison, your yia yia—my devoted mother, sacrificed so much to see her children well cared for, and nourished with love and affection. From her, I inherited the ability to display that affection. She taught me what it is to love your children. She provided countless domestic efforts benefiting everyone in our family and all guests invited into our home. Her work ethic of teaching herself to read and write English, keeping busy by completing her projects such as knitting sweaters, socks, and even gloves, was something to see. She could knit, sew, and crochet just about anything. From my mother I learned the joy of music, singing, and dancing. Her artistic creativity lives in me. Your mother and I see those same talents in you my son.

The treasures from my father are living inside of me every day. His quiet personality; love of animals; his consideration and generosity for his friends and others—even strangers who had less; his sense of loyalty to his family; his selflessness and love for us; calm understanding; his strength of character in knowing right from wrong; recognizing evil in his world and responding with a hand guided by God's goodness; all these noble values, he demonstrated to me through his actions and few words. I pray I've learned his lessons and live them to the best of my ability. Sometimes I succeed, sometimes I fail. Now, I pass them along to you my son. Like your papou, you have a love for animals and a deep love for your family. You've always been wise beyond your years. Do you have a quiet personality? Well, basically no, but we love that about you.

Harrison, as a boy, if something wasn't right, I complained to make it better. When I recognized humor, I cracked up. If something made me sad, I cried. When something or someone made me angry, I fought. If I didn't understand something, I usually responded by thinking about it—internalizing it. People often thought of me as being shy or even timid because of that. Maybe they were correct, but I really did think all the time. Not a prolific questioner, I tried to figure things out on my own. If I couldn't, then I'd ask questions. I'm still that way.

Uncle Nick gave me my first philosophy lesson while sitting in his barber chair. As he cut my hair, he spoke about the great Greek philosophers, especially Socrates. Uncle Nick made a simple point, in words I could understand. He wanted me to open my mind and think.

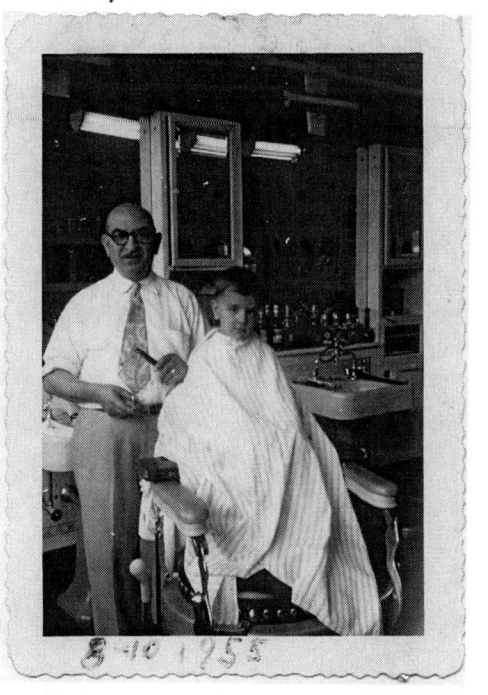

"Philosophy," he said, "is thinking and asking questions."

He taught me to use my thoughts as tools for solutions.
"Keep searching. Keep looking for answers like Socrates," he used to say.
I'm always looking for Popsicle sticks. I'll never stop.

Dear Prudence,

Good morning good morning from me to you.
There's a place across the universe,
Let it be good day sunshine when I get home.
Here there and everywhere, I want to tell you—two of us getting better.
Girl,
You've got to hide your love away in my life—strawberry fields forever.

Oh darling,
Please, please me because I'm happy just to dance with you.
I've got a feeling it won't be long—hold me tight.
Oo you—I'll keep you satisfied eight days a week.

It's for you—
Every little thing any time at all, flying like dreamers do from a window.
Do you want to know a secret?
Tomorrow never knows you can't do that.

Little child,
Tell me what you see, what you're doing, when I'm sixty-four.
That means a lot honey pie.
Magical mystery tour? Yes it is something.
Ask me why you won't see me cry baby cry,
I feel fine. I'm in love. Goodnight.

All my loving, Michelle
P.S. I love you

In 1963, I learned of The Beatles and the music that would influence my life in a profound way. I assembled this poem of Beatles song titles for Jan when we were married in 1991. I found my California Girl.

978-0-595-48531-4
0-595-48531-6